INDEPENDENT BUSES IN NORTH WEST ENGLAND

Neville Mercer

This book is dedicated to the memory of Roy Marshall (1928-2013), the man whose photography inspired this series of books on independent bus operators

© 2013 Neville Mercer and Venture Publications Ltd
ISBN 9781905304561

All rights reserved. Except for normal review purposes no part of this book may be reproduced or utilised in any form by any means, electrical or mechanical, including photocopying, recording or by an information storage and retrieval system, without the prior written consent of Venture Publications Ltd, Glossop, Derbyshire, SK13 8EH.

CONTENTS

Introduction	*3*
Acknowledgements	*42*
Part One Cumberland & Westmorland	*44*
Part Two Lancashire & Cheshire	*96*
Stop Press	*158*
Part Three North West England In Colour	*160*

FRONT COVER
This preserved PD2/40 Titan with lowbridge Weymann Orion bodywork, 528 CTF, was new to Fishwick in 1958 as fleet number 5. A regular attendee at events organised by the British Commercial Vehicle Museum in Leyland, it is seen here in Leyland *(John Senior)*

REAR COVER
Ocean Port Service Ltd of Liverpool used this lowbridge Bristol KSW5G/ECW double-decker, JDL 34, as a staff bus. The vehicle had been new to Southern Vectis in May 1952, and passed to OPS in 1969. It was sold for scrap in 1973. *(Alan Murray-Rust)*

TITLE PAGE
This picture displays the craft of that masterful photographer Roy Marshall, who will be sorely missed by all who knew him, and shows Viking's 1946 PS1 Tiger/Burlingham bus ARN 528 (fleet number 14) in Starchhouse Square, Preston. The blind shows 'Preston via Fylde Road'. All of Viking's services left Preston via this road, which was crossed by a low railway bridge. *(Roy Marshall)*

INSIDE FRONT COVER
In Congleton (Cheshire) and Biddulph (just across the border in Staffordshire) the local bus operators banded together into a Bus Owners' Association to co-ordinate their fares and frequencies, and to defend themselves against incursions by the two BET affiliates in the area, North Western and Potteries. Despite this alliance all of the operators listed at the top of this 1930 timetable except one had disappeared before the end of the decade. The exception was Ernest Wells of Biddulph, who sold out to PMT in 1953. *(John Dixon Collection)*

INTRODUCTION

In the Northwich area of Cheshire – where I lived until the age of nine – there were no independent bus operators at all. The few which had existed had either long since ceased operations or had been taken over by 'Combine' subsidiaries before the Second World War. In fact, such businesses were as rare as hen's teeth in the entire county of Cheshire by the 1950s, the only survivor of any real substance being Naylor Motor Services of Stockton Heath which had clung on to its daily service from Warrington (then across the border in Lancashire) to Appleton Thorn and Arley. Their Massey-bodied Guy Arab III was the only independent double-decker in use on 'unrestricted' stage-carriage services in Cheshire.

Naylor had sold its other routes to the North Western Road Car Co before the war, including year-round services from Great Budworth to Northwich and to the Stockton Heath terminus of Warrington Corporation's tramway (except on Sunday mornings when the trams didn't run and Naylor was allowed to operate into the town centre). A licence for a seasonal operation from Stockton Heath to Pickmere Lake, on summer Sundays, also passed to North Western although it seems that the latter company abandoned the service after just one summer. This was a great pity as the lake was then a popular leisure destination and was less than a mile away from the village which would become my childhood home.

As a precocious six year old, armed with paper and pencil, Pickmere Lake was a natural attraction. One could only record the same North Western vehicles on the local stage services so many times before the boredom became tangible, and trips to the lake on Sundays would usually produce something of interest to a young bus enthusiast.

In most cases I had no idea what I was looking at, but I did make an accurate record of the visiting vehicles registration marks. Some (such as 'breakfast parties' from the more urban parts of the North Western empire and excursions from Chester and Crewe by Crosville) were regular customers, but others were far rarer – I only found out how rare in later years. To give just one example, on the first Sunday in July 1960 the two vehicles noted down (both owned by Taylor's Tours of Castleton near Rochdale) were GDK 348, an AEC Regal III with Gurney Nutting bodywork – unusual in the North West, and GDK 936, a Morris Commercial with bodywork by Trans-United - which may well have been a unique combination. If I could go back in time I would give a decent camera to my younger self!

Despite the pre-war connection I never saw any of Naylor's fleet at Pickmere, but their Arab III double-decker was frequently sighted on family outings to Warrington, much to the relief of my parents as its appearance would end the mind-numbing refrain of 'are we nearly there yet?' If the aforementioned possibility of time travel could be realised in some form involving a large return payload this is the one bus above all others which I would rescue from oblivion. In real life it was thanklessly scrapped after Naylor sold their Arley route to Warrington Corporation in December 1964.

Early trips to Blackpool brought other North West independents into my field of vision; two-tone green Fishwick and red, black, and white Bamber Bridge double-deckers on the southern approaches to Preston, and the magnificent off-white, maroon, and black fleet of Scout Motor Services on the roads between Preston and the Fylde coast. All three of these independents were successful enough to be early customers for the revolutionary Leyland Atlantean, although my experience of the Scout examples was cut painfully short by Ribble's acquisition of the business in 1961. Ribble continued to use the Scout name until 1968, but the vehicles were rapidly repainted into standard Ribble group cherry red and cream. None of them looked better as a result, and I hope to live long enough to see one of the surviving Scout Atlanteans back on the road in its original colour scheme.

Further North

As mentioned in an earlier volume in this series, my 'Gran' was the village coach trip organiser, employing vehicles from Albert Bowyer & Sons of Northwich until 1959 and then from North Western. At least once a year the destination for an outing would be the Lake District. The earliest trip that I can remember (in the summer of 1959) went to Bowness on Windermere, and although there were no independent buses to be found there by that time I did manage to record dozens of visiting coaches, including JTU 244 of Pride of Sale. Three years later my family moved to Sale and one of my first expeditions in my new home town took me to Pride of Sale's garage. Sadly, 'JTU' had already gone but later research revealed it to have been a Maudslay Marathon III with fully-fronted Duple bodywork.

The 1960 Lake District trip (to Keswick) and the 1961 outing (to Penrith) proved to be more entertaining. At Keswick I first came across the bonneted Bedfords (and at least one Commer) of the Keswick Borrowdale Bus Services, although there was no opportunity to ride on them. Infuriatingly, I never did sample this service – I was planning to do so in the summer of 1967 when I discovered that it was already too late. A month after the company's absorption by Cumberland Motor Services I made up for this faux pas by spending an entire day riding Hawkey's OBs between Wadebridge and Polzeath (in Cornwall). I became an instant fan of the OB and many more such rides followed, but mainly in Derbyshire (with Silver Service), North Wales (Whiteways) and Shropshire where old OBs seemed to carry on forever. I am, however, still angry with myself for missing the Borrowdale examples. As Joni Mitchell once sang 'You don't know what you've got till it's gone'.

The high point of the Penrith outing was a visit to the Sandgate premises of Ernie Hartness, chosen in preference to a boat trip on Ullswater. My grandparents considered me eccentric, but in those days it seemed perfectly safe to leave an eight year old boy on his own to explore a bus garage. To use a slightly later phrase, Ernie Hartness's operation blew my mind. Here was a relatively small independent operator with his own bus station virtually in the middle of town. Almighty Ribble had no such facility in Penrith at that time and used some nearby street stands located on the former site of the town's pig market. I remember sitting there for half an hour or so, marvelling at the concept. There were nine vehicles on the premises, the most impressive being a Daimler CVD6/Roe double-decker although the fully-fronted CVD6/Roe saloons were also notable. I promised myself that I would return and ride on these buses which apparently operated long distance stage services to Carlisle and Wigton as well as more local routes.

It took longer than I had imagined, but in May 1967 a relative was making a day trip to Carlisle (by car) and offered me a ride. Cheekily, I asked her to drop me off at Penrith on the outward leg and arranged a place to meet her in Carlisle at tea-time for the return journey (Lowther Street bus station, in case you were curious – I was wringing every last drop of satisfaction from this journey!). Deposited outside Hartness's bus station at 9.30 in the morning I found a slightly different selection of vehicles, but surprisingly little had changed in the six years since my first visit. Discovering that I had quite a bit of time to spare before Hartness's next departure for Carlisle, I went outside to explore and came across a Morris Commercial with ACB bodywork belonging to another local independent. To be honest, what was actually entered into my notebook was 'KRM 444 Morris Commercial *Titterington*'. The name of the operator was underlined twice so as a teenage boy I had evidently found something vaguely comical about the first three letters.

I was probably still chuckling to myself in a prurient fashion when it became time to return to the bus station. I had hoped for one of the double-deckers but the departure was actually operated by a Plaxton-bodied Commer Avenger IV, VRM 836. The disappointment was soon diminished by securing the seat at the front next to the driver, affording first class views of the landscape and a chance to talk to both members of the crew as few passengers boarded en route.

Now, you have to remember that this was 1967. Not only was there no Internet, but the generally available reference books (Ian Allan's BBF series) contained no mention of independent operators in Cumberland and Westmorland. When the driver asked me if I was on my way to visit Blair & Palmer I had no idea what he was talking about. All became clear upon arrival in Carlisle. Ernie Hartness was not the only independent operator in Cumberland to have his own bus station.

By 1967 I had become quite adept at identifying the products of most of the big bodywork manufacturers (although the ACB body on KRM 444 had left me mystified), but many of Blair & Palmer's vehicles looked like nothing else on the surface of the planet. A friendly fitter who had allowed me access to the Drovers Lane depot saw me staring (open mouthed) at two single deck buses, NHH 482 and UHH 877, the former about to depart for Newton Arlosh on the company's main stage route. He grinned. "Do you like them? We made them ourselves."

I was flabbergasted. Big companies such as London Transport, Midland Red, Barton, and Northern General made their own buses, not medium sized independents with no more than 20 vehicles. As NHH 482 departed it became obvious that it had a Commer TS3 engine, although the noise seemed to be coming from amidships rather than at the front. The fitter confirmed this and pointed at UHH 877, "and that one started off as a Commer too, but we put an Albion 8-cylinder engine in it. It can't half go when you put your foot down."

Other highlights of my first visit to Blair & Palmer were a former Ribble 'White Lady' double-decker (DCK 221) and a Scottish-registered Atkinson Alpha with Duple Elizabethan bodywork (VS 6440). These two vehicles (along with UHH 877) are now long gone, but NHH 482 has survived and after a long hibernation in Herefordshire is now being restored by preservationists in Stoke-upon-Trent. By a strange coincidence this same preservation society also owns the more widely known Bedford SB5/Yeates Pegasus 951 UVT (ex-Beckett of Bucknall, PMT, and the Shetlands) and I hope to ride on both vehicles again before my mortal frame is sent to the human equivalent of Wombwell Diesels.

Going South

Returning from the dizzying heights of Cumberland and Westmorland to the flatlands of Cheshire, I should perhaps make brief mention of that unfortunate county's remaining independent bus operators. After Naylor sold out (it continued as a coach operator) these were all on a very modest scale. Reliance of Kelsall operated a Saturday evening service (two journeys) from Cotebrook to Chester which I never managed to sample due to the timings, although I visited their garage on several occasions. In the same part of the county Webster of Alvanley connected the railway stations at Helsby and Frodsham to the hilltop hospitals at Kingswood. Yes, there are a few hills in Cheshire, but not very many and not very big ones. As the Kingswood Hospitals were used in succession as tuberculosis sanatoriums and then as psychiatric institutions I was cowardly and decided to stay away.

In the far south of Cheshire, hard up against the Staffordshire boundary, Hollinshead of Scholar Green ran two stage services, a twice daily (Monday to Friday) route from Dales Green to Congleton and a Thursday only market run from Mow Cop to Sandbach. The former was originally restricted to mill-workers but began to carry members of the public during the Second World War. Its limited timings meant that most passengers went by the far more frequent PMT services from the Scholar Green area to Congleton. The Sandbach route was discontinued in 1964 and replaced by a local excursion.

And this, in a way, brings us back to the beginning of this personal reminiscence as Hollinshead also operated regular excursions to Pickmere Lake where I noted their fully-fronted Foden PVSC6/Metalcraft MMB 861 on multiple occasions in 1959-62. On weekdays the elderly Foden was the regular vehicle on the Congleton stage service and it is believed to survive in preservation although it has not been seen in public for a long time. A far more famous Hollinshead Foden, the rear-engined PVR/Metalcraft coach NTU 125, is roadworthy and a frequent attender at rallies. Connoisseur preservationist Roger Burdett has spent a fortune on this vehicle and deserves our gratitude and respect for saving such a rare and fascinating machine.

THE PIONEERING ERA

Some readers, especially those from the London area, might still believe the frequently repeated falsehood that George Shillibeer operated the first scheduled horse-bus service in the United Kingdom in 1829. This assertion has been made by many writers who should really know better and the claim is without any justification whatsoever. In fact, Manchester had already been enjoying regular horse-bus services for five years before Shillibeer began operations in London. The pioneering John Greenwood company in Manchester (in a sense the very first North West independent) was soon joined by others which contributed to a comprehensive network across the city, doing so for almost 70 years until superseded by corporation-owned trams.

The beginning of the 20th century brought the motor-bus to the region. Most of the early examples were conversions of petrol powered car and lorry chassis, but steam powered buses were chosen by a small minority of operators, including the Lake District Road Traffic Co which used at least one Clarkson in the Windermere area. The superiority of the internal combustion engine soon became apparent.

The Railway Company services

As elsewhere in the country, railway operators had a significant share of the earliest motor-bus services. The GWR began a cross-border route from its railhead at Wrexham to several Cheshire villages in 1904 and would later operate a service from a selection of the better hotels in central Liverpool to its railway station at Woodside in Birkenhead. The bus and its passengers crossed the Mersey estuary on a ferry boat until the opening of the railway tunnel under the river made the service obsolete. The new train service was operated by the Mersey Railway which duly established a network of motor-bus feeder services to bring Wirral-dwelling commuters to its Birkenhead Central station.

In 1905 the Great Central Railway started a bus service from 'Mottram' station (actually located in the neighbouring village of Broadbottom – a name that the GCR apparently found unacceptable) to Mottram, Hollingworth, and Tintwistle. This service eventually passed to the North Western Road Car Co which extended it at the Broadbottom end to Charlesworth in Derbyshire.

The Lancashire & Yorkshire Railway also tried its hand at bus services in the region. In 1907 they started a feeder route to their Liverpool to Southport railway line, connecting the stations at Blundellsands, Crosby, and Thornton. This was less well used than had been imagined and before the end of the year the vehicles were transferred to Chorley to operate a new bus service to Whittle-le-Woods and Bamber Bridge. The Chorley operation lasted until 1911.

A more unusual railway bus service could be found upon the shores of Lake Windermere. The Furness Railway operated a steamboat service along the lake, starting at Lakeside station at the southern end and sailing along the full length to Ambleside in the north via Bowness. This service made a substantial profit from tourist patronage in the summer months, but made a correspondingly substantial loss during the winter. The railway decided to place its steamboats into storage for the colder half of each year and to substitute a boat-replacement bus service. This was operated by railway owned vehicles in the winters of 1920/1 and 1921/2, but in April 1922 the railway abandoned its 'in house' operation in favour of an arrangement with the Lake District Road Traffic Co – at that time the second largest bus operator in the region with a fleet of Thornycroft char-a-bancs.

Independent Pioneers

The Lake District company had actually been established in January 1904, several months before the GWR began its service into Cheshire from Wrexham. Founded by Bruce Rigg, the company started operations with a fleet of three small Thornycroft char-a-bancs (EC 109/115/116) in the spring of 1905. These vehicles, along with a larger Clarkson steam-bus (EC 131), opened the company's premier route from Windermere station to Grasmere via Bowness and Ambleside. The service was an instant success as tourists raised in the horse-drawn era flocked to sample the newfangled horseless carriages. As ever, success brought imitation and various small companies soon emerged to operate motor-buses along the shores of the other major lakes.

Penrith & District Motor Services began operations from its home town to the western shore of Ullswater in 1906, offering joint bus/boat ticketing with the Ullswater Navigation & Transit steamboat concern. After the bankruptcy of the Penrith & District company in 1916 the bus element of this joint offering was taken over by Armstrong & Siddle of Penrith, founded by two Penrith hoteliers who already operated char-a-bancs along the lake for their own guests along with a courtesy service to Penrith railway station. Their enterprise would become the major independent bus operator in the Penrith area with trunk routes to Carlisle and Appleby.

Independents were also emerging in central Lancashire, depending on workers and shoppers for their custom rather than tourists. In 1910 James Hodson of Gregson Lane (a village as well as a road) began a service from Hoghton to Preston via Gregson Lane, Higher Walton, and Walton-le-Dale. Hodson prospered and by 1919 was operating a double-deck fleet of Karriers and Leylands. Meanwhile the British Electric Traction group (through its subsidiary BAT) was

One of the second batch of The Lake District Road Traffic Co's Thornycroft char-a-bancs, EC 224 (delivered in 1906), is seen here in Kendal awaiting its departure to Keswick. A similar, unidentified, vehicle is parked behind and both are well-loaded with cheerful customers. *(M Jones Collection)*

This Great Central Railway Milnes-Daimler single-decker (which appears to be registered N 1154) was the regular performer on their service from the GCR station in Broadbottom to Mottram and Hollingworth. This started in 1905 and was later revived by North Western, eventually becoming the western portion of SELNEC/Greater Manchester Transport's circular services 392/393. The Broadbottom to Mottram section is currently served by Stott's Optare Solos on route 341. *(M Jones Collection)*

The Manchester District Motor Omnibus Company started operations in March 1906 and was bankrupt before the end of that year. Their Milnes-Daimler double-decker H 1962 is seen here in a 'posed' shot at an unknown location. The postcard's original caption proclaims it to be the 'First double-decker bus in Manchester', which may or may not be true as the corporation took delivery of three Leyland-Crossleys in the same year. *(M Jones Collection)*

also planning to start operations into the Preston area and decided that the acquisition of Hodson's company would provide a perfect basis for such a venture. James Hodson & Son became Ribble Motor Services and by 1922 was operating frequent services from Preston to Blackburn (via three different routes), Chorley, Ormskirk, and Southport; and from Chorley to Blackburn, Bolton (via Westhoughton), Horwich, and Wigan. By then Hodson's pioneering route had been extended through to Blackburn and had somehow become services 7/7A - route number 1 was given to the Preston-Chorley run.

A few miles to the south of Preston John Fishwick had left his job with the Lancashire Steam Motor Co of Leyland (later better known as Leyland Motors) to start his own business in 1907. For the first four years this was mainly a haulage firm, but in common with many other hauliers at that time Fishwick saw that a flat-bed lorry could easily be converted into a primitive bus and make money at weekends when not required for goods traffic. In 1911 he began a timetabled bus service between Leyland and Eccleston, and while this was not a huge success the service from Leyland to Preston which soon followed was. Unlike Hodson, Fishwick and his descendants vigorously defended their independence, and as a result the company is still with us a century later and still providing the majority of services between Leyland and Preston.

Back in Cumberland one transport entrepreneur attempted to negotiate a middle way between the instant capitulation of James Hodson and the enduring stubbornness of John Fishwick. In August 1912 Henry Meageen founded the Whitehaven Motor Service Co to provide bus services along the Cumberland coast. The company was moderately successful but found it hard to raise further capital for expansion. Somebody suggested that Meageen should contact the BET Group and its subsidiary British Automobile Traction as they might be willing to help. After a short period of negotiation it was agreed that the company should change its name to Cumberland Motor Services (to reflect a wider ambition) and that BAT would acquire a 50% share in the restructured enterprise. Meageen would remain as Chairman and thus have the casting vote in the event of any disagreement with BAT/BET. It seemed like a very good deal.

Buoyed up by the financial input of his new allies in London, Meageen soon wanted to expand beyond the Cumberland littoral. In July 1925 he formed a separate limited company, Westmorland Motor Services, to acquire the assets of the trailblazing Lake District Road Traffic Co and two smaller operators in the county. To clinch this deal he needed further capital and shares in Westmorland were offered via what would now be called an Initial Public Offering. Meageen was delighted to see his allies at BET buying shares in the new company, but less delighted when he realised that they were acquiring far more shares than he could afford to buy himself. Nevertheless, he retained two seats on Westmorland's board, had the funding to extend LDRT's established main-line to run all the way from Keswick to Lancaster via Grasmere, Ambleside, Windermere and Kendal, and began to plan further geographical expansion. In February 1926 the company acquired two operators in the Lancaster area and renamed itself Lancashire & Westmorland Motor Services Ltd.

At this point somebody at BET/BAT (probably WS Wreathall, who was also a director of Ribble) decided that Meageen's semi-independent empire needed to be quarantined before it became any larger. In August 1926, without any warning, the London-based conglomerate acquired almost all of L&WMS's previously unissued shares, giving it outright control of the company. Meageen appointees were swiftly marginalised and the Lancashire & Westmorland company began to take its instructions from Ribble executives. In December 1927 it was merged into Ribble, taking the Preston company's routes all the way to Keswick where they connected directly with those of Meageen's Cumberland Motor Services for the first time.

Meageen was forced to eat even more humble pie by his nominal allies. Armstrong & Siddle of Penrith had approached Cumberland Motor Services in 1925 and again in 1926, offering to sell them the company as not that much money

Left: H 4208 was another Milnes-Daimler double-decker and is shown here while operating for Frank Clayton of Offerton on his Marple-Offerton-Stockport service. This ran from 1908 until 1912. The presence of a branch of the Whaley Bridge Co-operative Society at the rear of the vehicle suggests that it is on a private hire into Derbyshire, and the fact that Margaret Jones found the postcard original at a collectors' fair in Buxton seems to support this theory. *(M Jones Collection)*

was being made and Tom Siddle was anxious to retire. Meageen had turned them down on both occasions as he thought the asking price was far too high. Negotiations began for a third time in June 1927 and according to one insider (an elderly CMS inspector) it appears that Meageen had been given the impression that A&S would be his reward for showing good grace over the loss of Lancashire & Westmorland. The amazing thing is that he believed it.

What happened in the real world was a repeat of the previous situation. A&S was acquired by CMS in the spring of 1928 (along with the business of George Taylor, another important Penrith operator) and a new company was soon created to acquire the assets from Cumberland. The new company issued £16,250 of shares, of which £15,000 was taken up by BAT (in its own new incarnation as Tilling & British), £750 by the Meageen interests, and £500 by A&S co-founder Fred Armstrong. In due course the inevitable happened. Meageen was frozen out again and Armstrong & Siddle was merged into Ribble. It could easily be inferred that Ribble's relentless expansion was also meant to include Cumberland Motor Services, to give the Preston company almost complete domination over North West England, but this would never occur as the Meageens had become both vexed and defiant. Nonetheless they were still making a lot of money from their alliance with the BET Group which must have eased the pain.

Monopoly Money

In the latter half of the 1920s it became obvious that the four major railway companies were preparing to invest enormous amounts of money into the bus industry, determined to exercise enough influence to render the new sector incapable of genuine competition with their own services. The two leading private enterprise owners of bus companies, the Tilling group (with its foundations in the horse-bus trade) and BET (originally created by investors in the Brush electrical engineering group to promote new tramways as a market for their products), were relatively under-capitalised in comparison to the all-powerful railways and feared that they might be ruined if the 'Big Four' rail operators made a concerted effort to drive them off the road.

A dreadful compromise was reached in 1928. Tilling's investments in the bus industry (with a few exceptions) would be combined with those of the BET Group's British Automobile Traction subsidiary. There was already an interaction between the two bus giants as Tilling had co-operated with BET in several parts of the country to rationalise their separate holdings into single companies (East Kent being one example), and Tilling had also taken a minority interest in BAT itself. BAT's parent company, BET, retained direct control of several bus companies which were burdened with tramway debt (which Tilling had no intention of sharing), but most of the bus companies controlled by both groups were transferred to the new holding company Tilling & British Automobile Traction Ltd.

In most parts of England and Wales (outside of London and the inner Home Counties) Tilling & British now controlled almost all of the inter-urban and rural bus services and thus became a (potentially) more powerful threat to the railways' plans if the Big Four decided to opt for direct confrontation. Faced with this *'fait accompli'* the railways agreed to a bloodless compromise. They would abandon their tentative plans to become large-scale bus operators and in return were allowed to buy 50% of the shares of each of the bus operating subsidiaries of the Tilling & British company and of several major operators still owned separately by either Tilling or BET. The chairmanship of each subsidiary would remain in the hands of the bus companies, giving either Tilling or BET (depending on the original ownership) the casting vote in the event of major disagreements between the 50/50 owners.

From the railways' viewpoint it was an acceptable arrangement (despite the ultimate lack of control) on several counts. Firstly, they gained the expertise of people who already knew how to run profitable bus services, a completely different proposition to running a railway business. Secondly, they gained a geographically diverse portfolio of investments in an industry with consistently higher profit margins than their own. And thirdly, with the 1930 Road Traffic Act already being written by legislators, they could present a united front against all other applicants for Road Service Licences. As the Big Four were, by nature, overgrown bullies who preferred weaker targets to stronger ones, the concept of 'all

The front cover of the January 1929 edition of Armstrong & Siddle's timetable, showing an unidentified Albion – one of several acquired in 1926/7. The company had newer vehicles it might have displayed but used the same photograph for several years. The colour scheme of the vehicles was dark green and cream. *(Malcolm Wheatman Collection)*

Kirkby Stephen—Appleby—Penrith—Carlisle.

Depart.	a.m.	a.m.	a.m.	p.m.	p.m.	p.m.	p.m.	p.m.	p.m.	p.m.	p.m.	p.m.	p.m.	p.m.	p.m.
									Sat	S		S	S	S	S
Kirkby Stephen	7-0	8-50	...	12-15	...	2-0	...	4-15	6-0	...	...	1-0	...	6-0	...
Winton ...	7-9	...	...	...	...	2-9	...	4-20	6-9	...	...	1-9	...	6-9	...
Brough Sowerby	7-15	9-0	...	12-25	...	2-15	...	4-27	6-15	...	...	1-15	...	6-15	...
Brough ...	7-20	9-5	...	12-30	...	2-20	...	4-32	6-20	...	...	1-20	...	6-20	...
Warcop ...	7-35	9-20	...	12-45	...	2-35	...	4-47	6-35	...	...	1-35	...	6-35	...
Coupland Beck	7-45	9-30	...	12-55	...	2-45	...	4-57	6-45	...	...	1-45	...	6-45	...
Appleby ...	7-55	9-40	11-0	1-5	2-0	2-55	4-10	5-5	6-55	9-50	1-0	1-55	5-30	6-55	7-35
Crackenthorpe	8-5	9-50	11-10	1-10	2-10	3-5	4-20	5-15	7-5	9-57	1-10	2-5	5-40	7-5	7-45
Bolton ...	8-12	9-57	11-17	1-17	2-17	3-12	4-27	5-22	7-12	...	1-17	2-12	5-47	7-12	7-52
Kirkbythore	8-20	10-5	11-25	1-25	2-25	3-20	4-35	5-30	7-20	10-3	1-25	2-20	5-55	7-20	8-0
Temple Sowerby	8-27	10-12	11-32	1-32	2-32	3-27	4-42	5-37	7-27	10-10	1-32	2-27	6-2	7-27	8-7
Culgaith R. E.	8-30	10-15	11-35	1-35	2-35	3-30	4-45	5-40	7-30	10-12	1-35	2-30	6-5	7-30	8-10
Whinfell School	8-37	10-22	11-42	1-42	2-42	3-37	4-52	5-47	7-37	10-17	1-42	2-37	6-12	7-37	8-17
Carlton ...	8-47	10-28	11-48	1-48	2-48	3-47	4-58	5-57	7-47	10-23	1-48	2-47	6-18	7-47	8-27
Penrith ...	8-50	10-30	11-50	1-50	2-50	3-50	5-0	6-0	7-50	10-30	1-50	2-50	6-20	7-50	8-30
									Sat						
Carlisle ...	...	10-0	11-30	1-15	3-0	4-15	6-0	6-0	7-0	9-0	11-30	3-30	6-30	8-0	11-0	11-0

Sat—Saturdays. **S**—Sundays. Appleby Depot G. S. Evans, Market Place.
Kirkby Stephen Depot, Armstrong's Café, Market Place.

The timetable for Armstrong & Siddle's Kirkby Stephen to Penrith service makes no mention of the fact that passengers had to change at Penrith (often with lengthy waiting times before the connection) if they wished to continue to Carlisle. *(Malcolm Wheatman Collection)*

Penrith—Lazonby—Kirkoswald.

Depart.	a.m.	a.m.	a.m.	a.m.	p.m.	p.m.	p.m.	p.m.	p.m.	p.m.
		T	DT	T		TS		Sat	S	S
Penrith ...	7-5	9-0	9-15	10-30	1-30	3-20	5-0	9-0	1-0	6-0
BeaconEdge	7-10	9-5	9-20	10-35	1-35	3-25	5-5	9-5	1-5	6-5
Golf Course ...	7-15	9-10	9-25	10-40	1-40	3-30	5-10	9-10	1-10	6-10
Maiden Hill ...	7-20	9-15	9-30	10-45	1-45	3-35	5-15	9-15	1-15	6-15
Salkeld North Dykes	7-30	9-25	9-40	10-55	1-55	3-45	5-25	9-25	1-25	6-25
Salkeld South Dykes	7-35	9-30	9-45	11-0	2-0	3-50	5-30	9-30	1-30	6-30
Great Salkeld ...	7-37	9-32	9-47	11-2	2-2	3-52	5-32	9-32	1-32	6-32
Lazonby ...	7-47	9-42	9-57	11-12	2-12	4-2	5-42	9-42	1-42	6-42
Kirkoswald ...	7-52	9-45	10-2	11-15	2-17	4-5	5-45	9-45	1-45	6-45
*Melmerby ...	...	...	10-30	...	2-45	...	...	...	...	...

T—Tuesdays. **DT**—Daily except Tuesday. **TS**—Tuesdays and Saturdays.
Sat—Saturday. **S**—Sunday. *****—Thursdays only.

The Penrith to Kirkoswald and Melmerby service was less frequent, but still impressive by today's standards. There were no evening journeys, however, even in 1929. *(Malcolm Wheatman Collection)*

other applicants' was in practice applied to small, vulnerable independents rather than to municipally owned operators which had the resources to fight Tilling & British in the Traffic Courts.

Independent bus-men referred to this unholy alliance between the railways and the bus groups as 'The Combine' and, true to its nickname, it harvested them like wheat in a field. As recorded in my earlier book 'Independent Buses in North Wales' Crosville Motor Services (which had joined the Tilling & British consortium after a brief spell of direct ownership by the LM&S Railway) was particularly ruthless and energetic in its extermination of potential competitors. In the North West of England the other three Combine affiliates operating in the region, Cumberland,

Ribble, and North Western, were less gung ho and (as a rule) preferred to agree a generous price with a willing vendor rather than to cajole, undermine, and threaten their competitors into a sullen acquiescence born of the fear of imminent ruin.

Cumberland Motor Services

The Meageen family continued to be the major force at CMS, despite the dilution of their shareholdings occasioned by the agreement between the bus groups and the Big Four. Uniquely amongst the Combine subsidiaries, the shares of CMS were split evenly between three parties rather than just two with the founding family retaining a third of the equity plus the chairmanship. Henry Meageen and his son Tom spent the next twenty years playing an elaborate game of metaphorical chess with the other shareholders, deliberately pitching the railways' interests against those of the bus groups to ensure that his one third share would always be crucial in key decisions. As one might expect, he also displayed little (if any) enthusiasm for the Combine's 'Engulf and Devour' policy towards independent operators.

Between 1929 and 1942 (when the ruling triumvirate at BET decided that they could no longer share a board-room with Tilling's authoritarian Frederick Heaton, even if there was a War in progress in the outside world) CMS acquired less than a dozen businesses and none of those acquisitions involved more than eight buses. Several had just a single vehicle. Meageen's reluctance to go out of his way to make any purchases (Blair & Palmer would have been an obvious target) was further accentuated by the fact that there were so few potential acquisitions to be found. CMS had already become a virtual monopoly in its home area on the Cumberland coast simply by waiting for its rivals to abandon any hope of a reasonable return on their investment. There were very few money-making routes in western Cumberland and CMS had made most of them its own long before any competition had arrived on the scene.

A classic example of Meageen's lack of commitment to the Combine's policy can be found in his company's purchase (in 1936) of the business of Smith & Rose of Penrith. This operator held the licence for the only direct route between Penrith and Wigton – potentially a profitable service at that time – but within a year Meageen had decided that he couldn't be bothered, especially as Ribble was demanding a share in the service. He passed the route voluntarily (and for a token amount) to the well-known independent operator Ernie Hartness. Such behaviour would have been unthinkable elsewhere in the Combine.

Ribble Motor Services

Ribble, on the other hand, was voraciously acquisitive even before the railway money poured into the company. During Major HE Hickmott's long tenure at the top Ribble's intention was unmistakable – to become the major operator of bus services all the way from Carlisle in the north to the Lancashire coalfields in the south. This ambition accepted, Ribble (in most cases) treated its independent competitors in a far more ethical way than a company such as Crosville did. In general, if a company had been operating in an area before Ribble's arrival on the scene its rights to the traffic were respected. Hickmott would do his best to persuade an operator to sell out, but he would not apply undue pressure to force the issue.

Any company which started its services after those of Ribble was seen as fair game and was pursued in an utterly ruthless manner. The moral justification for this schizophrenic attitude seemed to be that the operator who was there first had first claim to the traffic. If that was John Fishwick in Leyland or Pennine Motor Services in the Yorkshire Dales they would be accorded respect and invited to enter joint working arrangements. If it was Ribble then God help anyone who tried to steal the company's gold.

Hickmott, however, was no saint. He was heavily involved in the BET Group's decision to take Lancashire & Westmorland and then Armstrong & Siddle away from Henry Meageen and acted in quite a scurrilous and dishonest fashion during the events which led to the two companies' absorption by Ribble. If he were still alive he might justify his actions by claiming that he was only following orders from above, but Hickmott really, desperately, wanted Ribble to reach the Scottish border.

Apart from the Hodson business which metamorphosed into Ribble itself the company's first few purchases were relatively modest. A small Preston area operator was acquired in 1923 and another in June 1925. Between these two (in April 1925) Hickmott paid a rather inflated price for the Chorley Auto Co and its affiliate Parsons Motors, increasing its already considerable presence in the Chorley area. In December 1925 Ribble strengthened its position in the Blackburn area by acquiring the stage-carriage routes of KCR Services. KCR continued as a coach operator with valuable licences for express services to Blackpool, but these would also pass to Ribble a few years later. Another Blackburn operator, Lancashire Industrial Motors (trading as 'Pendle Motors') was taken over in September 1926, bringing important routes to Burnley and Clitheroe.

Pilot Motors of Preston was the other important acquisition of that year, being taken over in October 1926. The company had recently irritated Ribble by taking over Castle Motors of Garstang in July and thereby creating a through route from Preston to Lancaster in advance of Ribble's own planned route which began in September. Pilot was also active to the west of Preston and the agreed price of more than £40,000 (more than a million in today's money) reflected Ribble's desire to consolidate its position in the important Preston-Lancaster and Preston-Blackpool corridors. Unfortunately for Ribble, while Pilot's former owners had been bound by a 'no compete' clause its former employees could not be similarly bound and soon established a new company, Empress Motors, to operate rival services on many of the Pilot routes. Ribble then became very nasty indeed, feeling that they had somehow been cheated.

The purchase of Pilgrim Motors of Elswick in July 1927 added more routes on the Fylde peninsula to Ribble's timetable, but the major event of that year was the acquisition of Lancashire & Westmorland Motor Services in December. The less than transparent methods used to produce this result have already been mentioned. The transfer of the company into Ribble's hands extended its network northwards from Lancaster to Keswick and also gave Ribble a dominant position in the Lancaster to Morecambe market, where L&WMS had acquired important routes from Lancaster & District Tramways and Fahy's Ltd.

The acquisitions continued at breakneck speed. Others in 1927 included Collingwood Motors of Liverpool (a coach operator), the stage-carriage services of William Webster of Wigan (jointly with Lancashire United), and Belford Services of Darwen. The Belford purchase included a substantial fleet of Karriers and Vulcans and a well-patronised route from Blackburn to Darwen and Bolton which would become the foundation for Ribble's much-photographed 215/225 trunk services.

In January 1928 Ribble established a significant presence in the Liverpool area by acquiring Waterloo & Crosby Motor Services, while the purchase of the Eccleston Motor Company in August added to the company's critical mass in the area between Preston and Wigan. In the previous month a substantial shareholding had been acquired in County Motors of Lancaster, but overall control of the company was not achieved until February 1929. County was a major player in its home city with both local services and longer routes to Kirkby Lonsdale, Preston, and Skipton. The purchase price remains unrecorded in the public domain, but must have exceeded £50,000 (again, more than a million today). Unusually for Ribble, County Motors was retained as a subsidiary until December 1930, mainly so that it could be used to do the company's dirty work such as driving other companies out of business without causing a general outcry against London-controlled monopolies.

On April Fool's Day in 1929 the firm of Armstrong & Siddle of Penrith officially passed from Cumberland to Ribble control. Members of the Meageen family might well have taken offence at the date chosen for the transfer given the background to the event. As well as its extensive territory around Penrith A&S had acquired the former Carlisle & Country (de Melo) Carlisle-Penrith route whilst under Cumberland control and this would result in Ribble finally achieving its goal of reaching the border city. The company's presence in Carlisle was consolidated later in the year by the purchase of a small local operator (Adair), setting the stage for the far more important events of 1931.

The company was also on the take-over trail at the southern end of its empire. In December 1929 it bought Ideal Omnibus Services and Imperial Motor Services, more than doubling its presence in the Liverpool area. Early in the following year it also acquired the large Merseyside Touring Co (which despite its name operated a network of local routes as well as coach services) and its

Lancashire Industrial Motors of Blackburn (trading as Pendle Motors) took delivery of CB 6065, a 32-seat AEC 413, in March 1926 as fleet number 36. The Pendle operation was sold to Ribble six months later and the AEC became Ribble's fleet number 214. They sold it to the Merseyside Touring Company (itself about to be swallowed up by Ribble and Liverpool Corporation) in 1930. *(Roy Marshall Collection)*

Belford Bus Service of Darwen liked Vulcans but did not live long or prosper. TE 642 was a 32-seat VWBL, one of six delivered in the first half of 1927 for the company's trunk service from Blackburn to Bolton. At the end of that year Belford sold out to Ribble and the Vulcan became their fleet number 449. In 1931 it was sold to Bethesda Greys, passing with that company to Crosville in January 1932. *(Roy Marshall Collection)*

This normal control Leyland, EC 4640, was delivered to the Kendal Motor Bus Co in early 1923. It had gone before the Ribble take-over and its subsequent fate is unknown. *(Senior Transport Archive)*

Kendal displayed the letter 'K' prominently on the front of their vehicles, positioned on the radiator grille in the case of all-Leyland PLSC1 Lion EC 6916, fleet number 17. It was new in April 1926 and after the take-over became Ribble fleet number C910. The vehicle is seen here at Dalton Square in Lancaster with conductor Mathew Wilson and driver Jack Creighton, the father of the contributor. *(Ian Creighton Collection)*

And here's Lion EC 6916 again, in a Leyland Motors pre-deliver shot. Although a crisper photograph and showing the nearside arrangement of entrance and bonnet, it somehow lacks the atmosphere of the previous image. *(Senior Transport Archive)*

Kendal switched from Leyland to Thornycroft in 1928. EC 8757 (fleet number 30) was one of a pair of Thornycroft BCs with Northern Counties bodywork delivered in April 1929. In April 1930 it became Ribble's C922. *(Senior Transport Archive)*

17

A Leyland Motors shot of the Furness Omnibus Co's all-Leyland PLSC1 Lion TE 2901, delivered in February 1928. It passed with the company to Ribble in May 1930 as their fleet number 956. In 1939 it was sold to Crosville as fleet number A32 and three years later became a mobile staff canteen. *(Roy Marshall Collection)*

Another Leyland Motors image, showing Dallas Services fleet number 23 (APL 551) without a registration plate. The vehicle was an SKP5 Cub (built at Leyland's factory in Kingston, Surrey) with a 32-seat Burlingham body. Initially used as a demonstrator (hence the Surrey registration), it passed to Dallas in 1934. *(Roy Marshall Collection)*

associate Nor-West Bus Services. The size of this acquisition is reflected in the purchase price of £120,000 – by comparison Waterloo & Crosby and Ideal had each cost less than £20,000 while Imperial had changed hands for a paltry £1,250.

The remainder of Ribble's 1930 purchases were widely scattered but each gave added bulk to the company's body of services. The largest acquisition outside of Liverpool was that of the Rishton & Antley Motor Co in March for £45,000. The purchase price included important routes to the north and east of Blackburn, some of them recently acquired from the Calder Motor Co, and 42 vehicles. Because of potential licensing difficulties (Blackburn Council was beginning to worry about Ribble's increasingly monopolistic position) Rishton & Antley was maintained as a separate company until September 1930 and in the interim period acquired the Claremont Omnibus company with another seven vehicles.

Meanwhile, Ribble had gone to war in the Preston area, doing its best to crush an alliance of Empress Motors (the company founded by former Pilot employees) and Majestic Motors (owned by local councillor Matthew Wade who was no friend to Ribble's ambitions). The two operators had been challenging Ribble on key routes such as those from Preston to Blackburn via Hoghton, to Blackpool via Kirkham and Wrea Green, to Lancaster via Garstang, and to Longridge. Ribble threw every asset it possessed into the conflict, deploying County Motors vehicles on the Lancaster route to act as 'chasers' and cutting fares remorselessly until the two upstarts were on the edge of bankruptcy. Both still refused to sell out to the hated Ribble and eventually, in April 1930, a deal was brokered whereby the two firms would be acquired by the LM&S Railway which, in due course, would sell the assets on to Ribble itself. Despite the use of County Motors for the dirtier parts of the war, few in Preston were deceived by the ploy, and Ribble's reputation in the Preston area suffered badly.

With Empress and Majestic gone the company's gaze again turned northwards, resulting in the acquisition of the Kendal Motor Bus Co in April 1930 and the Furness Omnibus Co of Ulverston in May. The former, widely known as the 'K' company (the letter was displayed prominently on the radiators and front domes of its vehicles), had started operations just after the end of the First World War and had competed in turn with the Lake District Road Traffic Co, Westmorland Motor Services, Lancashire & Westmorland, and Ribble on the important routes from Kendal to Grange-over-Sands, Grasmere, Kirkby Lonsdale, Lancaster, and Newby Bridge. By the end of 1929 Major Hickmott had received reports that the directors of Kendal, disillusioned by the lack of profits, were squabbling like cats in a sack. He offered them just over £20,000 and they took the money and ran. The Furness company was in better financial condition, offered access to Barrow-in-Furness among its attractions, and its shareholders received £45,000 from Ribble. With the acquisition of these two operators the network of Ribble services to the north of Morecambe Bay was largely completed in a form familiar to those of us born after the Second World War.

Later in 1930 Ribble acquired Brunshaw Motors of Burnley in October and Freeman's Services of Chorley in November. Freeman's had already been in receivership once, resulting in its ownership transferring from the eponymous Freemans to the Green family, and seemed incapable of making a profit out of its trunk route from Chorley to Bolton. Its fourteen vehicle fleet included a Leyland TD1 double-decker. The Freeman's purchase was made jointly with Bolton Corporation and, as an indirect consequence, municipal double-deckers would later become a frequent sight on the marathon 122 service from Bolton to Southport, via Chorley and a selection of sleepy Lancashire villages which had never seen a corporation bus before.

The New Year of 1931 started with the introduction of the 1930 Road Traffic Act and a national system for the licensing of bus services. Existing operators (however large) had to apply for Road Service Licences and hearings to approve these – or not - began in March. In common with most of its Tilling & British sister companies Ribble held its fire on the acquisition front, waiting to see who would receive licences to avoid throwing good money after bad. One exception was made with the purchase of Lawrence Motor Services of Fleetwood in January 1931. It is believed that this deal had been arranged in the last quarter of 1930 but not finalised until the New Year. The attraction had been several local services in the Fleetwood and

Cleveleys area and a garage from which to service them along with Ribble's existing trunk services to Preston via Kirkham.

The Carlisle Joint Transaction

The temporary cessation of acquisitions finally ended in November 1931 when Ribble became a party to the Carlisle Joint Transaction. To cut a very long story short, by 1930 the city was being served by a tramway network which had seen better days (and was owned by the Balfour Beatty group which wanted to close it as soon as possible), four Tilling & British companies (Caledonian, Cumberland, Ribble, and United), and no fewer than 47 independents (but with only 74 vehicles between them). Most of the independents were small – Wrexham style – one man bands, which had sprung up to cover for the inadequacies of the tram system and Balfour Beatty's unwillingness to spend any money on its refurbishment.

Not for the last time, the Northern Area Traffic Commissioners displayed a harsh attitude to small independents, completely contrary to the sympathy shown by their North West area counterparts to 'micro' operators in Wrexham. Many of the Carlisle one-man bands were discouraged from making licence applications in the first place, and others (including the alliance of small operators known as Carlisle & District Motor Services) were given the distinct impression that if they did apply, then they would be refused.

The eventual upshot of the situation was a pact (rubber-stamped by the Traffic Commissioners) whereby Ribble would become the predominant operator of local services, despite having only reached the city less than three years previously. The existing rights of the other three Tilling & British companies were preserved, and Balfour Beatty gladly made plans for its tramway to be closed and replaced by Ribble buses. The remaining Carlisle area independents who had persevered with their licence applications were offered generous payments for their businesses and most decided to accept the inevitable. Exceptions included Blair & Palmer and EL Proud of Ainstable who declined to give up their independence for what they saw as 'a mess of pottage'.

Consolidation

Elsewhere in the Ribble empire more transparent and morally defensible tactics continued to be the norm. It seemed almost as if the company considered the area to the north of Morecambe Bay to be some kind of 'Indian Territory' where its normal rules of civilised behaviour need not be applied. The independent sector, of course, also included some less than moral businessmen. Some had gone through the licensing procedures not to serve the public, but merely to obtain a higher price from Ribble and its corporate kin in the Combine.

Between the end of 1931 and the beginning of the Second World War in September 1939 no fewer than 17 independent stage-carriage operators were acquired by Ribble. The larger purchases included Dallas Services of Preston in July 1935 (with routes to Chorley, Croston, New Longton, and Whittingham), Cadman's Services of Orrell in August 1935 (acquired jointly with the corporations of St Helens and Wigan along with its fleet of Maudslays and important services from Wigan to Billinge, Ormskirk, Rainford, St Helens, and Southport), and the Yarrow Motor Co of Eccleston in April 1939 (operating from its home village to Chorley, Ormskirk, Preston, and Wigan, the latter two towns connected to each other by a through service).

Other interesting acquisitions included De Luxe of Preston in June 1935 (the only surviving independent competing with Ribble on the original Hodson route to Gregson Lane), the stage-carriage services of Leyland based operators Parkinson and Singleton (both acquired jointly with Fishwicks in August 1935), and Parker Bros Malhamdale Bus Service in February 1937 (jointly with Pennine of Gargrave). It should be noted that in the last three cases Ribble co-operated with local independents when making its purchases. Such behaviour would have been seen as treasonous at Crosville, but after the implementation of the 1930 Road Traffic Act Ribble had no problem with treating independents as equals. Both Fishwick and Pennine continued to have an excellent relationship with Ribble all the way through to deregulation in the 1980s.

Three further purchases were delayed until after the end of the war as any decisions made by the wartime authorities might have been overturned once power was returned to the

Singleton of Leyland's LT5A Lion bus TJ 5048 was new in May 1934 and carried bodywork by local company WH Fowler. When Singleton's stage-carriage services passed to Ribble and Fishwick in August 1935 the vehicles were not included in the deal. TJ 5048 passed from Singleton to Martindale of Ferryhill (County Durham) in April 1936 and was last licensed in 1951. *(Roy Marshall Collection)*

This 1931 Commer Invader, seen here minus its registration plate, was TF 4365 according to the inscription on the back of this manufacturer's view. It wears the full livery of (and an appropriate destination blind for) the Barley Omnibus Co, but is not listed in the fleet history of that company in PSV Circle records. Barley's stage services went to Ribble and Burnley in November 1945. *(Roy Marshall Collection)*

Enfield 30-seater B 2287 was new to the Mid-Cheshire company in 1914 and is seen here outside their Northwich garage. When Mid-Cheshire was taken over by North Western at the end of 1924 the vehicle was scrapped. *(Roy Marshall Collection)*

Mid-Cheshire's B 5741 was a 1914 Leyland, sold before the North Western take-over. The location of this shot is unknown, but the destination blind reads 'Pickmere' and the road could well be the present-day B5391 which runs through that area. *(Senior Transport Archive)*

Traffic Commissioners. Two of these, Jones of Newchurch-in-Pendle and the Barley Omnibus Co, operated a joint service to Nelson town centre from the villages on the side of Pendle Hill. Small vehicles were employed, the newest of these being Bedford OWB utility buses. The transaction was finally completed in November 1945 with the Burnley, Colne, and Nelson municipal undertaking paying half but receiving two vehicles (Ribble declined to take any) and the lion's share of the timings.

The third post-war acquisition was Head of Windermere, a one-vehicle operator which (in the pre-war era) had run a local route under the 'Magnet Bus Service' banner. As this route was primarily aimed at tourists it had been suspended for the duration of the war, but Mr Head had found alternative employment for his vehicle by operating works journeys to the facility which assembled and test-flew Sunderland flying boats on the lake. He finally sold out to Ribble in February 1946.

North Western Road Car Co

The BET Group's British Automobile Traction subsidiary established a 'branch' at Macclesfield in Cheshire in 1913 (using the fleet-name 'British') and ten years later this metamorphosed into North Western. By the beginning of 1924 the company had around six dozen buses, additional depots in Buxton and Stockport, and a route network which reached out to Crewe, Biddulph (in Staffordshire), Glossop and Matlock (both in Derbyshire) and to the various tram termini on the southern edge of the Manchester conurbation.

In most of its territory the atmosphere was more rural and in its early years British/North Western encountered little real competition. The unfortunate corollary of this was that the absence of competition reflected a lack of traffic and little room for further expansion. The company's directors decided to rectify this situation by making strategic acquisitions of existing businesses. The first to be purchased was the Mid-Cheshire Motor Bus Co of Northwich, in November 1924. Mid-Cheshire had been formed in 1914, principally to provide works services to the various chemical and salt extraction facilities in the Northwich area. In the intervals between works journeys the company's fleet operated irregular scheduled services available to the general public from Northwich to Knutsford, Sandbach, Warrington, and Winsford.

During the First World War Mid-Cheshire established a second base at Flixton, to the west of Manchester, and works services into the huge Trafford Park industrial complex were initiated along with 'public' routes from the Flixton and Urmston area to Eccles, Sale, Stretford, and Warrington. An infrequent service also ran from Northwich to Flixton via Mere, Lymm, and Carrington, more to facilitate rotation of vehicles for maintenance purposes than in any hope of an economically viable traffic flow. A total of 20 vehicles was transferred to North Western along with the two garages and the services. The Taylor family of Crosville was particularly annoyed about the acquisition, as they had been negotiating with Mid-Cheshire and had seen the Northwich company as their gateway to the Manchester area. As ever they were offering a relative pittance and their niggardliness had cost them this major opportunity.

The next purchase came in January 1926 when North Western acquired Altrincham District Motor Services. Founded in 1922 by a local businessman with interests in the furniture removal trade, ADMS had been a thorn in North Western's side for several years as it competed with them on the Altrincham to Stockport road. Its other services radiated from Altrincham to Knutsford, Warrington, and Wilmslow, and there was a high-frequency local circular to Timperley, operated in both directions. The purchase also included a sizeable garage and 26 vehicles, although the condition of these is reflected in the fact that more than half of them were scrapped within a year of the takeover.

As might be suggested by this narrative, North Western was considerably more selective in its purchases than Ribble which tended to buy anything that was for sale in the 'Wild West' days before the 1930 Road Traffic Act. Only one more company's stage services would be acquired by North Western before the Act came into force. Tetlow & Collier of Davyhulme competed with North Western on the (ex Mid-Cheshire) routes from Flixton and Urmston to Stretford where both operators connected with the Manchester tramway network. After the sale of its local services (and six vehicles) in March 1928 Tetlow & Collier continued as a coach operator for several more years before that part of the business was also sold to North Western.

In the days before national road service licensing the necessary authorisation to operate bus services came (in most cases) from local councils, as an extension of their existing powers to regulate taxis. Many of these municipalities operated their own tramway systems and were understandably reluctant to issue licences to competing bus services. Worse yet, they were under no legal obligation to do so and as a result the likes of Manchester City Council could ensure that all bus routes ended at the point where their own trams came into the picture. This restriction was particularly onerous to a company such as North Western, where possibly as much as half of its patronage came from passengers ultimately bound for Manchester city centre. Strangely, the solution to this problem came as a result of activities by independent operators as we shall see in the next section of this Introduction.

After the Road Traffic Act came into force in 1931 the pace of North Western's acquisitions increased markedly. Outside of the Manchester conurbation they acquired most of the services of Naylor's Motor Services of Stockton Heath in May 1932 (qv), Stelfox of Alderley Edge in June 1933 (with local services in the Wilmslow area), Norman Knowles of Congleton in March 1938 (local routes in Congleton), Firth & Kirkpatrick of Marple in August 1938 (operating locally and to Stockport), Thompson of Norley in July 1939 (with a service to Northwich), and the stage services of Edwin Bostock of Congleton in August 1939 (with a daily works service to Bollington and market day routes from assorted villages to Congleton, Macclesfield, and Sandbach).

There were also many other purchases in Derbyshire and Staffordshire, outside of the scope of this current volume, but the most important acquisitions not mentioned so far were of enterprising independent operators which had penetrated Manchester's tramway *cordon sanitaire*. In every case these acquisitions were made jointly with municipal transport departments and are best considered in that context.

The Municipal Factor

During the General Strike of 1926 municipally owned transport ceased to function and in Manchester (as in most major cities) local coach operators stepped in to provide an alternative for the duration. Many of these operators found the replacement services to be extremely lucrative and – when the trams returned – were reluctant to give the traffic back. Several of the local authorities which encircled the City of Manchester itself (particularly those without a vested interest in tramways) were sympathetic to such bus services and allowed them to continue, so all that was needed was a legal loophole to permit access to the city centre. The independents found this loophole in the 'return ticket' principle.

Briefly put, this arose from earlier legal cases where coach excursion operators had established that no licence need be sought in any jurisdiction which was merely a destination and within the boundaries of which no money changed hands for 'hire or reward'. In other words a coach operator from say, Nottingham, could run an excursion into Manchester city centre, drop his passengers off, and then return for them later, without a licence from the City Council – provided that the fare had been pre-paid outside of Manchester's territory. In theory both the drop-off and the pick-up could be made on the public highway, but given Manchester's hostility (and its control over its own police force in those days) it seemed advisable to use private property as a Manchester terminus to avoid trumped up charges of obstruction.

Once these legal principles had been examined and tested the independents flooded into the city centre and a host of 'bus stations' came into being on empty lots and at existing garages and filling stations all over the city centre. The most important (and busiest) of these was to be found at the northern end of Lena Street in a yard owned by the Rochdale Canal Company and catered for vehicles belonging to a full spectrum of independents. The popularity of Lena Street was partly due to its use by Sharp's Motor Services of Longsight (an inner city suburb). Sharp's had a small out-station on Lena Street (to the south of the Canal yard) and managed the facility on behalf of the waterways company.

Sharp's blue and cream buses operated 'return ticket' services into the city from Poynton and Woodford (both via Stockport) and from Winton (via Eccles). Other occupants of the Lena Street bus station circa 1930 were Cash of Urmston (operating brown and cream vehicles from Partington via Flixton and Urmston), Organ & Wachter of West Didsbury (operating from Styal

This long wheelbase Renault MV with a 32-seat Horsfield body is one of two (MB 9036/37) delivered to Altrincham & District Motor Services in 1925. At the end of that year the pair went to North Western as fleet numbers 47/8 but both were withdrawn and scrapped in 1928 when only three years old. *(Senior Transport Archive)*

Leyland SG5 MB 769 was new to the Altrincham company in 1922 and carried a Leyland body with 32 bus seats and removable side windows. It became North Western's fleet number 29 after the take-over, surviving until May 1929 when it was sold for conversion into a lorry. *(Senior Transport Archive)*

Tetlow & Collier ran from Flixton and Urmston to the Manchester Corporation tramway at Stretford, trading as Flixton & Urmston Services. This AEC Renown with a 30-seat United body, TD 4054, was new to them in 1925. Three years later it passed (with the services) to North Western as fleet number 137, but was withdrawn and scrapped only four years after it was built. *(Roy Marshall Collection)*

An unidentified Goodfellow Services Thornycroft stands at the Greenfield Street, Hyde, terminus of the company's service from that Cheshire town to Manchester. Behind it are two of the vehicles which operated the competing 'Co-ordinated Motor Bus Scheme' service 8 to Manchester and Bolton, Lancashire United LT1 Lion TE 6673, and an unidentified Manchester Corporation Crossley Six. *(GMTS Archive)*

via Gatley and Northenden using green and gold Gilfords), and Sykes Motor Tours of Sale (operating from Halebarns via Altrincham and Sale with yellow and cream Crossleys). As well as these local companies the Lena Street yard also played host to vehicles from further afield, such as Ripponden & District, along with excursion coaches from all over the North seeking protection from the Manchester Constabulary.

If (in 1930) you had headed south from Lena Street, crossed Piccadilly, and then turned right into Aytoun Street, you would have discovered the Auburn Street 'bus station' of Goodfellow Services – actually a filling station with room for up to four buses at a time. Ben Goodfellow had started a service from his native Hyde in 1927 and had originally shared the Auburn Street yard with two other 'return ticket' operators, Duignan of Denton and Coopwood Express which operated services from Bramhall and from Macclesfield via Alderley Edge and Wilmslow. The latter service was particularly galling to North Western which had been forced to terminate its own service from Macclesfield at the Cheadle tram terminus for many years. In December 1929 all three Auburn Street tenants merged to create Goodfellow Services (1930) Ltd with an impressive network to the east and south of the city operated by a fleet of grey and green Thornycrofts.

From the north Yelloway came into the city centre from Rochdale via Royton and the newly opened 'Broadway' arterial road, continuing a service inaugurated by its predecessor Holt Brothers in November 1927. Its orange and pale yellow vehicles used a yard at Goulden Street (close to the southern end of Oldham Road) as a city terminus, but this was too far from the central area to be satisfactory and Yelloway became the first of the independents to challenge the local police by operating what it called a 'mobile terminus'. This was basically a circuit of nominated stopping points in the city centre, chosen for the unlikelihood of causing anything approaching a genuine obstruction to other traffic. Seeing that Yelloway's vehicles were rarely molested by the city's police force, Sharp followed suit and began to operate across the city centre from Winton and Eccles to Poynton and Woodford, to the benefit of passengers from both directions.

On the western side of the city centre JR Tognarelli of Bolton used two separate yards close to Victoria Station (at Long Millgate and Mayes Street) for its services from Bolton via Farnworth, from Little Hulton via Walkden, Worsley, and Eccles, and from Chadderton. The stage services were only part of a portfolio of Tognarelli interests which included ice-cream manufacture, restaurants, haulage, char-a-banc hire, and an express service from Manchester to Glasgow. Tognarelli's buses were described in contemporary accounts as being 'lavender and silver', a colour scheme which is hard to reconcile with the few surviving black-and-white photographs. Readers over the age of 90 with good memories are invited to comment on this conundrum.

Another significant facility was to be found just off Cannon Street, in a garage yard known as the 'New Cannon Street Bus Station' – long since buried beneath the Arndale Centre. This terminus was shared by Foster & Seddon (which operated a service from Swinton and later became a chassis manufacturer after Foster's departure) and Orr's Motor Services of Little Lever. Thanks to the efforts of Ron Barton, John Holmes, and others at the Manchester Museum of Transport, the story of Orr's is more adequately recorded than most of the independents of this period.

Orr of Little Lever

HG (Harry) Orr opened a garage and filling station in Little Lever, to the south-east of Bolton, just after the First World War. During the 1926 General Strike he started a tramway replacement service from Prestwich (Guest Road) via Bury Old Road to Exchange Station in the city centre and this continued after the end of the strike, although transferring to private land as detailed above. Other services followed and by 1930 Orr was operating from Little Lever and Prestwich to Manchester (via both Bury New Road and Bury Old Road), from Little Lever to Bolton and to Ainsworth, and from Prestwich to Sedgeley Park.

Orr's first bus was a 20hp Vulcan (BN 4261) acquired new in June 1920, followed by a new Guy (TB 8316) in January 1922. A new Leyland, TC 7502, arrived in April 1924 and impressed Harry Orr enough to warrant the acquisition of a second of the marque, 26-seat BN 6966, from Bolton Corporation in February 1925. The success of the Manchester service resulted in an order for a new Leyland PLSC1 Lion and this materialised as TD

7780 in October 1926. Arrivals during 1927 were TD 8970 (a 32-seat Vulcan), TE 910 (a 14 seat Guy), TE 1271 (a 32-seat Guy), and multiple pre-owned Leyland 20-seater EC 5929 (new to Fein of Ambleside in 1925 and passing to Westmorland Motor Services, Lancashire & Westmorland, and Ribble in the tempestuous two years before its arrival in Little Lever).

Having cleared out most of the older stock, only two vehicles were delivered during 1928, both of them new. TE 5554 was a 35-seat Lion, and TE 5922 an AEC with a 32-seat body by Lewis & Crabtree. By comparison 1929 was a bumper year, seeing the purchase of five new saloons plus the company's first (and only) double-decker. The saloons were four Crossley Eagles (TE 6739/6740/8078/8079 with bodywork by Eaton/Northern Counties/Hickman/Roe respectively) and Manchester-registered AEC/Craven B32F VM 6005. The double-decker was open-staircase Leyland TD1 Titan TE 8365, a former demonstrator which had operated on loan to Manchester Corporation amongst others.

As can be seen from these details Orr's was a thriving concern with a viable route network and a modern fleet. And so were most of the other operators in the Greater Manchester area. Unfortunately, this did not prevent a ridiculous and strident black propaganda campaign by local councillors and the managers of municipal bus operations, who constantly slandered Harry Orr and his contemporaries as 'pirates' who operated vehicles in poor condition, employed drivers who were reckless, and failed to provide adequate insurance cover for their passengers. It was all nonsense in most cases and the travelling public knew it.

The Co-ordinated Motor Bus Services

Henry Mattinson, the General Manager of Manchester's municipal transport department in the late 1920s, had quickly realised that telling lies about his new competitors would not get rid of them. The public liked the 'return ticket' services and the only genuine way to claw back the lost revenue was to offer similar options under a municipal banner. Mattinson decided to give his own services a competitive edge by colluding with surrounding municipalities to create jointly operated routes which ran across the city centre. All of the area's municipalities agreed to participate in the scheme which got under way in earnest in the spring of 1928.

From the private sector, both North Western and Lancashire United signed up to Mattinson's vision. To give two examples of how they participated, North Western's existing service from Flixton to Stretford was not only allowed into the city centre for the first time, but became just one segment in an express service from Flixton to Stretford, Manchester, Rochdale, and Bacup, operated jointly by North Western and Manchester, and Rochdale corporations. The express service from Bolton to Manchester, started by Bolton, Salford, and Lancashire United in 1927 in an unsuccessful attempt to eliminate Tognarelli, was joined to the Manchester to Hyde express route commenced by Manchester and the SHMD Board as a response to Goodfellow's operations.

As part of the same package of rapprochement between Manchester Corporation and the North Western company, the NWRCC stage services from towns in Cheshire and Derbyshire were allowed across the city's boundaries for the first time 'by arrangement' but had to surrender all revenues for local journeys to the corporation. This sudden attack of generosity might also have been motivated by a vain hope that North Western would then 'see off' unauthorised intruders such as Sharp and Goodfellow, or might have been designed to dissuade the Tilling & British operator from following the independents' example and operating 'return ticket' services of their own from their new bus station at Lower Mosley Street.

To Mattinson's political masters it must have looked very impressive on paper, but the continued survival of all the major independents proved that it was ineffectual. The underlying intention had been to drive them off the road before the 1930 Road Traffic Act came into force and they obtained licences from the new Traffic Commissioners. All except Tognarelli (who had been the victim of a particularly brutal campaign of vilification and had sold out to LUT and the corporations of Bolton, Manchester, Oldham, and Salford in December 1929) lasted long enough to get their licences, although Cash of Urmston was disappointed by the frequency restrictions imposed upon his service and subsequently gave up in disgust.

Tognarelli used this 1928 Harrington-bodied TS1 Tiger coach, WH 1299, on the express services advertised above the side windows. After Tognarelli sold out at the end of 1929 it went to Bolton Corporation and was converted into a 32-seat bus as fleet number 4. It was withdrawn from service in 1938. *(John Holmes Collection)*

This 1929 ADC 426, WH 1441, also carried advertising for Tognarelli's express services but was in fact a 32-seat bus with Burlingham bodywork, used on the local services from Manchester to Bolton, Chadderton, and Little Hulton. After the take-over it went to Oldham Corporation as fleet number 58, lasting until 1934 when it was sold to a dealer. *(John Holmes Collection)*

Meanwhile, the writing was appearing on the wall for Mattinson's grand plan. Ironically enough, it was a pronouncement by the city's own police force which provided its final kiss of death. The police had been concerned for some time about congestion in the Market Street area of the city centre, mainly caused by slow-moving and inflexible trams, but made even worse by the sudden surge of 'Co-ordinated' buses en route from one side of the conurbation to another. Similar concerns had dictated that North Western's new coach station would be built at Lower Mosley Street, well to the south of the city centre, so that inbound vehicles from the north had alternative routes to Market Street on their approach to the terminus.

Technically, it's a terrible photograph (even after computer enhancement), but it does present a mystery. Why is Orr's fleet number 15 (TD1 Titan TE 8365) back at the Leyland factory and operating on trade plates but carrying a full load of passengers? And what was the occasion being celebrated by the decorations and the crowds? The vehicle later passed to Bury Corporation and had its staircase enclosed by Massey. *(GMTS Archive)*

An atmospheric shot of Orr's 1929 Northern Counties-bodied Crossley Eagle TE 6740 (fleet number 13), leaving the New Cannon Street bus station in Manchester for Prestwich. *(Ron Barton Collection)*

Another of Orr's vehicles, a Leyland Lion, reverses on to its stand at New Cannon Street alongside a Foster & Seddon machine on their service to Swinton. Also visible on the left is an Orr Crossley Eagle, and the vehicle protruding into the left foreground also appears to be a bus. *(Ron Barton Collection)*

Another shot of Orr's Crossley TE 6740, this time a few minutes after its departure from New Cannon Street bus station. As can be seen, traffic congestion was already becoming a problem in Manchester city centre. *(John Holmes Collection)*

ORR'S MOTOR SERVICE.

SPECIAL NOTICE.

Little Lever to Manchester route

(via Radcliffe, Whitefield, Prestwich—via Bury New Road).

Alteration of Time Table.

WEEK DAYS
Monday to Friday (inclusive).

From Little Lever (Coronation Sq.)	From Manchester (Cannon St.)
7 55 a.m.	9 15 a.m.
9 50 "	10 30 "
11 20 "	12 0 p.m.
1 20 p.m.	2 0 "
2 50 "	3 30 "
4 20 "	5 0 "
5 50 "	6 30 "
7 20 "	8 0 "
8 50 "	9 30 "
10 20 " (Last Bus).	11 0 " (Last Bus).

SATURDAYS ONLY.

From Little Lever (Coronation Sq.)	From Manchester (Cannon St.)
7 55 a.m.	9 15 a.m.
9 50 "	10 30 "
11 20 "	12 0 p.m.
1 20 p.m.	2 0 "
1 50 "	2 30 "
2 50 "	3 30 "
3 20 "	4 0 "
4 20 "	5 0 "
4 50 "	5 30 "
5 50 "	6 30 "
6 20 "	7 0 "
7 20 "	8 0 "
7 50 "	8 30 "
8 50 "	9 30 "
9 20 "	10 30 "
10 20 " (Last Bus).	11 0 " (Last Bus).

SUNDAYS ONLY.

From Little Lever (Coronation Sq.)	From Manchester (Cannon St.)
1 20 p.m.	2 0 p.m.
1 50 "	2 30 "
2 50 "	3 30 "
3 20 "	4 0 "
4 20 "	5 0 "
4 50 "	5 30 "
5 50 "	6 30 "
7 50 "	8 30 "
8 50 "	9 30 p.m.
9 20 p.m.	11 0 "
10 20 " (Last Bus).	(Last Bus).

The above times will come into operation on and after Sunday, August 24th, 1930, until further notice.

☞ PLEASE CUT OUT!

Friday, January 22nd, 1932.

ORR'S MOTOR SERVICES.

Important Notice.

Ladies and Gentlemen,

I beg to reply to the circularisation of the various rumours in connection with the above Services, and I sincerely desire to inform the Public of Prestwich, that all our local services, to and from Prestwich, will definitely continue to operate as usual until further notice, with the exception that the Bus Station in Manchester will be transferred from Cannon Street to "HANGING DITCH" in Cateaton St. (Corporation Street end), near the Taxi Station, on and after Sunday next, January 24th, at least until the result of the decision of our "Appeal" to the Ministry of Transport becomes known.

SECONDLY:—I also wish to assure the Public of Prestwich that all our Drivers and Conductors ARE paid the Trade Union rates of wages, and anyone either circulating or causing to be circulated anything to the contrary, I am afraid, will be prosecuted—in fact, we are under sealed agreement of the Transport and General Workers' Union specially to comply with those conditions.

THIRDLY.—I also desire to sincerely thank the Public of Prestwich for their continued and loyal support during the past year again, and to assure them that we shall certainly endeavour to give the continuance of the same efficiency and courtesy in the future as I hope we have rendered to them in the past.

Yours respectfully,
(Signed) HARRY G. ORR.

Orr's timetable for the Little Lever to Manchester service, dated August 24th 1930. This route was reinforced by other Orr services between Prestwich and Manchester, making the independent a major force in that corridor and a major annoyance to the local municipal operators. (Right) A letter from Harry Orr which appeared in the Prestwich & Whitefield Guide, a local newspaper. He sold out to a cartel of Bolton, Bury, and Salford Corporations in the following year, claiming then that all was sweetness and light between himself and the municipal purchasers of his business. *(Ron Barton Collection)*

Strangely though, little evidence was produced to back up the police's claims that the 'Co-ordinated' express services had made the congestion worse. One could almost suspect that (with Mattinson gone – he had died shortly after his scheme was introduced) the corporations had realised that it was all a gigantic and expensive mistake and that it would be cheaper to get rid of the independents by offering them big bags of money to go away. Whatever the motivation, most of the cross-city services were cut into two and handed back to their original operators before the end of licensing hearings by the new Traffic Commissioners, and most of the independents received a lot of money from the former 'Co-ordinated' partners in exchange for their routes.

Goodfellow Services was the first to accept the devil's shilling, selling out to a consortium of North Western, Manchester Corporation, and the SHMD Board in December 1932. The service to Hyde was merged in with existing municipal services, while those to Bramhall and Macclesfield were replaced by North Western with some Manchester participation as far south as Handforth on the Macclesfield route. As mentioned earlier, Charles Cash's service from Partington via Urmston had already ceased in April 1932 after an unsuccessful appeal on the matter of frequency. The route as licensed went to North Western as the almost mythical 12A.

May 1933 saw two more well-known names disappear. Sykes Motor Tours of Sale sold out to a combination of Manchester Corporation and North Western, with the latter taking the mileage between Altrincham and Hale Barns while the Altrincham-Manchester sector was subsumed into the corporation's existing main-line between the two. It will be noted that a direct link from Hale Barns to Sale and Manchester was lost in this division of spoils. On the other side of the city Harry Orr sold his company to the corporations of Bolton, Bury, and Salford. Surprisingly, given that most of Orr's routes crossed the boundary, Manchester was not involved.

In July 1933 Organ & Wachter decided to take the money and stay in bed until a civilised hour, selling to North Western and Manchester Corporation. Their service from Styal became jointly operated route 64, later modified so that some journeys turned west at Moss Nook to serve Manchester's Ringway Airport. The basic route, minus the Styal section, is currently service 43. John Sharp of Longsight made the municipal vultures wait a little bit longer for their expensive meal, eventually selling his stage routes to a concert party of North Western, Manchester, Stockport, and Salford in August 1936. The sections from Manchester to Poynton and Woodford went to the first three of the purchasers (becoming services 20/20A, later renumbered as the 157/158) while the mileage from Manchester to Eccles and Winton was transferred to Salford.

It took the privations of a World War to get rid of Yelloway. The company's main business was the operation of long distance express coach services from Lancashire to London via Derby, Leicester, and Northampton, and to Torquay via Cheltenham and Bristol. In common with most such services these were suspended indefinitely after the declaration of war and Yelloway was left to depend upon military contract work for most of its coaching income. The profit margin on such contracts was minimal (if it existed at all) and by the beginning of 1944 the company was desperate. As a result the stage service from Rochdale to Manchester passed to an alliance of Manchester, Oldham, and Rochdale in June, just as the D-Day landings were taking place. If the Allen family could have held out for another year or so things might have been very different. As it was, when Yelloway finally returned to the local service market after deregulation the company had already passed into the incompetent hands which would soon carry it to its grave.

Attentive readers will have noticed that this survey of Manchester independents has so far omitted any reference to Mayne of Droylsden, who became the last survivor of all the 'return ticket' operators. The company is (as you would expect) given a lengthy section of its own in Part Two.

The Edges of the Conurbation

It is easy to forget the operators out at the fringes of the area later known as 'Greater Manchester County'. One of the earliest contenders was the Whitworth Vale Motor Omnibus Co (trading as 'Pioneer') which started operations from Bacup via Britannia and Whitworth to the Rochdale tram terminus at Healey in 1906. The extension of the tram route to Whitworth brought the end two years later. In the same area Holt Brothers (the

33

company which was reborn as Yelloway Motor Services Ltd) was an early participant in suburban stage-carriage routes, starting a service from Bamford to Heywood in 1921. A combination of low demand and corporation hostility made this a short-lived venture, but the Holts were intrigued by the concept of stage-carriage work and soon made a second attempt. In May 1923 they started a network of services to the north and east of Oldham, the most important route being from the Oldham boundary at Waterhead to Delph, Uppermill, Grasscroft, and the Oldham boundary at Lees. As will be noticed immediately, this carefully avoided Oldham Corporation's jurisdiction and (at that time) the Saddleworth area villages it served were all in the West Riding of Yorkshire despite being to the west of the highest parts of the Pennines.

Holt Brothers' main service was an instant success, connecting with Oldham's tramways at both ends, but its other routes in Saddleworth (High Crompton-Shaw-New Hey-Denshaw-Delph-Uppermill and Denshaw-Moss Moor-Ripponden-Sowerby Bridge-Mytholmroyd) were often passengerless. In March 1924 the North Western Road Car Co opened a depot in the area and began to compete with Holt Brothers on their key Waterhead to Lees route. Worse yet, the BAT subsidiary applied to Oldham Council for permission to extend the service into the town centre, and although Holts instantly applied for a similar licence North Western won the day. The Rochdale company then withdrew all of its services to concentrate on coaching. Its next adventure in the stage-carriage arena would be with the Rochdale-Manchester route already mentioned.

Further west William Lees of Radcliffe operated services from his home town to Farnworth via Stoneclough and Kearsley, and to the Three Arrows crossroads via Black Lane, along with a third (geographically separated) route from the Bury boundary at Blackford Bridge to Hollins, Unsworth, and Whitefield. In March 1930 he sold out to a combination of LUT (which took the Farnworth route) and Bury Corporation (which absorbed the other two services).

Heading westwards again, Henry Martin of Astley Bridge (trading as 'The Rocket') opened services connecting Bolton Corporation's Tonge Moor Road tramway to the outlying villages of Harwood and Affetside. This was a one-man band and the 'Rocket' in question was a Bedford WHB at the time of the Bolton Corporation takeover in July 1934. One can only presume that the allusion in the trading name was to Stephenson's Rocket rather than to any airborne device of a swifter nature! Mr Martin must have kicked himself in later years, for while Affetside remained an isolated village, Harwood became a major suburb of Bolton, and his routes formed the basis for the corporation's high frequency circular services to the area (6/7 in Corporation days, renumbered as 506/7 in the SELNEC era). As the sitting operator he would surely have been entitled to at least half of the workings and have required a fleet of around half a dozen double-deckers.

Crosville Motor Services

Although better known as an operator of services in Wales, Crosville was based in Chester on the English side of the border and its territory included the western half of Cheshire and the extreme south-western portion of Lancashire between Warrington and Liverpool. Readers of the 'North Wales' volume in this series will already be familiar with my (low) opinion of Crosville's founding Taylor family and their attitude to independent bus operators. Say the word 'Exterminate!' in a Dalek accent and you have the gist.

The company's tactics in its English territory were no less ruthless than those used in Wales. Crosville was particularly aggressive in the Nantwich and Crewe area of Cheshire where it habitually employed 'chaser' buses to shadow the vehicles of its independent competitors. It has also been pointed out to me that the Taylors were often to be found wining and dining local councillors and other officials in exchange for them listening to various slanderous accusations made against local bus operators. No doubt the Taylors would have justified such activity as their public duty. Satan, in his Peter Mandelson persona, would agree.

Right: Later in 1938 Yelloway acquired a third TD5, but with Burlingham bodywork. DDK 441 passed to Manchester Corporation in 1944 as fleet number 394. In 1947 its original body was damaged in an accident and it received a 1937 MCCW body removed from a Crossley Mancunian. In this guise it was renumbered as 3601, lasting until 1951. *(Senior Transport Archive)*

Leyland-bodied TD5 Titan DDK 256 was one of a pair delivered to Yelloway in 1938. After the Manchester service was sold it went to Oldham Corporation as fleet number 227 and was withdrawn in 1952. Sister vehicle DDK 257 passed to Rochdale Corporation as part of the 1944 carve-up. *(GMTS Archive)*

35

Because of the AV Roe aircraft factory at Chadderton, along its route to Manchester, two Leyland TS11 Tigers were allocated to Yelloway in 1942. They had Burlingham bodies to wartime specification. EDK 726, seen here in its original form, received a new Burlingham coach body in 1947 and was sold two years later. *(Senior Transport Archive)*

The other TS11 Tiger, EDK 740, was given a new coach body by Trans-United after the war as shown here. It stayed with Yelloway until 1953. *(GMTS Archive)*

Crosville's very first acquisition in Cheshire took place in 1911, less than a year after the Taylors opened their own original bus route. The seller was Lightfoot of Kelsall, whose pioneering service to Chester (opened by an 18-seat Lacre char-a-banc) had inspired Crosville's transformation from a failed car manufacturer to its more familiar form as a predatory bus operator. Next, in 1915, came two bus companies active in the Crewe area. Ward Brothers operated two open-top Tilling-Stevens double-deckers on local services within Crewe, while Gregory ran a more ambitious route connecting Nantwich, Crewe, and Sandbach.

There was then a pause until January 1922 when JM Hudson's service from Ellesmere Port to Chester (which competed with Crosville's original route) was acquired. Two years later a much more significant purchase was made when the Taylors bought the network of services on the Wirral peninsula operated by John Pye of Heswall. The deal included some extremely remunerative routes into Birkenhead and 18 vehicles with chassis made by Albion (five), Straker-Squire (four), Ford (two), Pagefield (two), Bristol, Dodge, Fiat, GMC, and Tilling-Stevens. Pye used the money to expand his coaching fleet in the Colwyn Bay area of North Wales.

In April 1925 it was the turn of Gibson of Crewe, another operator on the Nantwich-Crewe-Sandbach route, and in November of the same year Harding of Birkenhead sold his stage service between there and Heswall to Crosville, reinforcing the Taylors' presence on a route they had acquired from John Pye. The Hardings also continued in business as coach proprietors and later accumulated a fleet of time-expired double-deckers for use on contract works services.

English acquisitions resumed in 1927. In February Crosville acquired the services of Trevor Garner of Runcorn and James Rogers of Malpas, and in November the jointly operated services of AV Peach and Don Taylor from Haslington to Crewe, eliminating another source of competition on the road towards Sandbach. There was then a brief respite while the Taylors concentrated on Welsh acquisitions and then finalised the sale of their own company to the London, Midland & Scottish Railway Co. They remained in charge both under railway ownership and after the LM&S passed the company into the hands of the Combine a year later.

Next came an assault on the independents in the Tarporley area. Barton's 'Tarporley Motor Co' route to Chester was absorbed in July 1930, Pascoe's service to Northwich in January 1931, and in February 1931 Crosville acquired the business of Zacchaeus Woodfin of Tarvin with three Vulcan buses and routes from Chester to Tarporley and beyond. The company now held a virtual monopoly on services to the small villages between Northwich and Chester, the only survivors being George West of Kelsall and Norman Webster of Alvanley (both covered in Part Two of this book).

There were still two major independents in the Crewe and Sandbach area to be eliminated. James Warburton & Sons, a Sandbach based haulage contractor which operated buses as 'Sandbach & District Motorways', had established a route network connecting Sandbach to Alsager, Crewe (two routes, one via Haslington, the other via Coppenhall), Holmes Chapel, and Middlewich. The company was a particular source of irritation to Crosville as it imitated the larger operator's 'chaser' tactics, undercut its fares, and frequently operated more buses into Crewe than its licence from the council allowed. The Taylors filed an official complaint with Crewe Council in April 1930, but were told to make their complaint to the new Traffic Commissioners instead. Sandbach & District were subsequently given the 'thumbs down' to their licence applications after Crosville's representatives filed objections based on their past history of illegal operations. The Warburtons' premises on Bradwall Road later became the depot of Coppenhall's Coaches.

Similar tactics failed to work against the other important independent in the area. The business of Samuel Jackson & Son of Wistaston was already well-established in the motor engineering trade before commencing local bus services in December 1929 under the name of 'Malbank Services' (Malbank is a district of Nantwich). By 1931 the company was running from Crewe to Nantwich, Sandbach, and Willaston, and from Nantwich to Winsford. Road Service Licences were granted despite Crosville's strenuous objections, and Jackson continued to give the travelling public an alternative until June 1934 when the Combine company's escalating offers finally became irresistible. The 'Malbank' fleet at the time of the takeover included five Crossleys (one of them a Condor double-decker), a Daimler CF6, and a Leyland TS2 Tiger. One of the single-deck Crossleys, LG 2367, survives and might one day be returned to roadworthy condition.

By the end of 1934 the only independent stage-carriage services left running in the Crewe, Nantwich, and Sandbach areas were market-day runs operated by Roberts Coaches (outbound from Crewe to Market Drayton and Whitchurch – both in Shropshire), Salopia (inbound to Nantwich from Whitchurch), Sergent of Wrinehill in Staffordshire (inbound to Nantwich), Bostock of Congleton (inbound to Sandbach from Swettenham), and Hollinshead of Scholar Green (inbound to Sandbach from Mow Cop in Staffordshire). It was a very far cry from the thriving competition in the area witnessed only five years previously.

Crosville's later acquisitions in Cheshire might almost be considered a mopping up exercise. In July 1934 Maddocks of Tattenhall sold out, bringing Crosville new services from Chester to Tattenhall, Broxton, and Bunbury, and from Tattenhall to Whitchurch. A month later it was the turn of Lowe of Audlem with routes from that village to Nantwich, Market Drayton, and Whitchurch. Finally, in January 1935, Crosville bought out the two surviving independents in Runcorn, JW Garner's 'Weaverside Road Services' and Frederick Watson & Co. Western Cheshire had become Crosville country by the systematic removal of every native competitor.

In the relatively small but disproportionately lucrative enclave of Crosville territory on the northern side of the River Mersey the company was uncharacteristically inclined to keep its money to itself. One obvious candidate for Crosville's attentions, the Pusill family's Suburban Motor Services which ran into Warrington from both Penketh and Sankey, continued to compete with Crosville until February 1939. Mr Pusill, it seems, didn't like Crosville, and eventually sold his profitable operation to Warrington Corporation. Suburban's seven-vehicle fleet was particularly modern (the oldest bus at the time of the take-over was built in October 1934) and included three Leyland double-deckers, two Dennis Lancets, an LT7 Lion, and a coach-seated Bedford WTB. All except the Lancets had bodywork by Waveney of Lowestoft, a rather odd choice for an operator in Warrington. The explanation for this anomaly was apparently that Mr Pusill took a holiday in Suffolk each summer and had become friendly with Waveney's Managing Director.

In other circumstances Crosville might have been expected to howl like a banshee about the Suburban take-over, and to object to the transfer of licences until the company received a share. As it was, past experience had taught Crosville to be very careful about annoying Warrington Council and Mr Crosland-Taylor kept his mouth shut.

Why no LUT?

Lancashire United Transport is excluded from the present volume for three reasons. The first is entirely pragmatic in that LUT has recently featured in Venture's *Super Prestige* series in an excellent book written by the late Eric Ogden. I really could not produce a better account of the company's history so why bother? The second reason is practicality – to describe LUT at any kind of suitable length would take this book's 'page count' over the maximum which can be accommodated in the Super Prestige format. The only alternative would be to reduce the amount of space given to the other operators, and as many of them have received little (if any) attention from earlier authors this is an unacceptable option.

The third reason is the most important one however. I do not believe that LUT should be classified as an independent bus operator. It fails to 'jump the hurdle' in several key respects, not least the test of ownership and control. To my mind a true independent is controlled by local investors, whether a single proprietorial family (as was the case with Barton Transport) or a group of unrelated shareholders (as with Bere Regis & District). In my view these were the two largest independents before deregulation, not LUT and its Yorkshire doppelganger the West Riding Automobile Company. Both LUT and West Riding were former tramway companies, and as such the majority of their shares were owned by London-based conglomerates and investment funds.

Almost all of the (non-municipal) tramway networks in this country were brought into being through stock offerings on the London market. Small investors had recently received an unpleasant shock from the failure of umpteen railway companies previously considered to be

(J. Warburton & Son, Proprietors.)

Sandbach and District Motorways.

TIME TABLE.   TIME TABLE.

SANDBACH---ALSAGER.

		Mon., Tues., Wed., Fri.				Thurs. only.				Sat. and Sun.			
										N.S.			N.S.	S.O.
		a.m.	p.m.	p.m.	p.m.	a.m.	p.m.	p.m.	p.m.	a.m.	p.m.	p.m.	p.m.	p.m.
SANDBACH	dpt.	9 15	1 15	5 30	9 15	9 15	1 15	4 30	9 15	9 15	1 45	5 30	9 15	9 45
THURLWOOD	,,	9 30	1 30	5 45	9 30	9 30	1 30	4 45	9 30	9 30	2 0	5 45	9 30	10 0
LAWTON ARMS	,,	9 37	1 37	5 52	9 37	9 37	1 37	4 52	9 37	9 37	2 7	5 52	9 37	10 7
ALSAGER	arr.	9 45	1 45	6 0	9 45	9 45	1 45	5 0	9 45	9 45	2 15	6 0	9 45	10 15
										N.S.			N.S.	S.O.
ALSAGER	dpt.	9 55	1 55	6 10	9 55	9 55	1 55	5 10	9 55	9 55	2 25	6 10	9 55	10 20
LAWTON ARMS	,,	10 3	2 3	6 18	10 3	10 3	2 3	5 18	10 3	10 3	2 33	6 18	10 3	10 28
THURLWOOD	,,	10 10	2 10	6 25	10 10	10 10	2 10	5 25	10 10	10 10	2 40	6 25	10 10	10 35
SANDBACH	arr.	10 25	2 25	6 40	10 25	10 25	2 25	5 40	10 25	10 25	2 55	6 40	10 25	10 50

25/11/30.   N.S.—Not Sundays   S.O.—Sunday Only.

The Proprietors beg to announce that it is their intention to maintain a reliable service. Any suggestion from the public, to create efficiency, will be welcomed. They do not however, take any responsibility for loss of time through any unavoidable circumstances, but every effort will be made to maintain the times as set out in the Time Table. Any alteration in the Time Table will be notified, but they, however, reserve the right to alter the Time Table without notice.

Eachus & Son, Printers, Sandbach

James Warburton & Sons of Sandbach traded as 'Sandbach and District Motorways', and this timetable for their service to Alsager is dated 25th November 1930. The company closed down at the end of the following year. *(John Dixon Collection)*

TW Pusill traded as Suburban Motor Services and operated from Penketh and Sankey to Warrington. The company was sold to Warrington Corporation in February 1939. ED 9468, an LT7 Lion bus with Waveney bodywork (new to Suburban in November 1935), became Warrington fleet number 86 and the regular performer on the corporation's share of the service to Arley. In 1948 they sold it to South Notts of Gotham. *(Roy Marshall Collection)*

rock-solid investments and were understandably reluctant to be stung again in a 'tramway bubble'. On the other hand the various companies in the wider electrical arena which had been floated in the 1880/90s had proven to be outstandingly successful and investors did not want to be excluded from the profits to be made in electricity-related industries such as tramway manufacture and operation. The solution was to give their money to professional investment managers who would spread the risk across a wide portfolio of companies.

The Leon family (who dominated West Riding for most of its existence) ran one such group of investment funds, although they might be better known to the general public as the original owners of Bletchley Park, later donated to the nation as a centre for code-breaking during the Second World War. The financial *eminence grise* behind LUT was another London-based fund manager, John Soame Austen, brought in to the company as early as 1906 by LUT Chairman Arthur Stanley. The aristocratic Stanley (he was the third son of the 16th Earl of Derby) had been the major force in assembling LUT – originally Lancashire United *Tramways* – from a bankrupt group of predecessor companies previously controlled by the Atherton family of Rainhill.

Stanley also invested in electrical and tramway stocks further afield, and rented a small London office in Dashwood House – a building which specialised in tenants who were investing in the new industries. Austen's Omnium Group of investment funds (which invested in such projects as a telephone company in Venezuela and a power generation company in Russia as well as tramways) was based in the same building, and Stanley soon came under Austen's spell.

Austen specialised in shares related to electricity. In 1896 the Brush group (created in 1879 to buy the British patent rights to American inventor Charles Francis Brush's electrical dynamo, and a leading manufacturer of all things related to tramways) approached Austen to create a market for the shares in a new associated company, British Electric Traction. BET had been spawned by Brush to finance, build, and operate tramway systems and its chairman was Brush director Emil Garcke. After the successful floatation of BET shares Austen became the new company's Deputy Chairman and in 1920 would replace Garcke at the top. The directors of Brush and BET trusted him completely and took his advice regarding investments in new opportunities.

Despite the bankruptcy of two of its progenitor companies (this was par for the course in the tramway business) Austen considered LUT to be a good bet and advised his friends at Brush and BET to buy. He also sold some of the shares to the National Electric Construction Company (then part-controlled by BET and bought outright by them in 1931), and a sizeable block to the Balfour Beatty group, another construction and tramway conglomerate, with much of the balance of the floatation being distributed among London-based investment funds under Austen's control.

Directors associated with either BET or Balfour Beatty would remain the dominant force at LUT until the final days of the company, and although neither of the two groups ever held more than 10% of LUT's shares each, these shareholdings were buttressed by those of associated families such as the Adams (Scottish solicitors who worked for Balfour Beatty), the Birches, and the Leons of the West Riding company (who sent Harry England across the Pennines to sit on the LUT board). After Austen's death in 1942 (Arthur Stanley would continue as chairman until 1947) the BET interest in the company was represented principally by John M Birch.

Mr Birch was the managing director of his family's famous Birch Brothers company, where his older brother Raymond W Birch was the chairman. Now, as Birch Brothers' services were entirely in the London-Rushden corridor (where they competed only with London Transport and United Counties) it was deemed permissible for Raymond Birch to simultaneously be the chairman of Birch Brothers and also to be the chairman of British Electric Traction and of its subsidiaries PMT, Hebble, and Yorkshire Woollen District. In truth the Birch family had been in alliance with the BET Group since 1912 when the Birches agreed not to compete with BET bus services in the London area in exchange for a steady supply of orders for bodywork from the Birches' workshops.

Sadly the shareholders register of LUT seems to have disappeared after the company's demise – so no concrete figures can be given - but a senior manager at the company's Atherton head office once told me that less than five percent of LUT's shares were owned by people in the North West of England.

Now, I can already hear the nit-pickers getting their combs out. "But, Neville," they might say, "you included the Llandudno & Colwyn Bay Electric Railway in your North Wales book, and they were a former tramway operator with a big Balfour Beatty presence". Yes, I did, but for a very good reason. By the time that L&CBER became a bus operator the Balfour Beatty shareholding had been reduced to almost nothing (they knew how to abandon a sinking ship!) and the shares had been sold to wide-eyed local investors. I rest my case.

So I would argue that the question is not so much, "Why no LUT" but, "Why was LUT ever classified as an independent in the first place?" It can't be because there was no railway shareholding (several BET subsidiaries were in that position and nobody calls them independents). It can't be because they were in fact dominated by two of the big bus-owning groups rather than just the one (were Black & White Motorways and Timpsons independents?). And it certainly can't be because of their operational characteristics (they had area agreements with all of their Tilling & British neighbours, were on extremely friendly terms with North Western, and rubbed along in an adequate fashion with Ribble and Crosville). None of this is meant as a criticism, it was a fine company. It just never was an independent one.

Author's Notes

As with previous volumes in this series, the main focus of attention is upon enterprises which operated stage-carriage services, available to the general public, between the early post-Second World War era (in this case the 1st of January 1950) and the advent of deregulation in 1980-86, with a separate history for each operator. These are presented in two parts, the first covering the traditional counties of Cumberland and Westmorland (nowadays the northernmost 80% of Cumbria), the second the traditional counties of Lancashire and Cheshire.

The old boundaries (which prevailed for most of the period under study) are also used in the text so Barrow-in-Furness, Ulverston, Hawkshead, and Grange-over-Sands are in Lancashire (now in Cumbria) while at the other end of the region Warrington is still in Lancashire where it belongs as are Southport, Liverpool, St Helens, Wigan, Bolton, Salford, Manchester, etc. The Wirral peninsula is entirely in Cheshire as are Altrincham, Sale, Stockport, Stalybridge, Hyde, Dukinfield, and the Longdendale panhandle pointing towards Yorkshire. To the north of this Yorkshire spilled over to the Manchester side of the Pennines and the Saddleworth area (now in Greater Manchester County) was in the West Riding, although reference to it will still be found in this book as it was within the North West Traffic Area even when still part of Yorkshire.

Methodology reasonably established, the baton passes to parameters. Operators which began their bus services after the 1980 Road Traffic Act (introducing partial deregulation) came into force are excluded as they represent the beginning of a different history to the one attempted here. Fans of Yeowart Brothers of Whitehaven may like to look at my fellow Venture author Harry Postlethwaite's book on Cumberland Motor Services which includes full details of this fascinating operator along with a colour photo gallery of their vehicles. Due to the fact that there is so little of any interest to say about them, minibus operators are not given their own separate entries but reference to them will be found in the histories of the full-size bus operators whose abandoned services they replaced.

These basic rules are generally quite easy to apply from my viewpoint, but in the North West of England one operator – Taylor & Hudson, trading as 'Mountain Goat' - straddles the boundaries of precise definition. Although the company began to operate in 1972 (that is, well before deregulation) and did operate a relatively tiny number of its stage-carriage departures with larger vehicles, it was in essence a leisure-oriented operator of minibus excursions. Because these excursions operated on a daily basis during the summer season and the company offered all-day tickets valid for all of their services, they required stage-carriage licences to comply with the letter of the law. These were not in any way, shape, or form normal stage-carriage services, and the occasional heavy load carried by a Bedford VAS, Bristol LHS, or (if you were very lucky) the company's 'heritage' Bedford OB, instead of the usual community transport style minibus, could not make them so. As you may have guessed by now, I decided to leave the Mountain Goat outside. It won't starve.

41

This series is targeted at two different audiences, those interested in local history, and those with a specific interest in the history of the bus industry. To avoid alienating readers in the 'local history' category I have (in previous volumes) been sparing in the provision of registration numbers and other fine details of the fleets involved. However, I have decided to be more liberal with such information in the present volume after receiving many letters from readers of the 'North Wales' book asking for more specific vehicle information.

In this book registration marks are given (where known) for operators whose fleet details are not freely available elsewhere. In practice this means that nearly all of the operator histories in Part One (Cumberland & Westmorland) contain registration details as do some of those in Part Two covering lesser-known companies. Where there are publications available which give such information (eg Fishwick, Mayne, and Scout) a footnote is included offering a source for further research. I hope that this is an acceptable compromise.

ACKNOWLEDGEMENTS

Most of the research for this book was done in the archive of the Greater Manchester Transport Society at the Manchester Museum of Transport, and my thanks go once again to the Museum's archivist, George Turnbull, for his generous help in this project. Several other members of GMTS made a significant contribution, including Ron Barton and John Holmes (who allowed me access to their material covering 'return ticket' operators in Manchester) and John Dixon (who was equally informative about pioneering operators in southern Cheshire).

John Kaye has, once again, allowed me access to the early records of the PSV Circle, and his advice in all matters has made this book more accurate than it could ever have been without his (tolerant!) assistance. Another stalwart of the enthusiast community, Alan Oxley of The Omnibus Society, has used his knowledge of the OS Photographic Archive to provide us all with some rare images of obscure independents' vehicles (and at fairly short notice after others let me down). Other rare photographs were provided by John Howie, Keith Johnson, Alan Murray-Rust, Ross Pattison, David Stanier, Peter Tulloch, Ian Walker, and Jack Williams and all of these gentlemen are thanked for their endeavours in searching through their voluminous collections. John Howie also provided some invaluable research material.

Two people I've forgotten to thank in previous volumes are Philip Lamb and Nigel Appleford of *Bus & Coach Preservation* magazine, for allowing me space for photographic appeals in the 'Busmart' section of their excellent magazine. Thanks are also due to the newspapers in Cumbria which printed similar appeals on my behalf, and to the people who contacted me as a result of those letters, including David Atkinson, John Box, Ian Creighton, Stuart Emmett, Tony Hutt, Tom Macan, Michael Nield, and Malcolm Wheatman.

My daughter, Helena Mercer, took responsibility for the computer enhancement of some very poor quality images. She is gifted and will go far! My friends Philip Cryer and Samantha Hardy were also supportive on the technical side and came to my rescue whenever my computer misbehaved (or, as they might put it, when the idiot pressed the wrong key again). Thanks go as always to my publishers, and in particular to Mark Senior, John Senior, and Ian Stubbs for their advice and encouragement during the creation of this book. I am also grateful to Mary and David Shaw for their diligent proof-reading. I hope that you enjoy reading it, as it was fascinating to write.

PKD 588 was the first of three late-model Regal IIIs with Roe service bus bodies acquired by the Belfast Steam Ship Co in 1954. The trio were used on a restricted service connecting Liverpool's main railway stations to the ferry terminal at Princess Dock. The third vehicle, PKD 590, is illustrated on page 174. *(Author's Collection)*

No, it never ran on stage-carriage services, but I don't care! Foden/Whitson observation coach EBN 898 was delivered to Hargreaves of Bolton in 1950 as a (Gardner powered) PVSC6 but was soon sent back to Foden to receive their own two-stroke engine. Several customers found these observation coaches too heavy for the Gardner 6LW – they weighed more than most double-deckers. *(Roy Marshall)*

43

The Middleton Tower holiday camp operated a private service for its visitors, offering connections to the railway stations at Heysham or Morecambe. The Bedford OWB used in the early 1950s was replaced by this Duple (Midland)-bodied Bedford SBG bus, 617 FTE, in 1958. *(Author's Collection)*

Part One

CUMBERLAND & WESTMORLAND

The traditional county of Cumberland was very much dominated by the City of Carlisle (population 71,000), an important centre since Roman times as it was the lowest bridging point across the River Eden which then snaked westwards through bleak marshlands to join with its Scottish cousin, the River Esk, to form the mighty estuary known as the Solway Firth. The Roman roads from the south were later paralleled by railway lines and Carlisle became an industrial city with large numbers employed in textiles (the city was in the middle of a million sheep), engineering (exploiting the iron and coal from the Cumberland coastal region), and food production (local companies included Carr's Biscuits).

In the 20th century the rapidly improving road network gave birth to a host of well-known motor hauliers, including Robsons of Carlisle and Eddie Stobart, although the route to the south – particularly the bleak section of the old A6 through Shap, between Penrith in Cumberland and Kendal in Westmorland – could still be treacherous in bad weather. The accident rate on this stretch of road remained frighteningly high until the opening of the M6 motorway section from Lancaster to Carlisle in 1970. Curiously, in view of the city's great distance from London and its importance as a regional capital, airline companies have always been rather scarce at Carlisle Airport.

Outside of the local metropolis the county divides handily into three parts from west to east. The western third is composed of the small fishing villages along the southern bank of the Solway Firth which lead from Carlisle to Silloth (several major airfields were built in this area during the Second World War, making use of the flat coastal plain), the coal and iron-ore mining towns and seaports on the West Cumberland shores of the Irish Sea, the most important of these being Maryport (population 11,600), Workington (28,500) and Whitehaven (26,700), and a more rural area to the south between the bulging headland known as St Bees Head and the Duddon estuary where Cumberland met Lancashire.

The central third of Cumberland rose steeply as you went southwards, climbing from Carlisle (virtually at sea level) to the highest of the Lake District mountains at an altitude of more than 3,000 feet. The southernmost end of this wedge was dominated by the market towns of Keswick (population 5,180) at its western extremity and Penrith (11,300) in the east. Both towns were also major tourist destinations due to their proximity to Derwent Water (Keswick) and Ullswater (Penrith). While Penrith was located on the main railway line from London to Carlisle and Glasgow, Keswick was catered for by a branch line which ran from Penrith to Cockermouth. The western section of this line was closed in 1968 and the Keswick-Penrith remainder in 1972.

The eastern third of Cumberland is defined by the valley of the River Eden which flows southwards from Carlisle, passing a few miles to the east of Penrith before crossing the old county boundary and running into Westmorland. The soil is good for agriculture and dairy farming is widespread. The Eden effectively divides the Lake District Fells from the Pennines and on the eastern side of its fertile valley the ground rises rapidly into the county's sparsely populated moorlands. The largest community in this Pennine upland area is Alston (population 1,200), which lays claim to be the highest town in England at more than 1,000 feet. There are extensive lead and zinc mines in the Alston area and the town (which spans the south branch of the River Tyne) might more naturally have been administered by Northumberland as it is on the eastern side of the Pennine watershed.

The county of Westmorland included the eastern shore of Lake Windermere (the western shore was then in Lancashire), and such well-known tourist destinations as Ambleside (population 2,800), Bowness (3,800), and the town of Windermere (8,100). In the summer months the population of these resort towns could easily double and then double again if day visitors were included in the total. The town of Windermere, incidentally, was given its name by the railway company to emphasise its closeness to the lake. The location was originally a village known as Birthwaite. Say it out loud to see why the railway didn't like it.

Kendal, seven miles to the south-east of Windermere, was the largest town in Westmorland with a population of more than 21,000. In the Victorian era it replaced Appleby as the county town and also became famous for its mint-cake and snuff factories. The town's location on both the railway line and the A6 trunk road made it easily accessible to tourists who would often combine it with Windermere as a good day out.

The most important urban areas to the south of Kendal were Milnthorpe (population 2,100 and known for Duralon combs) and Arnside (a seaside resort with 2,300 permanent inhabitants). To the east of Kendal the market towns of Appleby (pop 1,950) and Kirkby Stephen (1,630) were the largest communities in the Westmorland portion of the Eden valley. The latter is now best known to bus enthusiasts as the home of Will Hamer's 'Cumbria Classic Coaches' business, which organises a major vintage vehicle rally in the town every Easter weekend, and also operates a small network of stage-carriage routes with preserved buses.

Blair & Palmer of Carlisle

There are three important roads to the west of Carlisle. The northernmost of these is an unclassified lane which leads to the Solway Firth villages of Bowness-on-Solway and Cardurnock. The bus service along this road passed to Ribble in the early 1930s and tended to be the preserve of oddments within the fleet such as Dennis Aces in the 1930s and Sentinel STC4s in the 1950s. The vehicles of Cumberland Motor Services left Carlisle for Wigton and the coast via the 'A' road which ran several miles inland, and between the coast and the 'A' road there was a third string of small villages situated along the 'B' road to Kirkbride and Newton Arlosh. At the beginning of 1928 the bus traffic along this 'B' road was shared by Hughes & Beattie (a local haulier specialising in livestock transport) and two small one-man bands, Parker and Larkspur. The latter two ran past Newton Arlosh to the port and seaside town of Silloth, but this extension was less remunerative than might be thought due to competition from the railway and from the CMS service to Silloth via the 'A' road.

On the 9th of January 1928 the Hughes & Beattie service passed to a new partnership of Hedley Blair and Jack Palmer. Broadly speaking, Blair provided most of the capital while Palmer (who had driven for Hughes & Beattie) was the expert on all things mechanical. Within a year the new partnership had acquired the competing services of Parker and Larkspur and established control over the route as far as Newton Arlosh. The first known vehicle, a 20-seat Vulcan 3XB (TY 2123), was soon replaced by a succession of Crossley Alphas during the early 1930s. Some were new (such as Roberts-bodied HH 6009) but most were acquired from operators in Scotland and the English Midlands (including VA 9498, RF 8347, VT 7960, and BNN 625).

The extension from Newton Arlosh to Silloth was discontinued during the mid-1930s due to a fares war with the railway company, but by then another service had been started (on market days only) from Newton Arlosh to Wigton. Business on the main service was booming and the profits made were quickly reinvested into the partnership. The Carlisle departure point for the Newton Arlosh route had originally been at a roadside stand in Market Street, but city centre congestion led to pressure to establish an 'off street' terminus. Blair & Palmer went one better and on the 1st of June 1935 opened their own bus station and depot on a site between Drovers Lane and East Tower Street.

With war against Germany clearly inevitable in the near future, the Royal Air Force and the Fleet Air Arm began to expand their assets in all parts of the United Kingdom. Northern Cumberland was not forgotten and in 1938 construction began on two major new aerodromes, at Kirkbride for the RAF and at Anthorn for the Navy. Both sites were in Blair & Palmer territory and necessitated the purchase of the company's first double-deckers, two Massey-bodied Daimler CP6s acquired from Birkenhead Corporation (BG 746/749). Once the two air-bases became operational the traffic increased still further and in 1939/40 the CP6s were joined by four more double-deckers, on this occasion Crossley Condors from Manchester (XJ 2241/48/52/58).

Hedley Blair's health had taken a turn for the worse in the late 1930s and in 1940 he decided to retire from business and leave the partnership. Jack Palmer became the sole proprietor of the firm, a difficult task for a man without many resources at a time when profits were low and everything was hard to find. Blair agreed to leave his capital in the business (as a loan to Palmer) until the end of the war. A fifth Condor, DJ 5407, was acquired from St Helens Corporation in 1941, and this was followed by an influx of vehicles from Scotland. The first were two Albion Valkyrie saloons with 39-seat Cowieson bodies (XS 4410/11) and a Northern Counties-bodied Albion Venturer double-decker (XS 3232), acquired from Young of Paisley. The remaining wartime arrivals were another Northern Counties-bodied Venturer (WS 7808) which came from W Alexander & Son, and a Leyland TD1 Titan with Croft bodywork (WE 8776) which arrived from Young's associated company Paisley & District but had been new to Sheffield.

All of these additional vehicles (which had swollen the fleet from six in 1937 to 14 in 1945) required further garage and parking space. A small out-station was established at Newton Arlosh in 1938, and this was supplemented by a second facility in Carlisle itself in 1941. The new premises in the city were located at Church Street in the Caldewgate district and consisted of a filling station, a large yard, and two structures suitable for housing vehicles. Maintenance continued to be the province of the original Drovers Lane depot which already had the inspection pits and equipment required.

After the war had ended, Hedley Blair wanted his money back. The problem was solved by the establishment of a new company, Blair & Palmer Ltd, on the 22nd of November 1945. A major stake in this new company was held by Ernie Hartness (qv), the Penrith bus operator, who had apparently come into money at the end of the Second World War although details of this remain obscure. The windfall had enabled Hartness to order a large number of Daimler CVD6 chassis from the manufacturer, and some of these were diverted to Blair & Palmer. The first two to arrive in Carlisle were Roe-bodied double-deckers (BHH 798/9) and were painted in two-tone blue (to represent the Hartness influence) rather than in Blair & Palmer's traditional two-tone green. A third double-decker chassis (CHH 162) followed in early 1947 and was originally fitted with a second-hand Burlingham L53R body originally from a pre-war Ribble Titan. This was soon replaced by a new Roe H56R body identical to those on the 'BHH' vehicles.

The next two CVD6s from the Hartness order were single-deck chassis and were fitted with pre-war ECOC bodies which came from mechanically exhausted North Western machines. The first of

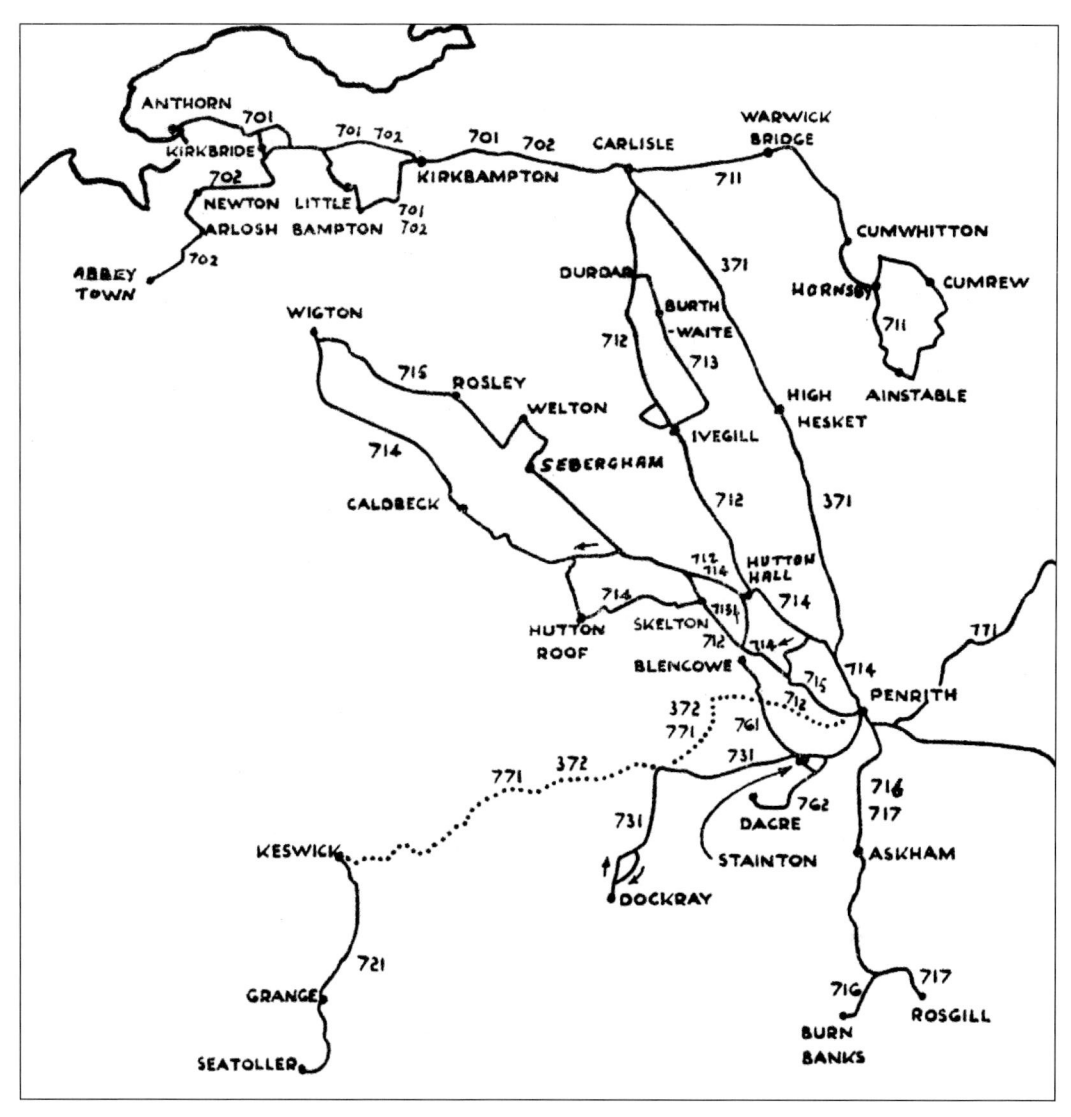

This map was included in The Omnibus Society publication Northern Independent Bus Operators 1964. It shows all of the independent routes in Cumberland at the end of that year, Sim of Boot (whose services would have been off the bottom left corner of the map) having abandoned their stage-carriage work in October of that year. The numbers shown here are entirely unofficial and were intended for ease of reference to the text of the original publication. Routes 701/702 were Blair & Palmer. Route 711 was operated by Proud of Ainstable until 1953, Blair & Palmer from 1953-57, and Ernie Hartness of Penrith (from 1957-71). Routes 712-717 were operated by Hartness throughout the post-war period, although all except one had been acquired from other operators before 1945. Route 721 was operated by Keswick Borrowdale Bus Service, 731 by Mandale of Greystoke, and 761/762 by Titterington of Blencowe. Route 771 is Wright Bros of Nenthead's main service from Newcastle to the Lakes via Alston. Other Wright Brothers services operated in the Alston area, off the right hand side of this map. Services 371/372 were operated by GNE Motor Services of Darlington, County Durham, and are included on the map as the (fundamentally) express routes were allowed to pick up local traffic in the Pennine highlands to the east of Penrith where no other bus service existed. *(The Omnibus Society)*

these, CHH 298, received a Plaxton body in 1953 while the second, GRM 365, was rejuvenated by the addition of a new body made by Associated Coachbuilders (ACB). A third Hartness CVD6, GRM 461, was fitted with a Plaxton body from new. The final new vehicle of 1947 was a Bedford OB/SMT coach, CHH 508.

Factory-fresh vehicles acquired during 1948 included another CVD6/Roe double-decker (CHH 725), and two Albion Valkyries with Duple coach

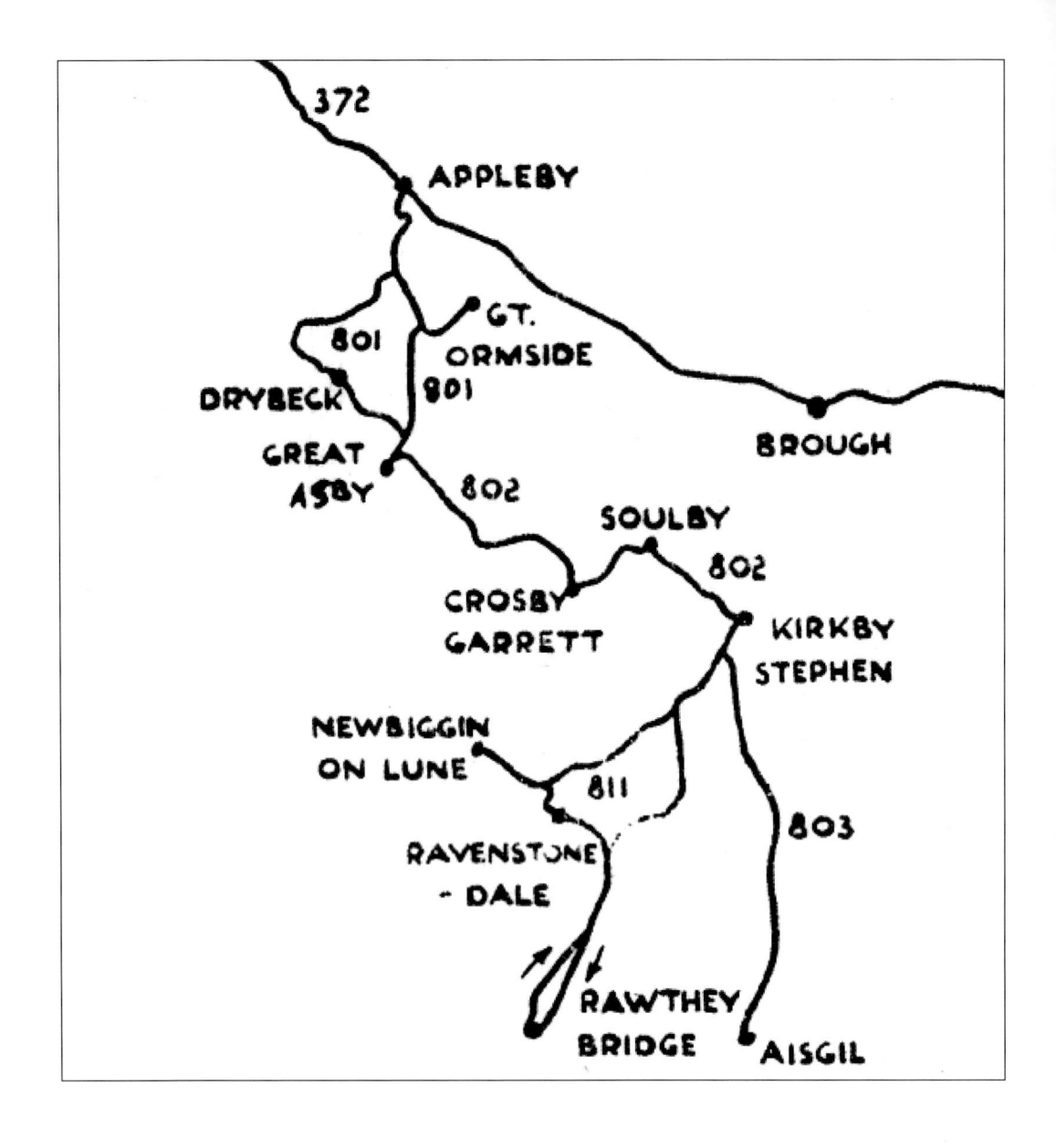

The 1964 Omnibus Society publication also yielded this map of Westmorland's independent bus services. GNE Motor Services express route to Darlington and beyond (Map Route 372) runs along the top of the diagram through Appleby and Brough. Routes 801 and 802 were operated by Sowerby of Great Asby from 1932 until 1940, then by Ernie Hartness until 1957, and then by Robinson of Appleby. Route 803 was the last remnant of the substantial local network operated by Walton of Kirkby Stephen until 1931. Walton revived the route to Aisgill in 1934 and ran it until 1963 when it passed to Robinson of Appleby as their third post-war stage service. Route 811 operated on schooldays only and was first recorded as operated by John Dargue from 1928-35. It then passed to WE Reed of Newbiggin, and to Walton of Kirkby Stephen after the war. When the Walton family sold off its bus and coach interests in 1963 the schools service went to Jackson of Kirkby Stephen. The total mileage of these services was very meagre, even after Robinson increased the frequency of its Great Asby to Appleby route. The loss of Dallam Motors to Ribble in 1950 had drastically reduced the county's independent bus sector, as Dallam had been the only Westmorland firm to offer an hourly frequency to its customers, or a service of any kind on all seven days of the week, since the Ribble take-over of the Kendal Motor Bus Co in 1930. *(The Omnibus Society)*

bodies (CHH 740/1). The Valkyries were sold within months, suggesting that they were less than acceptable. Second-hand purchases in that year were of a pre-war AEC Regent/Weymann double-decker from Sheffield (CWA 493), two ageing LT5A Lion coaches with Brush bodywork from Western SMT (VD 3422/52) which lasted just over a year, and another pre-war Condor double-decker – this time from Barrow-in-Furness (EO 5242). The latter vehicle never received a Blair & Palmer fleet number and it is believed that it was acquired as a source of spares for the Manchester examples which continued in service as 'back-up' machines for the new CVD6 double-deckers.

Ernie Hartness's huge order for Daimler CVD6s had almost been completed (the last two would enter the Hartness fleet in 1950), but in 1949 Western SMT placed a large batch of (virtually unused) CVD6/Burlingham coaches on the market. The Scottish operator had deliberately over-ordered at a time when new coaches were still difficult to find, perceiving (correctly) that it could always sell surplus vehicles at a profit given the state of the market. Four of these (CAG 786/795/7/8) were snapped up by Blair & Palmer, with two of them remaining in service until 1962. With the arrival of these fine coaches the pace of acquisitions began to slow down as most of the fleet was now relatively modern. Over the next two years the only arrivals were another Bedford OB (DHH 886), two Albion Victor/Duple coaches (FHH 488/571) and a second-hand AEC Regent/MCCW double-decker from Glasgow Corporation (BUS 159).

Life after Ernie

Jack Palmer and Ernie Hartness were both engineers at heart, but both men were also rugged individualists and any observer who thought that their alliance would be the first step towards the creation of a major independent bus operator in Cumberland would have soon been disappointed. By 1951 they had agreed to go their own separate ways again. Jack Palmer had accumulated a nest-egg from his share of the post-war profits and offered to buy the 50% share held by Hartness since 1945. Ernie was more than willing as he felt that his involvement with Blair & Palmer had seriously restricted the amount of time he could spend looking after his own beloved company in Penrith. After Hartness's withdrawal the Palmer family reigned supreme, with directors including Jack Palmer's wife Hannah and his brother Michael. They would later be joined by Jack Palmer's children John (born 1931), Alan (born 1937), Barbara (1938) and George (1939), all of whom became active in the company as they reached adulthood. The experiment with a blue livery was rapidly brought to an end and the traditional colour schemes of two-tone green (for service buses) and green and cream (for coaches) were restored.

In 1952 Proud of Ainstable (qv) abandoned his stage services from his home village to Carlisle (daily) and Penrith (on market days). Blair & Palmer agreed to replace Proud on the Ainstable-Carlisle route, but whereas the original proprietor had used a 'driver only' Bedford OWB on the route, B&P decided to use double-deckers with two crew, particularly on the last journey of the day. This left Carlisle along the Newcastle road half an hour later than the last United Auto departure and so did very well as far as Warwick Bridge. At this point the route turned south to the villages, passengers evaporated, and an echoingly empty double-decker headed for Ainstable. It couldn't last and in 1957 Blair & Palmer withdrew the service. Fortunately for the locals, Ernie Hartness agreed to take over, using one-man-operated CVD6 saloons which quickly reduced the losses to manageable proportions.

The first new acquisition after the amicable split with Hartness was a new Commer Avenger III/Plaxton coach, HHH 301. Six years would pass before the next new vehicle but second-hand purchases during those years included an assortment of half-cab coaches. Daimler CVD6s were still the favourites. Two Burlingham-bodied examples came from Stockland of Birmingham (HOJ 425/7) while Duple built the coachwork on KTC 985 and FFY 959, and rare Margham bodywork was fitted to FDL 67. Other half-cab arrivals were of AEC Regal/Trans-United KTC 458 (from Lowland Motorways of Glasgow) and PS1 Tiger/Whitson AGR 5 (from Cowell of Sunderland).

In 1958 the (Tuesday) market-day service from Newton Arlosh to Wigton was withdrawn due to a lack of traffic. The main routes from Carlisle to Newton Arlosh and Anthorn were also suffering as a result of the decline of the aerodromes at

Anthorn and Kirkbride, both of which would soon be abandoned by the military. The number of double-deckers in the fleet declined at a corresponding rate, with the first two CVD6s being sold to AA Motor Services in August 1959. All of the pre-war double-deckers had already gone by then and the other two post-war CVD6s would be withdrawn in 1961. Double-deckers continued to feature in the fleet, but the few second-hand examples subsequently acquired were mainly employed on works services, many of which were of a military nature.

To compensate for the loss of revenue from Anthorn and Kirkbride aerodromes, Blair & Palmer had been awarded a share of the services to RAF Kingstown – previously operated exclusively by Western SMT. Kingstown, formerly a training airfield, had become No 14 MU (Maintenance Unit) after the war and held large stocks of everything the RAF could require from aircraft engines and spares to uniforms and office furniture. It was a very large site with hundreds of civilian employees and the services bringing them to work required two double-deckers and a coach. Another major source of military contract work in the Carlisle area was provided (from 1958 onwards) by the Spadeadam testing range in the thinly populated border region to the north-east of the city. More details about this site are to be found later in this chapter under the Sowerby of Gilsland heading.

All of this new work kept the company alive, but did not solve the problem of the losses by then being made on the stage-carriage services. One obvious solution was to convert the routes to one-man-operation, but almost all of the Blair & Palmer fleet was made up of vehicles impossible to use without a conductor. In fact, the company started 1958 without a single underfloor-engined vehicle as Jack Palmer had considered them to be vastly inferior to more traditional machines. The need to convert to single-crew operation forced him to change his mind.

The company had already operated two Commer Avenger IIIs (a second example with unusual Strachan bodywork, PAO 784, had been acquired from Hamilton of Workington) and Jack Palmer began to look in this direction for the solution to his problem. In the mid-1950s Commer and bodybuilder JC Beadle had introduced their jointly produced T48 Rochester coach model with an entrance at the front directly opposite to the driver. Jack Palmer found two low-mileage examples on the second-hand market (630 BPF from the Caterham Motor Co and OVD 362 from Hutchison of Overtown) and gave them a makeshift conversion to 'driver only' configuration. The exercise was not entirely successful but inspired Jack Palmer to come up with a more radical solution.

In early 1959 the company took delivery of a brand-new Commer Avenger IV chassis. Like all of its breed this had its engine at the front, but Palmer and his fitters redesigned the chassis to accommodate the TS3 engine amidships, beneath the floor. The customised Avenger was then fitted with a 45-seat body built by Blair & Palmer themselves, using standard frames acquired from MetSec. For a homebuilt design with revolutionary features, NHH 482 (chassis no BP1) was rather splendid and gave many years of faithful service on the stage-carriage routes. As noted elsewhere in this book, it is now preserved. A more conventional Avenger IV coach with Duple bodywork (OHH 112) was delivered in November 1959.

An acquisition of a different kind came in January 1960 when Blair & Palmer bought the coaching business of Gibson of Carlisle. The purchase included three vehicles, an AEC Regal IV with Burlingham Seagull bodywork (JGE 423 – sold the following month showing that Jack Palmer still didn't like underfloor-engined vehicles!), a Regal III with fully-fronted Gurney Nutting bodywork (EHJ 433), and a CVD6 with Duple bodywork (KTC 986, sister vehicle to KTC 985 acquired some years earlier). The main attractions were the company's excursion licences as the Palmers were anxious to increase this part of their business to compensate for falling stage-carriage revenues. The only other vehicle purchased during 1960 was yet another Daimler CVD6, this time a Santus-bodied example (ORE 209) which had been new to a Staffordshire operator.

As mentioned previously, the final two CVD6/Roe double-deckers from the Hartness era were retired in 1961. Their replacements were an Alexander-bodied Daimler CVG6 acquired from Western SMT (BAG 102), and a pre-war Leyland TD5 with post-war Alexander bodywork to Leyland design which came from Ribble (RN

Blair & Palmer's Crossley Mancunian XJ 2241 (fleet number 18) was one of four acquired from Manchester Corporation in 1939/40. It is seen in Carlisle during the Second World War, awaiting another departure to Newton Arlosh. *(John Howie Collection)*

This Daimler CVD6, CHH 162, was new to Blair & Palmer in 1947 as fleet number D27 ('D' for Daimler). It originally carried a second-hand Burlingham body donated by a Ribble TD5 Titan, but this was soon replaced by the new Roe body shown here at Drovers Lane, Carlisle. In 1961 it was sold to Ernie Hartness and used as a source of spares for his own CVD6 double-deckers. *(Author's Collection)*

Another CVD6 from the same year, CHH 298 (fleet number D28) was initially fitted with a Crossley body from a 1936 Alpha. This was then replaced by a pre-war ECW body from a North Western vehicle, and this lasted until 1953 when the new Plaxton Venturer coach body shown here was fitted to the vehicle. *(David J Stanier)*

Blair & Palmer's Burlingham-bodied CVD6 coach CAG 798 (fleet number D40) was one of four acquired from Western SMT in 1949. The Scottish operator had never used them in service before selling them on. *(Author's Collection)*

8612). The only other purchase made during the year was of SY 9908, an Albion Valiant with Plaxton bodywork, which arrived from Whitelaw of Uddingston. It had gone by the following year, while the pre-war TD5 double-decker was sold for scrap in January 1963. BAG 102 would continue as the company's only double-decker until sold to Sowerby of Gilsland in December 1965.

The last two Daimler CVD6 coaches to be acquired by Blair & Palmer arrived in early 1962. OOC 200 came from Smith of Birmingham and FDL 65 from Hutchings of Oxley (although, like B&P's Margham-bodied FDL 67 it had been new to Shotter on the Isle of Wight). Both had Burlingham bodywork and replaced the last two 'CAG' CVD6s bought from Western SMT in 1949. The next arrival was absolutely unique, even by Blair & Palmer standards.

The vehicle which became UHH 877 started life (like NHH 482 before it) as a standard Commer Avenger IV chassis. As with its predecessor, the Palmers converted it to underfloor engine layout, but on this occasion the Commer TS3 engine was removed completely (to be held in stock as a 'spare' for the other Avengers in the fleet) and replaced by an 8-cylinder Albion power-plant – basically two 4-cylinder units 'glued' together. It received a home-made 45-seat body very similar to that on NHH 482, but some sources refer to this unit as being a rebuild of an earlier Scottish Aviation body. To me this seems unlikely. The completed vehicle (chassis number BP2) joined 'BP1' on the routes to Newton Arlosh and Anthorn in May 1962.

Newcomers during the next five years (all second-hand) included a good cross-section of the used coach market. A Plaxton-bodied Avenger III (YEH 220) arrived in November 1962, followed by a Bedford SB1/Burlingham in April 1963 (FJM 534). A far rarer acquisition, also in April 1963, was that of Duple Elizabethan-bodied Atkinson Alpha VS 6440, previously operated by Doig of Greenock. The only arrival during 1964 was 733 PRF, an Avenger IV with Duple bodywork, and in 1965 there were no purchases at all. Another Avenger IV, this time with Plaxton bodywork, was bought from a dealer in July 1966 (YUM 581) and was joined in September by a 13-seat Trojan 19 minibus (YRY 884). A new type of chassis arrived in the fleet in February 1967 when Ford 510E Thames Trader/Burlingham Seagull 60 XUX 812 was acquired. It came from a Brighton operator but had been new to Whittle of Highley. It apparently made a good impression as two identical vehicles (609/11 BOH) were acquired from Palmer's old friends Stockland of Birmingham in May 1967.

Double-deckers returned to the fleet in 1967, mainly for contract work. The first was the best. DCK 221, a former Ribble 'White Lady' PD2/3 with fully-fronted East Lancs bodywork, arrived from Bingley of Kinsley (United Services) in April. Sadly it only stayed at Carlisle until September when it was resold to Morris Bros of Swansea. The other double-deck acquisition of 1967 was RKP 907, a PD2/12 with Weymann 'Orion' bodywork, originally operated by Maidstone & District, which arrived at Drovers Lane in August. It was supposed to be one of a pair, with the other (RKP 911) replacing the Ribble 'White Lady', but events overtook this intention.

Palmer of Carlisle

In 1967 Jack Palmer's second son, WA (Alan) Palmer was 30 years old and although recently made a director of the company he was employed mainly as a driver. Appeals to his father for more managerial responsibility apparently fell on deaf ears and in November he decided to go into business on his own account using the fleet-name 'Palmer of Carlisle'. His first two vehicles were the former M&D PD2/12 RKP 911 (he had been handling negotiations with the dealership!) and ex-Northern General Tiger Cub/Weymann Hermes saloon DCN 886. Later acquisitions by this offshoot of the main business would include two Northern Counties-bodied Daimler CSG6-30s bought from Lancashire United (105/8 JTD), a Regent V/Northern Counties PCP 403 from Hebble, and Lodekka/ECW XAO 604 from Cumberland Motor Services, as well as a varied portfolio of second-hand coaches.

Alan Palmer's company was almost exclusively devoted to contract work, and is thus outside of the scope of this present volume, but for the record those contracts included taking construction workers from Carlisle to the section of the M6 being built between Penrith and Carlisle (usually operated by coaches), transporting workers to and from the Pirelli factory in Carlisle (requiring two

53

double-deckers), and carrying schoolchildren to their swimming lessons at the municipal baths.

Alan Palmer remained a director of Blair & Palmer, and was allowed to rent one of the two garage buildings on the Church Street (Caldewgate) site. He would eventually take his independent operation back into the main family company after the death of his father in the mid-1970s, although it would resurface again in 1986, using the same trading name.

The Ford Era

The 'lost' double-decker (RKP 911) was eventually replaced by ESD 217, a Guy Arab IV with Northern Counties bodywork acquired from Western SMT in March 1968. It would be Blair & Palmer's final double-deck acquisition. In the years between then and Jack Palmer's death all acquisitions were coaches, most were second-hand, and all were of either Ford or Albion manufacture. The Albions were all of one type, the VT21L Victor with Duple (Northern) Firefly bodywork. Six were acquired on the second-hand market between 1968 and 1972. It goes without saying that such vehicles were totally unsuited to stage-carriage work and the Fireflies were confined to excursion and private hire work.

The Fords were of a more varied nature. By 1972 there were eight of them (the majority of the fleet) including three 510E or 570E Thames Traders, two Ford 676E Thames 36s, two R192s, and an R226. None were that suitable for stage work, but the R192s and the R226 (all of which had driver-operated power doors) could be made to do the job if they had to, which they did. This situation was rectified to some extent in March 1972 when the company acquired its first new vehicles for ten years, a pair of Ford R192s (YHH 401K with Plaxton bodywork and YHH 444K with Duple). Although built to coach designs they were equipped with ticket machine holders and other accoutrements of driver-only operation.

Two more new Fords arrived in 1972 (DHH 44/5L) and another in 1973 (NHH 900M). All had Duple bodywork. As will be obvious, the stage-carriage routes were now considered to be a very small part of the business and coaching was very much the name of the game. It continued thus until the end, the only major difference being a change in vehicle policy after the founder's death. The Fords and Albions disappeared and were replaced by heavyweight chassis types. By 1984 the fleet was made up of six AEC Reliances (three of them with Caetano bodywork), two Leyland Leopards, a Leyland TRCTL Tiger, a Caetano-bodied Volvo B58, and a Van Hool T815 integral.

Deregulation and After

As deregulation approached it became obvious that different members of the family held irreconcilable opinions about how to react to the new legislation. Preparations were made to split the business into four parts to adequately represent these different threads within the family. Blair & Palmer Ltd would continue as a property company until the assorted 'legacy' assets were sold and the proceeds distributed. A new company, Blair & Palmer (1986) Ltd was formed to inherit the family's assets in overseas coach touring. This entity was based in Chelmsford, Essex, close to the home of John Palmer, and its other directors included John's eponymous son (born in 1962), George, and Barbara. George Palmer also became an operator in his own right, trading in the Carlisle area as 'Borderbus' and operating a small fleet of ex-Preston Leyland Panthers on schools contracts.

Alan Palmer, somewhat surprisingly, proved to be the family member with most commitment to the stage-carriage services. He re-established 'Palmer of Carlisle' and acquired three elderly Ford/Willowbrook DP45F saloons (FTC 849/50J and RSB 26K) from Bowman on the Isle of Mull for use on the Newton Arlosh routes. These services were not registered as commercial operations during the deregulation process and were subsequently lost to a lower bidder. Although buses operated by the Palmer family would no longer provide the traditional routes along the B5307, they continued to operate stage services as Alan Palmer was successful in bidding to operate from Carlisle to Longtown (just on the English side of the border) and Gretna (on the Scottish side).

By 1989 his resurrected company was operating Alexander-bodied Atlanteans (from Tyne & Wear), a Northern Counties-bodied Bristol VR (from Rhymney Valley), and a handful of Ford saloons on both tendered services and on commercial routes around Carlisle (in competition with Cumberland Motor Services). He had also reassembled a large coaching fleet, including six

Fleet number AEC44 went to another Scottish vehicle, Weymann-bodied Regent BUS 159, which came to Blair & Palmer after a career with Glasgow Corporation as fleet number 593. The Carlisle company sold it in March 1955 for use as a caravan. *(Roy Marshall)*

This Duple-bodied Albion Victor, FHH 571 (fleet number A46) was one of a pair delivered new to Blair & Palmer in 1951. It lasted for seven years before being sold to Kirkpatrick of Brigham. *(Author's Collection)*

Centre entrance Commer-Beadle T48 Rochester 630 BPF was new to the Caterham Motor Co in Kent in 1957. They sold it to Blair & Palmer in 1958 as fleet number BC52. *(Author's Collection)*

Daimler CVD6 coach FDL 67 carried rare Margham bodywork. It had been new to Shotter on the Isle of Wight but came to Blair & Palmer from Morley of Whittlesey (near Peterborough) in August 1958. It was allocated fleet number D54 but may not have worn it. *(Author's Collection)*

Fords, and in many ways was his father's natural successor despite their earlier rift.

At the end of 1989 he sold the Palmer of Carlisle operation to Cumberland (or 'Stagecoach Cumberland' as it by then preferred to be known). The original family company (latterly with Hannah and Barbara Palmer as its only directors) had been officially wound up in May after disposing of its fixed assets, including the Drovers Lane/East Tower Street headquarters. The Carlisle branch of Debenhams now stands on the site. George Palmer's 'Borderbus' operation was sold to Cumbria Coaches (a relative upstart when compared to the Palmers) in the mid-1990s. The only part of the family business still extant is the Chelmsford-based tour operator where George and John (the younger) remain as active directors.

Dallam of Milnthorpe

The small south Westmorland town of Milnthorpe (population 2,100) sits astride the A6 trunk road, roughly half way between the county seat at Kendal and Carnforth in Lancashire. Another important road leads westwards from the town to the seaside resort of Arnside (population 2,300). Arnside seafront (actually on the southern shores of Morecambe Bay) has impressive views of the Lake District fells and used to be one of the few places where you could look northwards from Westmorland to Lancashire rather than the other way around.

The most noticeable landmark along the road between Milnthorpe and Arnside is Dallam Tower, a stately home later converted into a major hotel, and when John Fawcett decided to start a bus service from Kendal to Milnthorpe and Arnside he named his new operation (Dallam Motor Services) after this well-known edifice. Fawcett had opened a garage and filling station in Milnthorpe shortly after the end of the First World War, followed the usual progression by operating hire-cars and then taxis, and then started his bus service in 1922.

The very first vehicle remains unknown, but fleet numbers 2 (EC 5413) and 3 (HN 3095) were normal control Vulcan 23-seaters acquired in March 1924 and April 1925 respectively. No 4 (EC 7137) was also a Vulcan but of the larger VWBL model with a 32-seat dual-door body. It was new in July 1926. The next delivery was of No 5 (EC 8368), a Leyland PLSC3 Lion which arrived in July 1928. This vehicle lasted with Dallam until the end of the company in 1950 and then saw further service with the Forestry Commission as a mobile office.

In October 1928 the company started a second service, from Arnside to Lancaster via Silverdale, the Yealands, and Carnforth. This operated three or four times each day, compared to the hourly frequency on the Kendal route, but still required the acquisition of further vehicles. Another new Leyland Lion, No 6 (EC 8765), arrived to ease the strain and would later be joined by two second-hand vehicles which remained unnumbered, 26-seat Vulcan TD 2921 (originally with Pilgrim of Elswick) and PLSC1 Lion CK 3865. Both came (via dealers) from Ribble. According to some sources TD 2921, which lasted until 1950, was later given fleet number 6. As there appears to be no photographic evidence of this I remain unconvinced.

The new service to Lancaster (Ribble already operated from Silverdale to Carnforth and Lancaster via a slightly different route) and Dallam's success on the Milnthorpe-Kendal corridor (where their service was faster and cheaper than Ribble's) irritated the larger operator's management into action. Both of Dallam's stage services were subjected to an intrusion by 'chaser' buses and Fawcett responded by buying two small Fords during 1929 to serve as chasers to the chasers. They remain unidentified and received no fleet numbers before their sale the following year after the Ribble threat receded.

Dallam returned to Vulcan for its major purchase in 1929, a 26-seat Duchess (fleet number 7, EC 8852) delivered in July. It would be the last Vulcan to join the fleet. The next delivery, fleet number 8 (EC 9694), was a 31-seat Leyland LT2 Lion which arrived in August 1930. Further Lions would arrive in October 1934 (No 9, JM 1464) and July 1937 (No 10, JM 3095). Another Leyland, on this occasion an LZ5A Cheetah, was scheduled for delivery in October 1939 but was delayed by the start of the Second World War. It eventually arrived in May 1940, sporting (?) a 32-seat Burlingham 'austerity' body and the expected fleet number 11 (JM 4898). The only new arrival during the remainder of the war was a Bedford OWB utility bus (fleet number 12, JM 5567) in July 1944.

When peace came in 1945 the company (by then J Fawcett & Sons, trading as Dallam Motor

57

Services) appeared to be in good shape. Two of the founder's sons (John Jr – known as Jack, and Harold) were active in the bus operations while a third son (Percy) ran the filling station, garage, and taxis. However, it seems that the bus services were making very little money. Most of the vehicles were quite old (1926 Vulcan No 4 was still in use, and 20+ for a Vulcan was the equivalent of 100+ for a human being!) and required intensive maintenance to keep them operational. The old-timers soldiered on until 1948 when the first post-war vehicle was finally delivered. This was JM 7697, a Seddon Mark 4 with Seddon's own bodywork, and was given fleet number 14 (13 was not used). A second Seddon Mk 4, JM 8122 (fleet number 15) arrived in 1949.

Three different correspondents have regaled me with stories about the Seddons, all agreeing that they were truly dreadful machines and responsible in no small part for the company's demise. Whereas the pre-war machines which they had replaced on the Kendal route were very old, they were also quite comfortable and – given Dallam's lower fares – a perfectly acceptable alternative to Ribble vehicles on the Milnthorpe-Kendal sector where Dallam made most of its money. The Seddons were brand-new but also noisy, smoky, and bone rattlingly uncomfortable. People began to plan their journeys to suit Ribble's timings.

There was very little that the Fawcetts could do about this state of affairs, having committed all of their available capital to the purchase of the vile Seddons. With hindsight they would have been better advised to buy good quality second-hand vehicles in their place. At the beginning of 1950 the service to Kendal went into the red for the first time, and as the Lancaster service had never made an annual profit this was a serious development. Fortunately the company still operated three lucrative schools contracts (from Arnside and Milnthorpe to the grammar schools at Kendal and Heversham, and from Arnside to the secondary modern school in Milnthorpe), but there had already been mutterings about the elderly vehicles used on these contracts. A family tragedy intervened to tip the scales. In June 1950 Percy Fawcett died from self-inflicted gunshot wounds. As can be imagined, the two surviving brothers were deeply disheartened by this event.

An approach was made to Ribble, who proved to be quite generous in the circumstances, and acquired the goodwill of the stage services (plus the schools contracts, although these were about to expire) for the staggering sum of £10,000 – more than £120,000 in present day values. The money changed hands on the 1st of December 1950 and Dallam Motor Services ceased to exist. The Seddons were sold for a pittance for service elsewhere and most of the pre-war vehicles were scrapped (although rumours persist that one of the Vulcans, probably EC 8852, survives). Jack Fawcett retired and Harold used his share of the money to buy a small factory to the south of Milnthorpe. My correspondents all agree that the firm is still fondly remembered, especially by the generation which made its journeys to school on ancient but well appointed Vulcans.

Hartness of Penrith

Ernie Hartness was a star – there is no other word which does the man justice. Born in the village of Skelton (to the north-west of Penrith on the edge of the area known as the Inglewood Forest) in 1893 to a farming family, he became a selfless benefactor to the local community, operating local bus services at a loss for years because the people needed them. If you place Stagecoach at one end of the spectrum, Ernie was at the other.

Invalided out of the army in 1916 he returned from the trenches to his native Cumberland and used his military pay-off to buy a horse and cart, operating a traditional 'village carrier' service into Penrith on market days. At the beginning of the following year he switched to petrol power with the acquisition of a nine year old Daimler taxi. This vehicle (AO 580) was converted into a primitive bus and began a timetabled week-day service from Skelton and other nearby villages to Penrith in January 1917. In May a second service was introduced, running from the villages to Carlisle each Saturday with enough time for shopping before the return journey.

In 1922 a second Daimler was acquired. CP 1508 was a former War Department lorry chassis and Ernie equipped it with a home-made (removable) bus body. When not needed for passenger work it returned to lorry configuration, providing the nucleus for the haulage side of the

Here is the first of Blair & Palmer's home-made 'Commer Specials', NHH 482. Jack Palmer and his fitters took a brand-new Commer Avenger IV chassis, shifted the TS3 engine from the front to underneath the floor amidships, and then built a 45-seat front entrance bus body to suit. It entered service in May 1959 as fleet number C59 and is now preserved in the Potteries. *(Author's Collection)*

AEC Regal III coach EHJ 433 was one of three vehicles acquired with the business of Gibson of Carlisle in January 1960. It carried a fully-fronted Gurney Nutting body and was sold to Prince of Cleator Moor in April 1961. Allocated fleet number AEC62 may not have been worn due to the vehicle's brief stay with Blair & Palmer. *(Author's Collection)*

business which continued (albeit on a relatively small scale) throughout the company's existence. The third passenger vehicle to enter the fleet, at an unknown date, was a 26-seat Tilling-Stevens char-a-banc, TB 1093.

Fleet details for the remainder of the 1920s are drastically incomplete, although it is known that Hartness operated three Morris-Commercials and a (Belgian built) Minerva. These were the vehicles used on a new daily service from Penrith to Carlisle via Skelton, Ivegill, and Durdar which began in April 1928. The route was already operated by William Smith and the passenger flow was far too modest to support two operators. Ernie Hartness was the loser and ceased operation on the route in September 1929. The Morris-Commercials and the Minerva were sold to pay off the accumulated debts, and the only thing that saved the Hartness business from ruin was a successful tender to operate contract journeys for Penrith Grammar School.

Ernie had learned his lesson. In such thinly populated countryside one did not compete with another. His ambitions became more humble and acquisitions in the early 1930s were limited to an (unidentified) Commer and a Star Flyer. The next arrival was a 20-seat Albion PK26/Roberts coach, SY 3308, which came from SMT in Scotland, and this was followed by a third Daimler in 1935. Like its two predecessors of this marque, GK 5415 had an interesting back-story. Built in 1930 as a CH6 double-decker for the London General Omnibus Co (part of a batch of three bought for comparison to the standard AEC-built ST design) it was discarded after just over four years when the trials came to an end. LGOC kept the double-deck body (which was of AEC-compatible measurements) and sold the chassis to a dealer who equipped it with a 30-seat saloon body and sold it to Ernie.

Building a Rural Network

The 'new' bus was required to operate a daily (except Sunday) Wigton-Caldbeck service which had been acquired from Barker & Owen. Ernie received permission from the Traffic Commissioners to extend this from Caldbeck to Penrith after convincing them that the route in its original form was unviable. Two years later he bought the other Wigton to Penrith service (via Sebergham) from Cumberland Motor Services. This route had been started by Wright of Nenthead (qv) but had changed hands like a burning coal, passing first to Smith & Rose, and then to CMS in 1936. At that point Ribble had demanded a share under its area agreement with Cumberland, and rather than allow Ribble into Wigton Henry Meageen sold the service to Ernie Hartness for next to nothing. Other new services introduced to the growing Hartness network in 1937 were market-day runs (Tuesday and Saturday) from Mosedale and Mungrisedale to Penrith. These were discontinued for the duration of the Second World War and never restarted afterwards. Five passengers had apparently been considered to be a good load.

In January 1938 the service from Penrith to Carlisle, which had nearly bankrupted the business ten years earlier, fell into Ernie's lap. In the intervening years the licence had passed from William Smith (who died in 1930) to his wife Kate, then to Rowland & Graham in July 1932, and to Frank Welch in September 1936. Welch then became financially embarrassed and the route was sold on for a fraction of its potential value. Hartness now held a trunk route to Carlisle as well as his existing workings to Wigton, but this sounded more impressive to the public than it might have seemed to his bank manager. Ribble still took the lion's share of the Penrith to Carlisle traffic on their more direct service via the A6, and the Wigton routes were only busy on market days.

Known vehicle purchases in the latter half of the 1930s were restricted to four Duple-bodied Bedford WTBs, one new and three second-hand (but with low mileages). These vehicles operated the stage services, a new contract service to take employees to the BBC transmitter station near Skelton, and on an increasing amount of private hire work. This part of the business blossomed after Hartness acquired the excursions and tours licences of Tom Fleming in May 1939 along with premises at 12 Sandgate in Penrith. Before this all of Ernie's vehicles had been kept at his garage in Skelton. The Sandgate connection would grow in time.

In March 1940 Ernie acquired the local bus services of William Sowerby of Great Asby in Westmorland (not to be confused with William D Sowerby of Gilsland). These included routes from Great Asby to Kirkby Stephen (on Mondays), to Penrith (on Tuesdays) and to Appleby (on

The next four views (of Dallam Motors vehicles) are reproduced from poor quality postcards, but the rarity of the subjects justifies their inclusion. This is Dallam's fleet number 8, EC 9694, an LT2 Lion with a 31-seat Leyland body delivered in August 1930. It gave 20 years of service to the company. *(Tony Hutt)*

Dallam's fleet number 9, JM 1464, was an all-Leyland LT5A Lion new in October 1934. It lasted until October 1950. *(Tony Hutt)*

Wednesdays, Thursdays, and Fridays, and on Saturday evenings), and a vehicle was permanently out-stationed at Appleby to cover the timings.

More expansion came in July 1942 with the purchase of the business of Richard Coulston. Coulston had services southwards from his Penrith base to Burn Banks (a new village created for workers on the Hawes Water reservoir project, served on a daily basis) and to the remote hamlet of Rosgill (served on Tuesdays only). The deal included three vehicles, a 20-seat Commer bus (WH 4104), a 20-seat Bedford WLB/Willowbrook bus (RM 8993), and a 25-seat Bedford WTL/Robson coach (ETN 645).

61

This 1937 Lion with an updated version of Leyland's bus bodywork, JM 3095, was Dallam's fleet number 10. It was also still in the fleet in 1950. *(Tony Hutt)*

Dallam's final new vehicle was its second Seddon Mk 4, JM 8122 (fleet number 15), delivered in 1949. Like its predecessor of 1948 vintage it carried Seddon's own bus bodywork, but with a forward entrance. The 1948 vehicle had a rear entrance. *(Tony Hutt)*

The ten-year old Commer had seen better days, but Ernie removed its body and placed it on a two-ton Bedford lorry chassis. In this guise it became DRM 617 and continued in service for another eight years.

The growing Hartness route network was of sufficient strategic importance to merit the allocation of five Bedford OWB utility buses during the Second World War (ERM 552/3, ERM 657, ERM 949, and FAO 500). Other wartime arrivals – in addition to the ex-Coulston vehicles listed above – were two vehicles previously operated by Robinson of Appleby (qv), Bedford WTB/Duple coach JM 3815 and OWB utility bus JM 5298, which were transferred to Hartness ownership during 1944. According to one source these vehicles had been operating a contract service to a mysterious 'top secret' RAF airfield in the Appleby area, used to train the pilots who flew Westland Lysanders into occupied France. When the contract ended after D-Day they were no longer needed by Robinson. However, I have been unable to find any details of this airfield and would welcome further information.

At around this time Ernie had been casting his gaze around Penrith town centre, looking for larger premises to replace his existing (rather primitive) facilities at Skelton and at 12 Sandgate. He found what he was looking for on the opposite side of Sandgate when a former Wesleyan chapel (which had been damaged in a fire and abandoned) came on to the market. The builders went in, and despite the privations of wartime managed to complete the work by May 1945. The Wesleyan chapel had become a bus station and depot, capable of holding all of Hartness' vehicles either undercover or in the large adjoining yard. At first the original premises in Skelton were retained for the haulage side of the business, but by late 1946 the lorries had also moved to Sandgate and the Skelton garage was sold. This may help to account for at least a part of the relatively enormous expenditure which followed.

An Armada of CVD6s

After six years of war the people of Britain wanted to have fun and coach outings were a cheapish source of excitement and pleasure. For most operators this was a one-way street which led from urban areas to the countryside or the beach, but for Ernie Hartness the traffic ran in both directions. People in rural Cumbria not only wanted to go to the seaside, but to the big cities such as Manchester and Newcastle for shopping trips and for cultural events. On the other side of the equation, urban visitors to the Lake District tended to stay for a week or more, unlike (for example) Blackpool where a lot of the visitors were day-trippers. Long stay visitors needed coach excursions and in Penrith Ernie Hartness was the man willing to provide them.

A large influx of pre-war vehicles began to arrive at Sandgate to cater for this trade. Acquisitions in 1945/6 included an Albion PM28 from Red & White (WO 6566), and three Albion Valkyries (XS 4766 from Young of Paisley and CS 7968/AAG 864 from AA Motor Services). These were followed by three Crossley Alphas from Ashton-under-Lyne (ATC 975/6 and CTD 788). All seven of these vehicles had bus seating, but the excursions which they operated were of a fairly local nature and the public was so eager to get out and about that they didn't really care. Nevertheless, Ernie was a canny enough businessman to know that they were a stop-gap solution and that more luxurious vehicles would be required.

In early 1946 Ernie Hartness placed an order for no fewer than 36 Daimler CVD6 chassis, to be delivered over the next four years. It would have been an impressive order for a major operator, let alone a small Cumberland independent, and Daimler would not have allocated the delivery positions without a substantial deposit on each vehicle. They didn't have to – operators were hammering at their doors, demanding new vehicles at more or less any price.

This raises the inevitable question of where all the money came from to finance this radical modernisation. Ernie had already made a large expenditure at the end of 1945 by buying Hedley Blair's share of Blair & Palmer, and should (in theory) have been 'on his uppers'. As mentioned above, the Skelton premises had been sold, but at the prevailing prices this would have realised less money than had already been spent on the purchase and rebuilding of the Sandgate premises. We seem to be left with the alternatives of a major win on the football pools or a pact with the devil. Both of these options seem unlikely.

In the immediate post-war era the acquisition of chassis was, to some extent, only half of the problem. Bodywork manufacturers were also hard-pressed to keep up with the enormous demand for new vehicles and waiting times were long. Ernie had already rebodied several of his vehicles and naturally saw this as a solution to the bodywork problem. When the first four CVD6 chassis were delivered in mid-1946 he fitted them with pre-war Alexander bus bodies which had started their lives on vehicles belonging to W

Alexander of Falkirk and Young of Paisley. FRM 492/493/615/649 would receive new Plaxton coach bodies between 1949 and 1952 when the market had returned to normal conditions. The other two 'new' vehicles acquired in 1946 were also rebodied. GAO 3 was based on a Bedford OLBD drop-side lorry chassis but received the 24-seat Duple bus body from pre-war WTB VN 7462, while GAO 81 was a Bedford ML chassis which inherited the Willowbrook body from (ex-Coulston) WLB RM 8993.

Delivery of the CVD6s accelerated in 1947 with 13 delivered to Hartness (and others to Blair & Palmer). To accommodate this sudden surge Ernie went out on a grand tour of dealers and scrapyards, looking for suitable bodies that might last for a few years. He returned having bought a large number of pre-war ECOC/ECW bodies which had been used to modernise much older chassis owned by North Western. The first 1947 CVD6, GAO 136, received the body from Crossley Alpha ATC 975. This was replaced by a new Plaxton coach body in 1949. The next two deliveries, GAO 152/3 were lucky enough to receive Plaxton coach bodies from new, but GAO 169 started life with an ex-North Western body and GAO 201 with the body from Crossley Alpha ATC 976. The next machine, GAO 399, also received a temporary ex-North Western body but was quickly rebodied as a double-decker by Roe. In that form it was Ernie's first ever double-decker and survived until 1965. Then came two non-Daimlers. GAO 400 was a new Albion Valkyrie chassis but received a pre-war Alexander body. It was later sold to Sowerby of Gilsland (qv). GAO 595 was a new Bedford OB which provided a platform for a Mulliner utility body donated by an unknown OWB.

Back in the Daimler arena GAO 951/2/3 were given ex-North Western bodies: 951 and 953 would receive new (fully-fronted) Roe bus bodies in 1954, while 952 would become the second Roe H56R double-decker. The fourth of this batch, GAO 954, got a pre-war Alexander unit and had to wait until 1955 to receive a new Plaxton coach body. At the tail end of the 1947 CVD6 deliveries, GRM 91 was the recipient of the body from Crossley Alpha CTD 788, while GRM 365/393 had ex-North Western bodies. GRM 365 was transferred to Blair & Palmer in this form while 393 was updated as a Plaxton coach. Two more Albion Valkyrie chassis were acquired during the second half of 1947. GRM 22/133 were both given pre-war Alexander bodies and later sold to Sowerby of Gilsland. The year's impressive list of deliveries ended with a brand-new (both chassis and body) Bedford OB/Mulliner bus, GRM 378.

The pace of deliveries in 1948 was only slightly less frantic. The first three of the six CVD6s delivered in that year (GRM 918 and HAO 138/9) had Plaxton coach bodies from new, but the other three (HAO 577/8 and HAO 987) had to settle for ex-North Western units. New Roe FB35F bodies were fitted to 577/8 in 1954, but the identity of the replacement body on 987 is unrecorded. It obviously received one as it remained in service until 1961.

Two more CVD6s arrived in 1949. JAO 50/749 started out with ex-North Western bodies but were soon rebuilt by Ormac of Preston as 26-seat coaches. The only other deliveries during the year were both 'all new'. JAO 748 was a solitary Commer Commando with a 29-seat bus body by Scottish Aviation, while JRM 112 was Hartness's first example of the ubiquitous Bedford OB/Duple Vista coach. By this time the Hartness fleet was thoroughly re-equipped and 1950 saw the arrival of the final two new CVD6s. KAO 158/9 were fitted with fully-fronted Plaxton coachwork from new.

Now, before anybody tells me that I can't add up, I do realise that the list of CVD6s given so far (including those previously mentioned under the Blair & Palmer heading) comes to a total of 33. What happened to the other three from Ernie's original order? I simply don't know. Perhaps Daimler asked if they might deliver them to other customers with a more pressing need, but this is guesswork.

The Shap Catastrophe

Just after 2pm on the 23rd of August 1953, Hartness CVD6/Plaxton coach FRM 649 departed for Morecambe with a full load of excursionists on board. The coach was being driven by Ernie's brother, John Hartness. Half an hour later the vehicle was on the A6 at Shap, stuck behind two slow-moving lorries in the southbound lane. John Hartness could see the road for a reasonable distance ahead and decided to overtake. As he

Ernie Hartness's fondness for Daimlers is mentioned at some length in the text. This one is GAO 953, delivered in early 1947 and originally fitted with a pre-war ECW body from North Western. In 1954 it received this new, fully-fronted, bus body by Roe and remained in service until 1966. *(David J Stanier)*

Daimler CVD6 HAO 577 was delivered in early 1948 and was also fitted with a pre-war ECW body new to North Western before being rebodied by Roe in 1954. Like its sister it also lasted until 1966. These Roe saloons were the work-horses of Hartness's deeply rural network. *(Author's Collection)*

Yet another CVD6, KAO 158, delivered to Hartness in early 1950. The vehicle carried this fully-fronted Plaxton coach body from new but was also withdrawn during the 'Great Daimler Cull' of 1966. *(Keith Johnson Collection)*

At first glance this might appear to be a Bedford SB with an early version of Plaxton's Consort bodywork. It is, in fact, a Karrier Gamecock with a 26-seat miniature version of the Consort design. TRM 345 was one of a pair new to Hartness in May 1957. *(Author's Collection)*

drew alongside the rearmost of the two lorries it's driver made the fateful decision to overtake the lorry in front of him. It seems that the lorry driver was completely unaware of the Hartness coach, or had presumed that it was still safely behind. The lorry side-swiped the CVD6, sending it across the northbound lane, through the dry stone wall beyond, and over an 80 ft sheer drop into the valley below.

Seven of those on board the coach died at the scene of the accident, including John Hartness. Local hospitals reported that they had received 33 injured survivors. This figure might seem suspect, as the coach was only a 33 seater (plus driver = 34, minus the dead = 27) but it should be remembered that there were toddlers on board who were sitting on adult laps, a common practice at that time and perfectly legal. The official report into the accident allocated two thirds of the blame to the lorry driver, and one third to John Hartness who they felt had been too ambitious in attempting to pass two lorries at once. I've read this accident report many times and I still don't understand this decision.

Fortunately for the business, local people also saw it that way and once the grieving was over they continued to give their excursion and private hire bookings to the firm. It was Hartness's only fatal accident in 54 years.

Retrenchment and Decline

No more new vehicles were delivered until 1957 when TAO 712, a Commer Avenger IV with Plaxton coach bodywork, joined the fleet. The next two deliveries, in May of the same year, were also Rootes Group products, but of a far more unusual kind. TRM 345/6 were built on the Karrier Gamecock chassis more readily associated with goods vehicles and carried Plaxton C26F bodywork. The first delivery during 1958 was VRM 835, a Bedford SB1 with Yeates Europa coachwork which arrived in July. A few weeks later VRM 836 materialised in the shape of an Avenger IV with Plaxton bodywork. Identical vehicle WAO 28 was delivered in September, along with a second-hand Bedford OB/Duple Vista, KUG 666.

The stage services, feeling the pressure from rising car ownership, began to decline. The services in Westmorland (acquired from Sowerby of Great Asby in 1940) were the first to go, passed to Robinson of Appleby (qv) in September 1957. By way of compensation Hartness acquired the route from Carlisle to Ainstable previously operated by EL Proud and then Blair & Palmer, and this provided work for the CVD6 bus previously deployed to Appleby. In January 1958 the magazine 'Commercial Motor' carried a news item stating that Ernie Hartness was to begin a new Penrith local service, but there seems to be no evidence of this either in the Traffic Commissioners' records or in the memories of local people. One change which definitely did take place, in January 1960, was the abandonment of Sunday services on the Penrith to Carlisle route. It was the first of many reductions to the traditional Hartness timetable.

The Bedford OB KUG 666 was sold in early 1962, but was immediately replaced with an identical vehicle acquired from Yates of Morecambe, KTF 235. The next arrival, in June 1962, was a brand new Bedford SB5, converted to suit Yeates Pegasus bodywork by having the leading axle set back. It could thus accommodate a front entrance and was capable of comfortable driver-only operation. The 44-seat vehicle, registered 979 GRM, was a regular on the service to Burn Banks during the summer months when the nine extra seats (compared to a CVD6 bus) were very useful in avoiding duplication. It was also Ernie's last new vehicle, another sign of the times. The next arrival at Sandgate, in November 1962, was Blair & Palmer CVD6/Roe double-decker CHH 162. Sadly it was destined to become a spares source for Ernie's two similar machines rather than to join them in service. In reality Ernie's third double-decker arrived in April 1965 when he bought Daimler CVG6/Northern Counties machine BSD 258 from Western SMT. It ran alongside the two original CVD6s until November, when they were both withdrawn, and the CVG6 became the only double-decker in the fleet.

The arrival of the CVG6 coincided with Ernie's application to the Traffic Commissioners to reduce the frequencies on most of his services. The Carlisle route was to be reduced from four full length journeys on Monday to Friday to three, and from six on Saturdays to four. Short workings at the Penrith end of the route were also reduced. The Penrith-Caldbeck-Wigton service had already

67

dwindled to one journey in each direction (timed to suit local schools) except on Tuesdays (market-day in both towns) when there were three round trips. In future it would run on Tuesdays only, and be worked by the same vehicle which already operated the Tuesday only Penrith-Sebergham-Wigton route.

On a more positive note, the Burn Banks service continued to produce an annual profit (most of it earned from tourists during the summer months) and kept its frequency of five times daily on weekdays and twice on Sundays. The contract to take employees to and from the BBC's Short Wave transmitter station at Skelton, first operated in 1939, also continued.

All purchases after the arrival of the Western SMT Daimler were second-hand coaches. These included Plaxton-bodied Avenger IIIs (such as XTO 806 and OWT 313), a Duple-bodied Avenger IV (VJW 881), and a Plaxton-bodied Bedford SB3 (6016 WU), but the most interesting were a quintet of elderly CVD6s, visually at least taking the company back to its post-war heyday. The first two to arrive were DMS 558 (in January 1966) and DMS 557 (in May of the same year). These were particularly fine examples of their type and had been fitted with fully-fronted ECW bodywork by their original owners, W Alexander & Son. A third example from the same batch, DMS 561, was acquired from Alexanders in April 1967. The last two CVD6s to arrive, BMS 416 in June 1967 and BMS 404 in November of that year, had also started their working careers with Alexander but came to Hartness from their second owner, Highland of Inverness. They carried Burlingham half-cab bodywork.

All five of the 'new' CVD6s retained their previous operators' liveries, a symptom of the company's rapid decline. In the case of the ECW-bodied machines, their previous colour scheme had been blue and cream, so they did not look too badly out of place at the Sandgate depot. The same could not be said of the Burlingham-bodied examples which appeared in service in Penrith in Highland's dark red and cream livery. Only the Hartness titles and legal lettering revealed the identity of their owner. It was a lacklustre way to celebrate Ernie's fiftieth anniversary as an operator of motor-buses, but repaints were expensive and the coffers were almost completely empty.

Ernie Hartness died in February 1971 at the age of 77 and the company he had founded ceased to trade. It had remained a sole proprietorship throughout its existence, and as Ernie had no children the business died with the man. His closest living relatives were his nephews, Richard, Ernest, and Joseph Robinson, who ran their own haulage company in Carlisle and had neither the time nor the inclination to become involved in the bus business. The goodwill of the stage services was sold by Ernie's executors to another haulage firm, Barnett & Graham of Penrith, who announced that they would run the bus services for a trial period of one month. Both partners in the firm had driven for Ernie on a part-time basis before starting their own company.

By the end of the trial period it had become obvious that the services to Carlisle and Wigton were losing money at a phenomenal rate, and that Ernie had only kept them going for so long as a charitable act. The losses more than counterbalanced all of the profits made on the Burn Banks service and from excursion, private hire, and contract work. Barnett & Graham reluctantly pulled out of the venture and went back to making a living. Ribble provided replacement services to Burn Banks and to the Skelton area, but the long routes to Carlisle and Wigton ceased to exist.

After the demise of the company the bus station/depot on Sandgate went through a variety of tenants, the last being a chicken hatchery which supplied new-born chicks to local poultry farmers. After this the buildings became derelict and were finally demolished in 1991 to make way for a new (council owned) bus station and a housing development called Sandgate Court. In a gratifying nod to the past the clock from the old bus station, complete with its 'Hartness Bus Services' lettering now hangs on the external wall of the Sandgate Court flats. Ernie would have liked that.

Hetherington & Renwick of Garrigill

The small town of Alston in north-eastern Cumberland is a fairly remote community by anybody's standards, but the local lead-mining industry was important enough to merit the construction of a railway branch line from the main Carlisle-Newcastle route. There were

Hartness also bought full-size coaches from the Rootes Group, including this Commer Avenger IV/Plaxton Consort VRM 836, new in August 1958. *(David Atkinson)*

Here is Ernie Hartness's well-known Yeates Pegasus, 979 GRM, enjoying a trip to the seaside. The modified Bedford SB5, new in June 1962, was more usually to be found on the service from Penrith to Burn Banks. *(Keith Johnson Collection)*

69

Hartness acquired this CVD6 with ECW 'Queen Mary' bodywork, DMS 557, from Alexander in May 1966. It was one of three from the same batch which came to Penrith in 1966/7. *(Author's Collection)*

This (petrol-engined) Bedford SB3 with Plaxton Consort IV bodywork, 6016 WU, had been new to Wigmore of Dinnington in 1958. It was acquired by Hartness in October 1967. *(Robert F Mack)*

even more remote places nearby. The village of Garrigill, high on Alston Moor to the south of the town, was one of these.

In the early 20th century Garrigill was connected, on demand, to Alston Station by a local village carrier, John Hetherington. A horse and cart was the equipment. By the end of the First World War this was proving inadequate and Hetherington went into partnership with young Horace Renwick, the son of a local farmer, who knew a lot about internal combustion engines. The two men bought a succession of convertible lorry-buses to continue the traditional mix of passengers and goods. A photograph exists of one of these early vehicles carrying a char-a-banc body, but there are so many people obscuring the machine that identification is impossible.

When the Traffic Commissioners and Road Service Licences came into the picture in 1930/31, the business was forced to make a commitment to a timetable for its passenger services. A daily licence was awarded, connecting Garrigill to Alston via both Howhill and Leadgate. Four journeys were operated on weekdays (timed to connect with the passenger trains) and two on Sundays (scheduled to suit churchgoers). A written account of life in Garrigill during the 1930s describes the bus then in use as a 'Model T Ford', but the accuracy of this statement is unknown. To many lay-people anything with a bonnet was a Model T.

The first known vehicle was a Bedford WLB with a 20-seat Waveney body, AAO 204, acquired from Bennett of Millom in January 1941. Bennett's services had just been acquired by Cumberland Motor Services. The WLB was replaced (at an unknown date) by a Mulliner-bodied Bedford OB bus, CTY 303. This vehicle had been new to Fox of Falstone in Northumberland in February 1948, later passing to Tait of Kirkwhelpington and then to Hetherington & Renwick. It would be the company's final bus.

Horace Renwick (by then the leading light in the venture) faced the usual quandary of a deeply rural bus operator. The population of Garrigill could not sustain a more frequent service than that already provided, but the increasing numbers of privately owned cars had raised public expectations that they should be able to travel according to their own timetable. The Sunday service on the Garrigill route was particularly poorly patronised and ceased in May 1958. The weekday services continued until the summer of 1959 when they were suddenly abandoned without prior notice to the Traffic Commissioners. No replacement operators were forthcoming.

Hetherington & Renwick Ltd continued in business as a small haulage contractor (the company usually had two vehicles) until 1965 when Horace Renwick died. Six years later a bus route (of a very modest kind) returned to Garrigill for the first time in 12 years, when Wright Bros of Nenthead (qv) began a fortnightly market-day service to Alston. This was funded by the local Rural District Council and by a support grant from the Garrigill School charitable trust. Unsurprisingly, this service is no longer in Wrights' timetable.

Keswick Borrowdale Bus Services

Attitudes towards tourism changed radically during the Victorian Age. At the beginning of Queen Victoria's reign most of her citizens would have regarded an area such as the Lake District as an uncivilised (and quite possibly dangerous) wilderness. By the time of her death the Lakeland poets and artists had alerted the nation to the natural beauty of the region, and the new railway companies had made it accessible to anyone with the train fare. Keswick, close to the particularly picturesque Derwent Water and the highest of the Cumberland fells, was well-positioned to benefit from this new influx of visitors.

Several luxury hotels were built in the town, including the well-known Lake Hotel, and almost all of them offered their guests a wide variety of excursions into the surrounding countryside. These outings were operated with four-horse carriages, the number of 'horsepower' being dictated by the steep hills encountered on most local roads. Lake Hotel Coaches became a separate company in 1904 (although still owned by the hotel's Wilson family) and operated horse-drawn vehicles for the first 20 years of its existence.

One of the most popular excursions ran along the eastern shore of Derwent Water, paused at the Lodore Falls, and then continued through Grange-in-Borrowdale to the village of Seatoller at the foot of the vertiginous Honister Pass. From here the visitor could explore the Borrowdale fells or the famous Haystacks ridge later popularised by Wainwright in his walkers' guides.

Things changed after the First World War when motor vehicles began to be more common than horse-drawn conveyances. Char-a-bancs were easier to house than horses, and the hoteliers found their dominance challenged by entrepreneurs who had returned from the war with mechanical knowledge and money in their pockets. By the end of the 1920s the road to Seatoller was being used by local motor-coach operators such as RW Simpson and the Weightman family. Simpson was also the licensee of the Oddfellow Arms public house in Keswick. Robert Askew of Grange-in-Borrowdale saw the Keswick-based vehicles passing his farm and decided that he too was going to have a piece of the action. Others came to the area from outside in search of profitable business. Thomas Young had operated in Aspatria before emigrating to Keswick along with his vehicle.

There were many others, but most were deterred from continuing their excursions by the 1930 Road Traffic Act which made it clear that such operations (being operated on a daily basis with several journeys each day) must in future be licensed as stage-carriage services, with the attendant bureaucracy and higher maintenance standards for the vehicles employed. Perversely this made the Seatoller route more attractive to Cumberland Motor Services (less competition = more potential profit) and CMS started to operate on the route at the beginning of the summer season of 1930. Despite their 'Johnny-come-lately' status they were awarded a licence for the route by the Traffic Commissioners along with Askew, Simpson, Weightman, and Young.

One peculiarity of the licences was that only Simpson and Weightman operated on a year-round basis, with the other three providing additional frequencies from Easter to the end of September. As only one vehicle was required to operate the winter timetable, Simpson and Weightman took it in turns with each operating for a week at a time before handing over to the other.

Details of early vehicles are lamentably few. It is known (from old photographs) that Commers and Fords were used during the 1920s, but maddeningly the individual vehicles are not identifiable as they tend to be in the background of such 'postcard view' images. By the late 1930s Commers and Bedfords predominated. Askew had two Bedford WLBs (RM 8699 and NV 5198) plus a Waveney-bodied Commer PLNF5 (BRM 198) which they had acquired from Weightman. Simpson was the odd man out, preferring to use two Ford AAs with 20-seat Willett bodywork (ARM 824 and CAO 505). Weightman was the largest of the independents on the route, with two Bedford WLBs (RM 9415 and ARM 554), an Encol-bodied Bedford WTB (DRM 330), and two Waveney-bodied Commer PLNF5s (BRM 199 and CAO 461). The WTB had replaced the Commer sold to Askew. Young had two WLBs (ARM 198 and ARM 712), a WTB/Duple coach (CRM 861), and a 20-seat Albion (FV 1922) which had been acquired from WC Standerwick.

These were all completely separate operations with their own licences, although they coordinated their timings and marketed the service jointly as 'The Keswick Borrowdale Bus Services'. Tickets bore the name of the individual operator, although return tickets were accepted by all five, including CMS. A skeleton (winter style) service was operated during the Second World War, and then operations re-started in earnest at Easter 1946, continuing to the pre-war pattern.

Vehicle purchases were also similar, with Bedfords and Commers still in favour. At the beginning of 1958 Askew had Bedford OB/Duple Vista GRM 914, recently acquired from Mandale of Greystoke (qv). Simpson had a Bedford OB/SMT 'Vista lookalike', GAO 861 (which had been bought from Lake Hotel Coaches), and a Commer Commando with Myers & Bowman bus bodywork, HRM 108. Weightman had a similar Commer Q4/Myers & Bowman bus (HAO 950), a Commando/Myers & Bowman coach (HAO 402), two Commer Avenger coaches (JRM 796 with Myers & Bowman bodywork, and Plaxton-bodied KRM 221) and a recently delivered Bedford SBG with Yeates Europa bodywork (SAO 394). By this time Weightmans had become a wholly owned subsidiary of Lake Hotel Coaches and gave up its share of the Seatoller service in October 1958 as LHC's proprietor had bought the firm for its excursion licences. Young had a Bedford OB/Vista (HRM 48), new to them in September 1948, and a Leyland PS2/3 Tiger with Burlingham Sunsaloon bodywork (CCB 291) which had been acquired from Wearden of Blackburn.

This photograph, taken in Ernie Hartness's yard in Penrith, is a bit of a mystery as Hartness never operated a Trojan 19 minibus. The vehicle is on (just unreadable) trade plates and seems to have had the 'Ten Lakes Tour' excursion board placed in front of it as an act of mockery. Neighbouring operators Blair & Palmer and Robinson of Appleby both had Trojans, so this machine might have belonged to one of them. *(Keith Johnson Collection)*

Burlingham-bodied CVD6 coach BMS 404 had been new to Alexander, but came to Hartness from Highland Omnibus in November 1967. It remained in Highland's deep red and cream livery and displayed their fleet number 'DA4' – quite appropriately given the name of the contributor. *(David Atkinson)*

73

A sunny day in Keswick, but not that many passengers for the Keswick Borrowdale Bus Service departure from the Moot Hall to Seatoller. The vehicle is CRM 861, a Duple-bodied Bedford WTB coach owned by KBBS partner Young of Keswick. *(Keith Johnson Collection)*

This Bedford OB coach with Duple Vista bodywork, HRM 48, also belonged to Young and had been new to them in September 1948. It lasted until the end of KBBS in 1967. *(Keith Johnson Collection)*

In February 1958 the Borrowdale arrangements were criticised by Mr JT Hanlon, the Chairman of the Northern Area Traffic Commissioners, who described them as 'old-fashioned and strange'. The criticism arose during a hearing precipitated by Weightmans who were arguing that all five participants should operate all year round so that two out of the five were not left to carry the loss-making winter traffic on their own. Mr JM Wilson, company secretary of both Weightmans (Keswick) Ltd and its parent company Lake Hotel Coaches), said that in the winter months takings on the route were four pence per mile while costs were more than five times that amount (one shilling and nine pence). Interestingly, a representative of Cumberland Motor Services was also present at the hearing and revealed that in the 1956 summer season their share of the Seatoller operation had cost one shilling and nine pence per mile to operate and had produced revenue of only one shilling and sixpence per mile. The difference in revenue shows the disparity between winter and summer loads, but the cost comparison is interesting as it suggests that Weightmans were singing from the same song sheet. It is hard to believe that an independent would really have costs as high as those of a state-owned operator.

Regardless of this collusion by two of the parties involved, Hayton demanded that something should be done. He left it to the operators to decide what that was, but he wanted to see a fairer distribution of the income. With Weightmans already a pariah in their own ranks, the other three independents on the route (Askew, Simpson, and Young) decided to form a jointly owned company, Keswick Borrowdale Bus Services Ltd, to 'normalise' the situation and to spread the winter losses between all three local proprietors. Cumberland were not entirely happy with this arrangement, as the new limited company then put pressure upon them to take a share of the winter operations. Things had somehow backfired.

The Traffic Commissioners declared themselves happy with the new situation, granted licences to Keswick Borrowdale as a corporate entity, and things continued much as before apart from the absence of Weightmans. The Commers gradually vanished and further second-hand Bedford OBs were acquired to take their place, including HAO 389 (from Brownrigg of Egremont) and JRM 651 (from Titterington of Blencowe).

By 1967 all three of the proprietors were reaching (or past) retirement age and started to negotiate with Cumberland Motor Services. CMS was reluctant to make an offer at first, but the alternative seemed to be that the proprietors would sell out to Ribble instead and so a relatively generous settlement was made. Whether or not Ribble was actually interested in the service is open to question. It could be that the proprietors made this up to hurry negotiations along, or it might be that Ribble's management was merely making mischief to embarrass their opposite numbers at CMS. The deal between KBBS and CMS was finalised in May 1967, and at the end of June the name of Keswick Borrowdale Bus Services disappeared. The three surviving OBs all found new homes and two of them still survive in preservation.

The service to Seatoller still operates under the aegis of Stagecoach in Cumberland (or whatever silly name they are using by the time you read this – I'm still disgusted by the sight of Ribble vehicles carrying legal lettering for 'Glenvale Transport'!) and has been operated by open-top double-deckers as well as more mundane saloons. You can still have the beautiful landscape, but to me it would be improved by a few Bedford OBs.

Mandale of Greystoke

Like so many of the young men in his generation, Bernard Mandale acquired his mechanical skills during the First World War. In 1921 he opened a garage in his home village of Greystoke, to the west of Penrith, and then took the familiar route through the hire-car and haulage sidelines often associated with such pioneering garages. In March 1926 he progressed to the bus business, opening a weekday service from Greystoke to Penrith via Blencowe, and Stainton. This operated five times per day on Mondays, Wednesdays, Thursdays, and Fridays, seven times on Tuesdays, and eight times on Saturdays. Tuesday and Saturday were market-days.

The original vehicle was a 26-seat normal-control Albion, but two respected authorities offer two different identities for the vehicle. PSV Circle records show it to be HH 4038, new in 1926. The Carlisle registration could be accounted for by it being registered to an Albion dealership before delivery. On the other hand,

David Grisenthwaite (who wrote the Ribble Enthusiast Club's definitive book on early bus operations in Penrith) states that it was *RM* 4038, an Albion PFB26 (?) first registered in June 1927. There is an obvious problem with the date given, but I leave it to the reader to decide which version has the most merit.

Mandale's main competitor on the Blencowe-Stainton-Penrith part of the route was Ernest Titterington of Blencowe (qv) who began his service in October 1926. The fact that both proprietors seemed to be making a profit out of the route attracted the attention of Armstrong & Siddle, the largest operator in the Penrith area. In June 1928 they bought Mandale's service along with the schizophrenic Albion. A&S had just moved into the BET/BAT stable although Fred Armstrong remained as a minority shareholder and director. As outlined in the introduction, A&S would soon pass to Ribble and then cease to be.

There was a 'no compete' clause in the contract signed with A&S, but Bernard Mandale soon identified the loopholes in the agreement. If A&S was not providing a particular service, then he could. In practice this meant that his best option was to run the kind of peripheral, marginal, routes which were unlikely to be attractive to A&S or its successors, but could still earn a decent crust for a local man. He used the money from A&S to buy a 24-seat Reo coach (given in some sources as RM 553), and started a Saturday only service (one round trip) from Greystoke to Carlisle, timed to suit shoppers and football fans in equal measure.

A Tuesday service from the village of Dockray (in Matterdale) to Penrith was inaugurated in June 1929, followed by a similar market-day service from Berrier. Mandale then decided to add a Saturday journey on the Matterdale route, and acquired a second vehicle to accommodate the increasing work-load. This was a 14-seat Chevrolet, but remains unidentified. PSV Circle records also suggest that a PLSC Lion was acquired in the early 1930s, but no identity is given.

The next two (verified vehicles) were both Bedford coaches. DRM 588 was a WTB/Duple, new in 1938, while EAO 177 was an unusual pre-war OB with Thurgood bodywork and was delivered two months after the start of the Second World War. The services from Greystoke to Carlisle and from Matterdale and Berrier to Penrith were suspended 'for the duration of the war'. In fact, the Matterdale service was the only one to be revived when hostilities came to an end, and that was reduced to run on Tuesdays only.

A second new OB coach, this time with SMT bodywork, was delivered in January 1948 and registered GRM 914. It would later pass to Askew of the Keswick Borrowdale consortium (qv). Two years later a bonneted beast of a different nature arrived in Greystoke in the form of Leyland Comet/Plaxton coach KAO 72. The next delivery (in early 1951) was KRM 589, a Bedford SB/Duple coach, and then there was a long gap until the arrival of SB3/Duple Super Vega coach WRM 331 in August 1959. The following year brought another OB to the fleet, this time one with the 'proper' Duple Vista body. JDA 298 had been new to Worthington of Wolverhampton in 1951. It replaced the Bedford SB built in the same year.

Less desirable was UOT 818, a 10-seat Morris/Wadham minibus acquired on the second-hand market (flea market?) in 1962. A more pleasing purchase, a new (and unusual) Bedford A2/Spurling 13-seater, arrived to replace it in October 1964 and was registered BRM 486B. In July 1965 a four-year old Bedford SB1/Burlingham coach (WAW 356) was acquired from Smith of Shepton Mallet.

For the next nine years all full-size acquisitions were second-hand Bedford coaches. Most of them were SB variants but there was also a 1958 vintage C4Z2/Duple Super Vista (VNE 362, acquired from Atkinson of Millom in September 1971) and, at the other end of the scale, a four year old VAL14/Duple (ECU 383E) which came from Kirkby of Harthill three months later. In 1974 the first new full-size coaches in fifteen years were delivered when Bedford YRT/Duple RRM 1M arrived in May, followed by YRQ/Duple SAO 900N in October. The new vehicles were bought to initiate a programme of extended coach tours, including both British and European destinations. Predictably the weekly market-day run from Dockray to Penrith was soon abandoned.

The founder's son, WB (Bill) Mandale had taken over by this stage and decided to segregate the coach business from the continuing haulage operations. The haulage side became a limited company (as Bernard Mandale Ltd) in July 1974 while the coaching business remained a sole

Commers were almost as popular as Bedfords with the KBBS partners. This Q4 with a 32-seat bus body by Cumberland bodybuilder Myers & Bowman, HAO 950, belonged to Weightman of Keswick and is seen at the Moot Hall terminus. *(Keith Johnson Collection)*

Mandale of Greystoke bought this Plaxton-bodied Leyland CPO1 Comet, KAO 72, in late 1949. After a few years of coaching work it became the regular vehicle on the stage service to Matterdale until its withdrawal in the late 1960s. It was later sighted wearing a 'psychedelic' paint job and in use as a static caravan. Its ultimate fate is unrecorded. *(Author's Collection)*

From 1955, when the last of the pre-war Commers was withdrawn, until 1960 the McGregor service from Ambleside to Hawkshead and Sawrey Ferry Landing was maintained by a pair of (post-war) Commer Commandos with coach bodies by Barnaby. They were actually registered to Stan Faulkner's main company, Brown's Luxury Coaches. This one is JM 8316. *(John Kaye)*

In March 1960 the two Commandos were replaced by this Mulliner-bodied Bedford SB bus, LXJ 318. The vehicle had been new to Mayne of Manchester in July 1951, passing to Harper & Kellow of St Agnes, Cornwall, in June 1955, and then to McGregor. After the stage service ended it passed to an operator in South Wales. *(RC Davis via The Omnibus Society)*

proprietorship trading as 'Mandale Travel'. When control passed to Bill Mandale's son WB (Ben) Mandale in 1991 the coaching business also became a limited company with Ben and his wife Janet as the directors. By then the company was operating a sophisticated fleet of four Van Hool T818s, a Van Hool T815, and a Volvo B10M, all equipped with toilets. This was handy, for in 1994 both Mandale companies went down the pan. Mr Mandale and his wife left the transport business and currently own two restaurants in Greystoke village.

McGregor of Ambleside

For 800 years before 1974 the eastern side of Lake Windermere was in Westmorland, while the western side was in Lancashire. The town of Ambleside, at the north end of the lake, was on the Westmorland side of the border. A few miles to the south-west, the large village of Hawkshead was in Lancashire, and it is on this side of the border that the story of McGregor begins.

James Airey (born in 1873) came from a family of farm labourers and followed in his father's footsteps for the first few years of his working life. In May 1894 he married Mary Kendall, a domestic servant and the daughter of another farm labourer, but the pair were destined for a very different life to their forbears. By 1899 James had become the licensee of The Sun Inn in Hawkshead, a well-known watering hole frequented by walkers and the artistic set who still favoured the Lakeland scenery. The couple's children included Frederick, born in December 1894, Mary Elizabeth ('Lizzie'), born in 1899, and James Jr ('Jim'), born in 1904.

In 1923 Frederick and Jim Airey started a timetabled bus service from Hawkshead (The Sun Inn) to Ambleside using a vehicle described in contemporary press reports as 'an eight-seat car'. The service was soon extended at the Hawkshead end to Sawrey Ferry Landing (for the ferry to Bowness on the eastern shore) and tourists joined the local people as regular passengers. The eight-seater soon gave way to larger machines, but these remain unidentified until the arrival of a 20-seat Waveney-bodied Commer PN3 Centaur in April 1933 (JM 647). A second Waveney-bodied PN3 arrived in March 1938 (CTF 397).

James Airey Sr died in 1938, leaving the two brothers to run the pub as well as the bus service.

Of the two businesses the pub was by far the more profitable, and they began to think about disposing of the buses. This feeling increased during the war when Frederick did all of the driving until hiring Bob Bunting in 1944. Bunting (born in 1884) had started his driving career with the Lake District Road Traffic Co on Thornycroft char-a-bancs. He would remain the regular driver on the service until 1954 when he retired.

In January 1945 the brothers persuaded Stan Faulkner, the proprietor of Brown's Luxury Coaches in Ambleside, to take the service off their hands. Faulkner had just bought JM McGregor's garage and filling station in Ambleside and decided to place the bus service into the limited company formed to take control of this enterprise rather than use the Brown's name on plain old buses. Coincidence is a strange thing. One of the artistic visitors to The Sun Inn had been Beatrix Potter, the children's authoress. She had been charmed by the young 'Lizzie' Airey and she became the inspiration for the little girl in her 1901 story 'The Tale of Peter Rabbit'. The villain of this piece is, of course, a Mr McGregor! Potter bought a farm in Near Sawrey in 1905 and later married a solicitor from Hawkshead.

Stan Faulkner kept the two Airey Commer PN3s and bought a third, Strachan-bodied, example to handle the heavy post-war demand. This additional machine, AGF 929, had started life with Rickards of London in April 1933. Seven years later it passed to the bullion dealers Johnson Matthey – presumably for staff transportation, and then to The Church Army in April 1944 for use as a mobile canteen for the homeless. It apparently kept its seats as it returned to passenger service with 'McGregor' in April 1946 having served both Mammon and the Lord.

In 1950 Stan Faulkner (wearing his 'McGregor' hat) had placed an order for a Duple-bodied Bedford OB bus, but seems to have thought better of it before delivery. The allocated vehicle (chassis number 140985) ended up with an operator in Dumfriesshire as LSM 335. Centaur JM 647 was withdrawn from service in October 1951 and used as a source of spares for the other two PN3s. By July 1955 the remaining two had reached the ends of their careers as PSVs. CTF 397 had a short after-life as a mobile shop. Their replacements on the Hawkshead route were two of the post-war

Commer Commandos with Barnaby bodywork operated by Brown's Luxury Coaches (JM 7316 and JM 8303). These remained in Stan Faulkner's ownership and should (technically) have displayed 'on hire to JM McGregor Ltd' notices in the front windscreen.

By the beginning of 1960 the post-war Commers were also ready for the knackers' yard, and Stan Faulkner had no other coaches which were suitable for 'driver only' operation. In March 1960 he bought a replacement vehicle, a 34-seat Mulliner-bodied Bedford SB bus. LXJ 318 had started life with Mayne in Manchester (qv) in July 1951, passing to Harper & Kellow ('Reliance') of St Agnes, Cornwall in June 1955 before returning to the North. The machine's stay in Ambleside was relatively brief. Local people were far from impressed by the spartan interior of the 'military spec' SB. The Commer Commandos might have been old, but they had been very comfortable.

Stan Faulkner was forced to conclude that his passengers might be happier in the hands of Ribble and on the 30th of June 1962 the licence was transferred. The SB lingered for a while before being dispatched to the Don Everall dealership in Wolverhampton. It ended up with Hoskins of Blackwood in South Wales operating contract services for coalminers.

Proud of Ainstable

At first sight this operator's name might seem to belong to the group which includes 'Pride of Sale' and 'Pride of the West', but in this case Proud was the name of the proprietor rather than an assertion of excellence. Ainstable, a medium-sized village of around 500 residents in the Eden Valley (traditionally dependent upon its woollen mill), was the birthplace of Edward Lancelot Proud. Mr Proud was in the army during the First World War and became a driver and competent mechanic. After serving in the Salonika region of Greece he returned home and spent his gratuity on a small lorry-bus. This 14-seater (identity unknown) inaugurated a stage-carriage service from Ainstable to Carlisle via Warwick Bridge in 1921, and this soon became a daily operation.

A Tuesday only service from Ainstable to Armthwaite and Penrith began in 1929, and Proud celebrated this expansion of the business by acquiring two new Dennis G 16-seaters (RM 5303 and RM 6021) to replace his existing vehicles. The Penrith market-day run was suspended for the duration of the Second World War, but the Carlisle route continued to operate as it provided a vital lifeline to the village.

In June 1950 the two Dennis Gs were finally retired after nearly 20 years of service, and replaced by two second-hand Bedfords. Pre-war Bedford WTB CPU 59 had been new to Ongar & District in Essex and carried a 26-seat bus body by Thurgood, while FAO 835 was an OWB utility bus. Both survived until 1952 when Mr Proud decided to retire and sold the Carlisle service to Blair & Palmer (qv). The market-day route to Penrith was of no interest to Jack Palmer, and the mileage was covered by the diversion of an existing Ribble service from the Eden Valley area.

Blair & Palmer abandoned the Ainstable-Carlisle route in April 1957 after incurring an average annual loss of £11,000 on the service – an enormous sum for one bus route to lose. Edward Lancelot Proud was active in the campaign to save the service (by 1957 he had become the Chairman of Penrith Urban District Council) and persuaded his friend Ernie Hartness to take over in B&P's place. Hartness managed to stem the losses by using more appropriate vehicles (driver-operated Daimler CVD6s rather than crew-operated double-deckers) and continued to ply the route until his death in February 1971.

Mr Proud died in June 1978. Ainstable's bus service has now degenerated to one journey to Penrith (on Wednesdays rather than the traditional Tuesday) and one journey to Carlisle (on Fridays). Both of these services are operated by Fellrunner with community transport minibuses.

Robinson of Appleby

Thomas Robinson, a native of the small village of Dufton to the north of Appleby, bought an unidentified lorry, which could be converted into a char-a-banc, in 1914. During the four years of war which followed the vehicle was mainly used in its 'goods' configuration, but when peace came it began to carry the villagers of Dufton on regular excursions. Appleby market day was an obvious destination (as there was no regular bus service at that time), and in 1924 Robinson moved the business to Appleby to provide a larger catchment area for his programme of excursions.

The next known (but unidentified) vehicle was a Guy 20-seater, followed by a 14-seat Chevrolet bus (EC 7655) in February 1927. Robinson wrote to the local newspaper shortly after the purchase of the Chevrolet to dispel rumours that he had sold out to Armstrong & Siddle who were then establishing a presence in Appleby. In June 1928 the larger company started a stage service from Appleby to Dufton, operating five times on each weekday and effectively killing off Robinson's existing local route which tended to operate 'on demand' on market days.

Fortunately for Robinson his firm had established a near monopoly of local excursion work, and also operated some valuable schools contracts. A new 20-seat Reo (EC 9220) was delivered in April 1930 and replaced the anonymous Guy, and was followed by a smaller 14-seat Reo (RM 7068), acquired second-hand, which displaced the Chevrolet. The final (known) acquisition during the 1930s was the company's first Bedford, 25-seat WTB/Duple coach JM 3815.

During the Second World War the company apparently operated a service to a top-secret airfield in the Eden Valley which was being used to train RAF Westland Lysander pilots. The pilots were destined for night-time missions into Nazi-occupied Europe, carrying supplies for the various Resistance groups and exporting agents of the Special Operations Executive – many of whom would be shot as spies after their capture by the Germans. A Bedford OWB utility bus (JM 5298) was provided for this airfield work, with the pre-war WTB acting as a back-up vehicle. When the contract came to an end after the D-Day landings in 1944, the two Bedfords were sold to Ernie Hartness and Robinson continued as a haulier until peace returned.

The Robinsons had no children, but their company's continuing existence was guaranteed by the arrival of John Lance Elliott as an apprentice and lodger. In several published sources Elliott is wrongly given the name 'John Lawrence Elliott' and equally wrongly described as the Robinson's 'son-in-law'. The first mistake is probably due to a mishearing of his preferred name (Lance), while the second error seems to be unsubstantiated hearsay. He actually married a local girl unrelated to the Robinsons in 1946. The Robinsons were, however, very fond of their lodger and employee, and regarded him as the son they never had. Elliott and his wife Phyllis continued to live in the Robinsons' house until being offered a council property in 1949.

The Robinson firm re-entered the passenger business in 1946 with three pre-war vehicles bought as a stop-gap measure. These were CK 4760 (a TS6 Tiger with a post-war Santus coach body), WS 8031 (an LZ2 Cheetah with coachwork by Duple, previously operated by SMT), and a 29-seat Dennis Lancet I (AYH 215). These were quickly replaced by three brand-new vehicles, an SMT-bodied Bedford OB coach (JM 6731) which arrived in July 1947, and two Ormac-bodied Commer Commando coaches (JM 7912/7944). The next two purchases were second-hand but relatively new. Arab III/Wilks & Meade coach DNL 255 came from Armstrong of Newcastle, and Foden PVSC6/Whitson FBU 456 from Robinson of Oldham (no relation!). Further variety was added by the acquisition of a new Leyland Comet/Bellhouse Hartwell coach, JM 8905. These latter three vehicles replaced the two Commandos.

The Robinsons decided to retire from business during 1952 and sold the firm to their young apprentice. Elliott kept the trading name of 'Robinson of Appleby', having already given his son the name Phillip Robinson Elliott. Interesting second-hand arrivals under the new proprietor were rear-engined Foden PVRF6/ACB coach NPT 903 and Regal III/Windover OEH 426. The latter would be particularly useful from September 1957 onwards when the company returned to market-day stage-carriage services.

In 1940 Ernie Hartness had acquired a group of such services from Sowerby of Great Asby, operating from Great Asby and surrounding villages to Kirkby Stephen (on Mondays), Appleby (on Tuesdays and Saturdays), and Penrith (on Tuesdays only). In September 1957 the licences for these routes were transferred to Robinson, and were mainly operated by the Regal III until its eventual retirement in December 1965. This left the succession of new Bedford SB coaches acquired from 1956 onwards free to concentrate upon the expanding excursion and tours programme. Two second-hand Bedford OB/Duple coaches (FEO 175 and DCS 981) acquired in 1958/59 were mainly allocated to schools contracts and local private hires. These two sources of income also accounted for the acquisition of a

This Seddon Pennine RU with a 45-seat Pennine Coachcraft body, KJM 187J, was new to Robinson of Appleby in April 1971. The vehicle qualified for the Bus Grant, but its poor quality meant that Robinson soon took little pride in its appearance. Its stay with Robinson was brief. *(Robert F Mack)*

Robinson bought this 35-seat Bristol SC4LK/ECW bus, OVL 497, from the Lincolnshire Road Car Co in October 1976. It went up hills very slowly and was withdrawn in June 1978. *(Keith Johnson Collection)*

chain of minibuses, starting with a Morris J2 in 1960/1 and continuing with a Commer VHD in 1961/2 and a Trojan 19 (HEF 754) from 1962-64. This is probably the anonymous Trojan depicted earlier while being mocked in Ernie Hartness's yard.

A further stage-carriage service came into the Robinson portfolio in February 1963 when Walton of Kirkby Stephen (qv) decided to cease trading in the bus and coach business. FH Jackson took Walton's schools services, while the market-day run from Aisgill Bridge to Kirkby Stephen passed to Lance Elliott's firm. It dovetailed nicely with the existing route from Great Asby. Robinsons also bought Walton's last coach, Avenger III/Plaxton DEC 404, but this was sold five months later.

The Avenger's replacement was the company's second AEC, two year old Reliance/Duple Britannia coach 44 CAA. This fine machine was itself replaced by a new Bedford SB13/Duple Bella Vega (LJM 920) in June 1964, but it appears that the AEC made a favourable impression as a brand new 36ft Reliance with Plaxton bodywork (BJM 361C) arrived in October 1965. This was, of course, for touring work. After the disposal of the Regal III at the end of that year almost all of the stage services were operated by the older Bedford SBs in the fleet.

Surprisingly, the stage services from Great Asby were doing quite well, and by 1965 the Great Asby to Appleby route had been increased from two days per week to six – although most of the extra journeys were timed to absorb traffic previously carried on contract schools services. Coaching was still the main business of the company and new deliveries during the late 1960s included Bedfords (a VAM and a VAL, both with Duple Viceroy bodywork) and a 36ft Leyland Leopard/Plaxton. As the coaches became larger they also became less suitable for use on the stage services, and this led to an order for a 45-seat Seddon Pennine RU 'dual purpose' vehicle in April 1971 (KJM 187J). Lance Elliott soon realised that this was not the best decision of his business career. In the opinion of most observers the Seddon RU was only suited to the dual purposes of chicken shed or bonfire fuel. Another new type, acquired in the same month, was a recent vintage Ford R226/Duple Viceroy coach which came from Simpson of Shap.

The 1970s also saw the first 'foreign designed' vehicles, beginning with the delivery of Caetano-bodied Reliance MEC 997K in July 1972. Sister Reliance MEC 998K had British-made Willowbrook Expressway bodywork, while the following year's new Reliance carried a Plaxton body. The new touring coaches in 1974 and 1975 both had Duple bodywork, but mounted on Volvo and DAF chassis respectively. The European floodgates had opened.

Meanwhile, the company had been successful in bidding for a large variety of schools contracts. The solitary Pennine RU was quickly shown the door and replaced by some far more interesting equipment. The first to arrive, in July 1975, was Bedford VAL/Willowbrook service bus UAO 755H which had been new to British Gypsum as a staff transport in 1970. Three months later it was joined by Bedford YRT/Duple B66F LNM 903P, which achieved its abnormal passenger capacity by offering five-abreast seating in its rear half. It seems that there were less fat schoolchildren in those days.

The schools contracts also brought about an influx of elderly Bristols. This began with the arrival of an SC4LK/ECW B35F (OVL 497) from Lincolnshire Road Car Co in October 1976, and an MW6G/ECW C39F (52 GUO) from Western National in November. Western National also provided a pair of RELH6G/ECW C45F coaches, ATA 104B in February 1977 and 393 TUO in January 1978. All the Bristols had gone by the end of 1980 except for ATA 104B which remained in service until December 1985 as a reserve coach.

None of Robinson's stage services were commercially viable in a deregulated environment, but the company was successful in tendering for much of its traditional mileage. Now under the ownership of Mr S Graham (the Elliotts sold the firm after Lance's retirement), Robinsons Coaches is mainly a touring and excursion business, but also finds time for schools contracts and tendered services. The latter (at the time this is being written) include a Tuesday service from Appleby to Penrith via Dufton and a Wednesday service from Appleby to Kendal via Orton and Tebay. In 2014 the company will celebrate a hundred years of service to the people of Westmorland.

83

Robson of Midgeholme

If you head eastwards from Carlisle along the main road to Newcastle you reach the small town of Brampton. Forking to the right onto the A689 (which would eventually take you to Alston and then Bishop Auckland) you might notice the two small villages of Hallbankgate and Midgeholme, the latter only a few hundred yards from Cumberland's border with Northumberland. For many years a market day service ran northwards from these two villages to the small town of Haltwhistle, back on the main Carlisle-Newcastle road.

Remarkably little is known about this operator. Thomas L Robson appears to have been from a family of coalminers. His first identifiable vehicle was a 14-seat Chevrolet, CN 4621, acquired from Fraser of Swalwell in April 1937. By this time the stage route to Haltwhistle had already been operational for at least seven years. In the post-war era Robson acquired some contracts from local collieries and the Chevrolet was replaced by a trio of second-hand Bedford OWBs (ASD 103, AJR 926, and FPT 169) which also handled the market service.

More unusual second-hand vehicles included an AEC Q (BXD 544, formerly London Transport Q23) which arrived in August 1953, and a pre-war TS6 Tiger with a post-war Ormac body (DRN 562) which came shortly afterwards. Both of these machines were quickly sold on (to G&B in County Durham). The next known purchases were two second-hand Commer Commandos (EF 9266 and GAY 844) in June 1956, followed by a Seddon Mk 4 (HYG 99) and another Commando (DNL 192) with rare NMU bodywork.

The construction of the Spadeadam military complex (see under Sowerby of Gilsland for further details) brought welcome extra work to several operators in northern Cumberland, including Robson. Vehicles bought to operate these contracts included LZ2A Cheetah WG 7629 (which came from W Alexander in June 1957), TS7 Tiger/Weymann HE 7671 (from Yorkshire Traction in September 1958), and pre-war Regal/Brush CN 9988 (from Northern General in 1959). Profits from the military work funded the purchase of a 'new' market day bus, Bedford OB/Mulliner MHU 915, during 1958. This machine had originally been ordered by the Bristol area's last surviving independent, Dundry Pioneer, but was delivered to Bristol Tramways in 1950 after it acquired that business. It replaced the last of the OWBs. Two second-hand AEC Regal III coaches were also acquired during 1958/59, Burlingham-bodied JVO 150 and Trans-United-bodied KTF 7.

At the beginning of 1961 the fleet was made up of the two Regal IIIs, the OB/Mulliner bus, and Commandos EF 9266 and DNL 192. The stage service to Haltwhistle ceased in March and the rest of the company's operations seem to have ended in May. In June 1961 the market day service was taken over by Mid-Tyne Transport (of Hexham in Northumberland), but the attempted revival was unsuccessful and the service was abandoned for a second time in January 1962.

Sim of Boot

The village of Boot is at the inland end of Eskdale, some seven miles from the Cumberland coast and the nearest standard gauge railway line at Ravenglass Station on the route from Carlisle to Workington, Whitehaven, and Barrow-in-Furness. A narrow gauge railway between Ravenglass and Dalegarth (at the southern end of Boot) was opened in 1875 by Whitehaven Mines Ltd, a company which had extensive iron ore workings in Eskdale. Passengers were carried on the line from 1876 until 1908. By 1913 the iron mines were beyond economic use and the line closed completely.

This left the people of Eskdale without any form of public transport and William Sim (a resident of Boot) stepped into the breach with an unidentified motor vehicle, variously described as a wagonette and a char-a-banc. Sim also offered light haulage services so it seems likely that the vehicle was some kind of small lorry with a demountable passenger section. Regular daily services were offered to Seascale (the next station northbound from Ravenglass) with an extension to the nearest major town of Whitehaven 'as announced'.

In 1915 the Eskdale railway line reopened, its gauge narrowed still further (from 36 inches to 15 inches) by its new owners, model steam engine manufacturers WJ Bassett-Lowke and Robert Proctor-Mitchell. Although now targeted at the tourist market it could equally well be used by local residents. Most stuck with Sim's bus service, which was cheaper and (for those intent upon the shops of Whitehaven) avoided changing at Ravenglass.

Details of Sim's early vehicles have long since been lost. The first machine recorded by the PSV Circle (and the only one from the era before the Second World War) was BRM 673, a 14-seat Commer PN3 which lasted until 1952. Immediately after the war this vehicle was joined by two second-hand Bedfords. RN 7849 was a Duple-bodied WTB coach, acquired from Wearden of Blackburn, while GZ 941 was one of the dozens of ex-NIRTB OWBs which returned from Northern Ireland to help satisfy the insatiable appetite for vehicles in the post-war years. Its utility bodywork was made more acceptable to Sim's passengers by the installation of 29 coach seats.

Ownership of the 'competing' narrow gauge railway changed after the war when it was acquired by the Keswick Granite Co. Standard gauge rails were laid to either side of the model-makers' tracks and the line was used to provide the company's quarries with a link to the national railway network. The quarries were exhausted by 1953 and the line was closed, not reopening again until 1960 when it was acquired by a preservation society.

Business was good in this era, and made even better in 1950 by the opening of an Outward Bound mountaineering school in Eskdale. Sim's services at the time ran from Boot to Seascale (daily except Thursday and Saturday), from Boot to Whitehaven (on Thursday/Saturday), and from Boot to Drigg via Seascale on Saturdays only. The extension to Drigg was abandoned in 1954, leaving the Seascale service to run on every day except Thursday until July 1958 when the Monday and Wednesday journeys were withdrawn due to dwindling levels of support.

In 1959 the ageing OWB was replaced by a slightly younger (1949 vintage) Bedford OB/Duple Vista coach. This vehicle, DNL 580, had been new to Armstrong of Westerhope but arrived at Boot from Fox of Falstone. Two years later a Morris J2 minibus arrived to cater for small private hires such as darts teams and rock-climbing groups. The WTB had been withdrawn in 1956, so this represented a doubling of the vehicle strength if not the seating capacity.

The stage services were still in headlong decline, as the vast majority of Eskdale residents now had access to a private car. The Sunday service on the Seascale route was withdrawn in October 1962, meaning that its operation was then restricted to Tuesday, Friday, and Saturday. Whitehaven services continued on Thursdays and Saturdays. A more positive note was sounded in October 1963 when the Morris J2 was replaced by a 29-seat Bedford C4LZ2/Duple Super Vista coach (60 BYB) which came from Winn of Whiston.

It came as no great surprise when all of the remaining stage-carriage services were withdrawn in October 1964. The Bedford OB (DNL 580) was sold at the same time, but was immediately replaced by a slightly newer example of the same combination (MHU 995) which had originally been delivered to Bristol Tramways in March 1950. The business continued as a coaching operation and still uses the same premises in Boot as its base. At least I presume that it does, as they failed to respond to all of my emails!

Sowerby of Gilsland

The village of Gilsland is around 15 miles to the east of Carlisle, and a similar distance from the market town of Hexham, across the border in Northumberland. It is close to the most scenic section of Hadrian's Wall, and so in every sense is a border community. After the fall of the Roman Empire it became a remote and little-known area, a neutral zone between the Kingdoms of England and Scotland ruled by the bandits known as the Border Reivers. Inevitably, the rise of the nation states put an end to such anarchy.

William D Sowerby followed the usual path for young men returning from the First World War with driving and mechanical skills by opening a garage and filling station in the village. Taxis came next and then a Ford char-a-banc (AO 5293), and this relative prosperity allowed Sowerby to marry. His son from this relationship, William Neville Sowerby, was born in 1922. In 1929 Sowerby married for a second time, to Caroline Pardoe Baxter, and they produced a daughter, Patricia, in 1934.

The original Ford was replaced by a Halley char-a-banc, RM 2705, in 1926. A second, unidentified, Halley chara followed in 1928. By the time of the Road Traffic Act of 1930 Sowerby was already operating a (Wednesday) market service from Gilsland to the small town of Brampton, half-way to Carlisle, and this was duly licensed by the new Traffic Commissioners. When not required for the market service, or for journeys to the coal mines in the area, the two Halleys operated excursions and private hires.

The first recorded vehicle with a permanent roof was 20-seat Reo coach RM 7900, delivered in 1931. This was followed by a Leyland Cub/Burlingham 20-seater, FV 2520, which had been new to Seagull Coaches in Blackpool but arrived in Gilsland from its second owner Wright Bros of Alston. In 1939 two Bedford WTB coaches were added to the fleet, a second-hand Duple-bodied example from W Alexander (WG 3586) and a new vehicle with Plaxton bodywork (DAO 21). During the Second World War the company's commitment to miners journeys and other works services led to the allocation of two Bedford OWB utility buses, FAO 822 and FAO 913.

In 1947 the sole proprietorship gave way to a limited company, Sowerbys Tours Ltd. The post-war boom in excursion traffic resulted in orders for four Commer Commandos and a Bedford OB. Two of the Commandos carried Plaxton bodywork (FRM 616 and GRM 203), and the other two (HRM 871 and JAO 273) were-bodied by Santus. The OB which came imbetween the two pairs of Commandos (GRM 910) had bodywork by SMT to the 'Vista lookalike' design. Second-hand purchases during the late 1940s were two post-war Albion Valkyries (GAO 400 and GRM 22), surplus to the requirements of Ernie Hartness who was standardising on the Daimler CVD6. Both were fitted with pre-war Alexander bus bodies by Hartness, but at some point GAO 400 had its bodywork rebuilt by Ormac of Preston. This probably saved it from the fate of GRM 22, which was cut down for further service as a lorry in 1952.

The next decade began with the delivery of a new Commer Avenger/Myers & Bowman coach (KAO 141) which replaced one of the Commandos, and this was followed by a third nearly-new Valkyrie from Hartness (GRM 133). The next new vehicle (in 1952) was an underfloor-engined AEC Regal IV coach with rare Yeates Sherwood bodywork, LAO 367. The Yeates body must have proven to be satisfactory as a third-hand Bedford SBG/Yeates Riviera (ECB 377) arrived in late 1955. It had been new to Ribblesdale in 1953 and had then passed to Wearden, also of Blackburn, before heading further north. It replaced another of the Commandos.

Missile Country

In 1957 a major opportunity fell into Bill Sowerby's lap. The government had ordered the design and manufacture of Britain's very own 'Medium Range Ballistic Missile', known as Blue Streak, and required a testing site suitably remote from large populations. A 9,000 acre site known as Spadeadam Waste, immediately to the north of the village of Gilsland, was chosen. Over the next two years a work-force of almost 600 (most of them Irish labourers) would build the testing range and be housed in temporary accommodation 'on site'. As the closest bus operator to the range Sowerby received a lion's share of the contracts to provide the workers with transportation.

The Sowerby fleet expanded dramatically, mainly by the addition of 'time expired' vehicles from major fleets. First to arrive were 12 LZ2A Cheetahs from W Alexander during 1958, followed by two more in 1959 and a further three in 1960. Other deliveries for Spadeadam duties during 1959 were four AEC-Beadle rebuilds from Maidstone & District, and four similar vehicles (but with Leyland running units) came from the same source in 1960.

With such relatively easy profits on offer, the market-day service to Brampton became a very low priority. The route was discontinued in October 1960. A replacement minibus service was provided by various members of the Moses family until October 1963 when the route was abandoned.

Meanwhile all was not well on the Spadeadam front. The Blue Streak missile programme was cancelled during 1960, although some testing continued to see if the system could be adapted to launch satellites. With most of the construction workers gone many of the contract vehicles were scrapped. All but one of the Cheetahs had met their fate by the end of 1962, while the Leyland-Beadle rebuilds were sold to a dealer in September of that year. Three of the AEC-Beadles went during 1963, although one remained in service until October 1966.

The replacements for the Cheetahs and Beadles, far fewer in number, were a succession of elderly double-deckers – Sowerby's first such

Robson of Midgeholme's KTF 7 was an AEC Regal III with a coach body by Trans-United, bought from Knightsbridge Coaches of Barnsley in 1959. In May 1961 it moved on to Mid-Tyne of Acomb, just across the border in Northumberland. Mid-Tyne also had a go at reviving Robson's recently abandoned stage service but this thankless experiment soon came to an end. *(Keith Johnson Collection)*

Photographs of vehicles belonging to Sowerby of Gilsland proved hard to find. This AEC-Beadle rebuild, NKT 951, came to Sowerby from Maidstone & District in November 1959. *(Keith Johnson Collection)*

Titterington of Blencowe bought this Morris Commercial OP/R with a 32-seat ACB coach body, KRM 444, in 1951. Replaced by a Bedford SB3 coach on excursion work during 1958 it spent its remaining nine years with Titterington as the regular vehicle on the Blencowe-Penrith service. *(Author's Collection)*

Titterington's older SBs took over from the Morris Commercial. This 1962 Bedford SB1 with Duple Super Vega bodywork, 631 UTD, was acquired in July 1971 for use on the stage services and schools contracts. *(Author's Collection)*

vehicles. Four pre-war Leyland Titans arrived during 1961, two from W Alexander and two from Ribble. One from each source survived until 1966, to be replaced by a former Western SMT Daimler CVG6 (acquired from Blair & Palmer) and two ex-Southdown PD2s.

The founder died in 1991, with the business continuing under the stewardship of his widow Caroline, his son from his first marriage (WN Sowerby) and his grand-daughter Muriel Proud (the daughter of Patricia). It ceased to trade two years later, and Caroline Sowerby died in 2004 at the age of 99. As a footnote, in 1988 some top-secret documents about the Spadeadam site were released under the 30-year rule. It seems that the plans for the area were rather more extensive than local people realised. If the Blue Streak missile programme had continued a large number of launch silos would have been built within five miles of Gilsland, making the village the prime target for a Soviet first-strike against the West.

The Spadeadam Range continued to be used by the RAF for training purposes, and over the years has played host to a range of 'enemy targets' including redundant aircraft, tanks, and mock villages and military bases. In 1976 it was officially reclassified as an 'Electronic Warfare Testing Range', so local farmers can probably no longer tell the wheat from the chaff. At least they survived the madness of the Cold War.

Titterington of Blencowe

In March 1926 Mandale of Greystoke (qv) began a bus service from their home village to Penrith via Blencowe, Newbiggin, and Stainton. One of the young men watching Mandale's bus pass through Blencowe was 19 year old Ernest Titterington, the son of a local gamekeeper. He decided that there was room for competition and in October 1926 he bought a second-hand Star 14-seater (CB 9358) to start a daily circular route from Penrith to Lamonby, Hutton Roof, Berrier, Blencowe, Stainton, and back to Penrith. Traffic was thin to the north of Blencowe, and by the end of the year the service had been cut back to operate Blencowe-Newbiggin-Stainton-Penrith.

In June 1928 Armstrong & Siddle acquired the competing Greystoke-Blencowe-Penrith service from Bernard Mandale and decided to get rid of Titterington by increasing frequency and cutting fares. By October young Ernest (still only 21) had been forced to reduce his service to run on Tuesdays and Saturdays only – Penrith market days. It looked as if A&S had won the battle, but in February 1929 Titterington came back fighting. The Star was placed onto a daily service from Greystoke to Penrith, operating slightly in front of the A&S timings on the route. To A&S (and their new masters at BAT) it probably looked like piracy. To Titterington it was about survival.

A peace treaty was agreed with Ribble (by then in control of A&S) in June 1929. Titterington would abandon his extension to Greystoke and return to operating from Blencowe village to Newbiggin, Stainton, and Penrith. In exchange A&S (Ribble itself from September) would use the main road between Greystoke and Penrith, would curtail their own Blencowe service at Blencowe station (which was actually in the neighbouring village of Newbiggin) and would cease to serve Stainton village on the way in to Penrith. It was a remarkable climb-down by the larger operator. By 1934 the Ribble service to Newbiggin had been abandoned and Titterington had the route to himself.

In 1930 a second, more modest, route was inaugurated. This was a Tuesday only market day service into Penrith from the small village of Dacre, to the south-west of Stainton. For the rest of the pre-war era the same modesty would also prevail in vehicle acquisitions. All were second-hand and included a bus-seated Leyland Cub from United Automobile (VN 2531), a 24-seat Eaton-bodied Reo coach from SMT (SY 4279), and a Bedford WLB coach from a Harrogate operator (YG 828).

Meanwhile, Ernest's cousin Edward Titterington (who lived in Laithes, the neighbouring village to Blencowe) had decided that he too wished to become a bus proprietor. In November 1933 he applied to the Traffic Commissioners for a daily service from Penrith to Penruddock, Mungrisedale, and Caldbeck. As the Penrith to Caldbeck market was already catered for by the trunk Penrith-Keswick service jointly operated by Ribble and CMS there was no chance whatsoever that a licence would be granted, but the Traffic Commissioners agreed to consider the rest of the application. This involved seven round-trips on market days, five on other weekdays, and two on Sundays. As no other operator was providing a service to Mungrisedale at that time, the Commissioners decided to grant a licence, even though they had grave reservations about the viability of the service. Their opinion proved to be correct and Edward Titterington ceased operations in October 1935.

Back at Blencowe, the only arrivals during the Second World War were a Bedford WTB/Duple coach from a Leicestershire operator (BBC 144) and a 36-seat Morris Dictator/Alexander bus from Hunter of Wishaw (GM 1969). The WTB replaced the Leyland Cub, but by the end of the war the Dictator had already died and the rest of the fleet was barely serviceable. For the first time Ernest Titterington bought new vehicles, four of them of three different makes. The first to arrive was Bedford OB/Duple Vista GRM 604 in November 1947, followed by Yeates-bodied Crossley SD42 coach JAO 223 in 1948. Another OB/Vista (JRM 651) was delivered in March 1950, and the last of the pre-war vehicles was eliminated by the arrival of 32-seat Morris-Commercial/ACB coach KRM 444 at the end of that year.

The fleet was further increased in the early 1950s by the purchase of a wartime OWB, mainly for school runs, from Gibson of Barlastone (DRY 778), and the acquisition of two more Crossley/Yeates coaches on the second-hand market (LWB 253 and ONU 547). The latter of these was replaced in August 1958 by a brand new Bedford SB3/Yeates Europa coach, VRM 730. From then until 1969 all vehicles purchased (both new and second-hand) would be Bedfords, most of them SB variants, but an interesting exception was VAL14/Harrington Legionnaire AWH 371B which was acquired from Leigh of Bolton in April 1966.

Ernest Titterington retired in 1967 and the proprietorship passed to his son Gordon. The Bedford monopoly was finally broken in April 1969 by the acquisition of a new PSU4 Leopard/Duple Northern coach, SRM 400G. The next new machine was bought specifically for the stage-carriage service, being a Bedford YRQ/Willowbrook dual-purpose vehicle (BAO 620J) which arrived in June 1971. In the following month another new type entered the fleet in the shape of Ford R226/Plaxton coach ARM 300J.

The founder passed away in 1978, and shortly afterwards Gordon Titterington decided to go after schools contracts in a more determined way. Second-hand service buses which arrived to perform these contracts included a PSU3 Leopard/Marshall from Southdown (BUF 139C) and a Bristol LH6L/ECW from Trent (BNU 673G). The coaching side of the business also began to experiment with different chassis types. Three Volvos at the end of the 1970s were followed by a pair of MANs in 1980/81. One of these German machines became the official team coach of Carlisle United football club until replaced in that role by one of a pair of (12 metre long) PSU5 Leopards the following year.

In 1982 the stage service from Blencowe (or Blencow as it was later spelled for no apparent reason) was still thriving, with ten round-trips on market days and six on other weekdays. After deregulation it was put up for tender, and at the time of writing is being operated by Alba Travel with just three round-trips per day. Such is progress. Fortunately, the Titterington business is doing well in its 21st century niche of up-market coaching and is currently controlled by three grandsons of the founder, Ian, Paul, and Colin.

Walton of Kirkby Stephen

Thomas Walton first went into business in 1909 as a painter and decorator. A few years later he bought a motor-van and realised that there was money to be made from such contraptions. In 1919 he opened the first garage and filling station in Kirkby Stephen and also bought the town's first motor taxi. Char-a-bancs followed, and during the late 1920s he developed a network of market day routes serving the surrounding villages on Mondays. Outbound market day services were also operated, travelling from Kirkby Stephen to Hawes on Tuesdays and to Barnard Castle on Wednesdays. A Chevrolet LQ with a 20-seat Robson body, EC 8958 (delivered in August 1929), is the only known vehicle from this period.

Walton was unimpressed by the 1930 Road Traffic Act, which he considered far too bureaucratic and restrictive. As a result he refused to apply for licences for his stage-carriage services and closed them down in December 1931. The company's coaching activities continued, and in 1934 Walton diversified by buying a furniture shop. In the same year the villagers of Aisgill Bridge finally persuaded him to restore their market day run to Kirkby Stephen, and this would remain as the company's only generally available stage-carriage service. A second route into the town, from Rawthey Bridge, was later acquired from Reed of Newbiggin-on-Lune, but this was essentially a schools service.

Notable vehicles of the post-war period included a WTB/Duple coach (DTB 230), an OWB utility bus (SN 9560), and a Leyland Comet/ACB coach (JM 8828). At the time of the company's closure in February 1963 the fleet was made up of three full-size coaches (Regal III/Plaxton JWU 709, Avenger III/Plaxton DEC 404, and Reliance/Duple ROU 808) and an Austin J2 minibus. The Regal III was sold to Harrison of Kirkby Stephen, the Avenger III to Robinson of Appleby (qv) along with the Aisgill Bridge stage service, and the other two vehicles went to FH Jackson (also of Kirkby Stephen) who took responsibility for the Rawthey Bridge school run. The furniture shop continued into the present century and was finally sold in 2012.

Wright of Nenthead

The remote Cumberland town of Alston, high up in the Pennines, has always been a mining community. The Romans extracted lead from the area almost 2,000 years ago, and others from a more recent age added zinc to the list of valuable natural resources to be found in the surrounding hills. The mining operations brought the railway to the town in 1862 when a branch along the South Tyne valley from Haltwhistle was opened, but inhabitants of the surrounding villages were still dependent upon horse-drawn vehicles or the power of their own feet. Nenthead, four and a half miles to the east of Alston, was one such mining village.

A peculiarity of the Alston region was its human geography, inside Cumberland but virtually surrounded by Northumberland to the north, County Durham to the east, and Westmorland to the south. Nenthead was located close to the Durham boundary, on the road from Alston to Weardale and Bishop Auckland which passed over the fearsome Killhope Pass (with a summit of 2,056 ft and a gradient approaching one in four at the steepest point).

At the beginning of the 20th century Ned Wright was a gamekeeper on a local estate. He had ten children, five sons and five daughters, but when the First World War started his innate patriotism compelled him to join up as a volunteer recruit to the new Royal Flying Corps (the predecessor to the RAF). His two eldest sons, Tom and Jimmy, also enlisted with Tom receiving a good mechanical background as a member of the Tank Corps. Before the three of them left Ned bought a pony and trap for his wife Mary, so that she could continue to make a living for the family while the main breadwinners were away. She used this combination to provide an 'on demand' service from Nenthead to Alston Station.

At the end of the war, in 1919, Tom used his demobolisation payment to buy a Ford Model T car which he and Jimmy used as a taxi to replace their mother's pony and trap. Jimmy soon went his own way, taking a job driving char-a-bancs with Armstrong of Ebchester, but Tom persevered. In 1924 he went into partnership with two of his younger brothers, George and John, to buy another Model T – this one equipped with a 14-seat bus body. In the following year the brothers bought a second bus, a 20-seat Guy, and started a more ambitious service from Penrith and Alston to Hexham in Northumberland.

A 14-seat Fiat (NL 7210) was acquired later in 1925 and was allocated to the Nenthead-Alston service. This meant that the Ford could be used on a new works service, carrying miners to Haltwhistle. Further expansion came in 1926 with new services from Nenthead to Hexham via the West Allen river valley, from Nenthead to Haltwhistle, and a local route in the Haltwhistle area using the vehicle despatched there on the miners' service. This brought Wrights vehicles into conflict with those of Haltwhistle bus operator JG Ridley.

Ridley caused further annoyance to the Wright brothers in March 1928 when he introduced a pioneering long distance service from Newcastle-upon-Tyne to Keswick via Hexham, Alston and Penrith. This service competed with the Wrights existing Penrith-Alston-Hexham route, but also pre-empted extensions at either end which they had been planning to make themselves. Instead, they found themselves unable to compete with Ridley on the lucrative sector to Newcastle as the city council would not grant licences to an operator from across the border in Cumberland to compete with a 'native' company. Ridley's base at Haltwhistle was, of course, in Northumberland. Another new service during the

91

year ran from Alston to Stanhope via Nenthead, the Killhope Pass, and St John's Chapel. This initially operated on a daily basis, but was soon cut back to run on Tuesdays, Saturdays, and (in summer only) Sundays.

On the 15th of June 1928 a fire destroyed Ridley's depot and the two vehicles inside. Fortunately, the Leyland Lioness he used on the Newcastle service (TY 3914) was out-stationed at the Keswick end of the route and so avoided destruction. His service continued for the rest of the 1928 summer season, and then operated throughout the season in 1929. In January 1929 Wrights acquired their own Leyland Lioness (1925 Commercial Motor Show exhibit UP 147) so they could at least compete on an equal footing between Penrith and Hexham.

At the western end of their (shorter) version of the Trans-Pennine service Wrights attempted to raise their profile by establishing a new service from Penrith to Wigton in May 1929. The vehicle used on this route spent the night at the Newlands Garage, owned by Penrith businessman Frank Smith. When the Wrights announced that they were going to abandon the Wigton route in November 1929, Smith formed a partnership with his friend Tom Rose to provide a replacement service. This later passed to Cumberland Motor Services and then to Hartness (qv).

Newcastle at Last!

The Wigton service had never produced a profit, but the real reason for its abandonment was the need to concentrate on a far larger potential prize. JG Ridley had indicated that he might be willing to sell his Newcastle-Keswick route to the Wright brothers. The timing was crucial, as the new Road Traffic Act was already being formulated and the indications from Parliament were that any 'sitting operator' would automatically be licensed for their existing services. The deal was done early in the new year, and when the route reopened in April 1930 it was under the ownership of Wrights, as was Ridley's Lioness.

Other vehicles acquired during the 1930s included an unidentified Bedford WHG in October 1931, a 14-seat Dodge (TY 4302) bought from United Automobile in 1934, and a Leyland Cub/Burlingham coach (FV 2520) from Seagull in Blackpool which was passed on to Sowerby of Gilsland (qv) after a year or so at Nenthead. A Leyland PLSC3 Lion with Leyland B36R bodywork (CM 8063) arrived from Birkenhead Corporation in 1935, but the biggest surprise of that year was the purchase of two SOS 'QLC' types (CH 8918/9) from Trent.

In 1938 Tom Wright decided to sell his share in the partnership and used the proceeds to buy the Nenthead Hotel and a share in a small local coalmine. George and John then formed a limited company, Wright Brothers (Coaches) Ltd. Their sister Frances Wright had been active in the business since 1928 (as a conductress) and in 1938 she married Wilson Reed, a driver for a company which collected milk from dairy farms. Both would play a significant role in the future of Wright Brothers.

Wartime acquisitions included four second-hand Bedford WTBs (JR 9938 and DRM 125 with Duple bodywork, and two Strachan-bodied examples, HPL 420 and ENY 20), and a wide variety of pre-war Leyland Tigers including four from the SMT group, three from Ribble, and one from Standerwick. The reason for all of these arrivals was a peculiarity in wartime legislation which resulted in the suspension of almost all express services (including the Northern General/Ribble route from Newcastle to the western side of the Pennines) but allowed services licensed as stage-carriage routes to continue according to social need. The Wrights' service was licensed as 'stage-carriage' despite running all the way from Newcastle to the Lake District, and mopped up the traffic left stranded by full railway trains or suspended express services. This left-over traffic was considerable as thousands of children from Tyneside had been evacuated to the Lake District.

Early post-war acquisitions included three Bedford OWBs from W Alexander in 1946 (one received a new Duple Vista body and lasted until 1967), and three more pre-war Tigers in 1947 (two of which were also rebodied by Duple). An unusual arrival for spares use was ex-SMT Leyland TD1 Titan SC 5226 – the only traditional double-decker ever owned (though not operated) by Wrights.

Deliveries of new vehicles began in 1948 with two Bedford OB/Duple Vistas (GRM 491 and HAO 487) and a Yeates-bodied Dennis Lancet III (HAO 656). Another OB/Vista arrived in 1949 (JAO 144) as well as two more Lancet III/Yeates

The bulk of Wright Brothers' post-war fleet was made up of bog standard coaches, latterly Bedfords with either Duple or Plaxton bodywork. This Saunders-bodied AEC Regal bus, CN 9958, was thus something of an exception to the rule when it arrived at Nenthead from Northern General in August 1960. It stayed with Wrights until November 1963. *(Ross Pattison Collection)*

Wrights bought a mixture of new and second-hand Bedfords. This SB5 with Duple Super Vega bodywork, 8270 PT, came from G & B of Quarrington Hill (County Durham) in June 1965. *(Robert F Mack)*

Wrights' next service bus after the ex-NGT Regal was this Bedford VAM70 with Plaxton Derwent bodywork, VRM 100H – seen here at the Newcastle terminus. It arrived in February 1970, courtesy of the Bus Grant, but had gone by the end of 1973. It passed to Hylton Castle Coaches in County Durham, and from them to Richards of Moylgrove near Cardigan in 1979. It was scrapped by Richards in 1985. *(Keith Johnson Collection)*

A later generation of Wrights' Bedfords is represented by SAO 466X, a 53-seat Bedford YNT with Plaxton bodywork bought new in March 1982. *(Keith Johnson Collection)*

(JAO 321 and JRM 946) and a Yeates-bodied Crossley SD42 (JAO 328).The Crossley, it seems, made a better impression than the Lancet IIIs as no more Dennises were ordered but two 30ft long SD42 with 39-seat Yeates bodies (KAO 472 and KRM 173) arrived during 1950.

The company's first ever Bedford SB arrived in 1951 in the guise of Duple Vega-bodied KRM 248. The only other delivery in that year was the first underfloor-engined vehicle, AEC Regal IV/Yeates Sherwood coach KRM 521. The fleet then stabilised and no more vehicles would be bought for six years. When buying resumed it was predominantly of second-hand coaches. The boom years had ended.

George Wright died in 1956 and his shares passed to his sister Frances Reed who had become the manager of the Newcastle end of the operation, running the kiosk which handled enquiries and advanced bookings, and also sold confectionery, newspapers, and tobacco. She still found time to act as the conductress on the late afternoon short-working to Alston. One of the strengths of the company was that all of its directors had daily 'hands on' experience at the sharp end. Frances' husband, Wilson Reed, was by this time working as a driver for the firm.

Two coaches joined the fleet in 1957. Regal III/Duple half-cab HTC 706 came from Battersby of Morecambe, while TAO 801 was a new Commer Avenger IV with Duple bodywork to the 'Super Vega lookalike' design. The next acquisition was more interesting from an enthusiast's viewpoint. ADO 513 was a Regal I/Harrington bus which came from Hylton & Dawson in Leicester in May 1957. It was mainly used for school runs. There was then a two year gap before the arrival of Crossley SD42/Burlingham coach FUN 319. The Crossley had been new to Peters of Llanarmon-yn-Ial (note the correct spelling – I stupidly misspelled the third component of the village's name as 'Lal' in my North Wales book!) but came to Wrights from Patterson of Beadnell. It would outlive all of the other half-cabs in the fleet, latterly being used as a 'heritage' vehicle.

From 1960 until April 1967 all acquisitions (both new and second-hand) were Bedford SB coaches except for two older vehicles. CN 9958 was a Regal I/Saunders bus which arrived from Northern General in August 1960 for the schools services. while SW 8039 was a Bedford OB/Duple Vista coach and came from Campbell, Gatehouse of Fleet, in April 1966.

The summer-only competition from the Northern General/Ribble express service from Newcastle to Keswick had always been a problem. Wrights served the route (as far as Penrith) during the winter, when traffic was low, but had to watch most of the tourist traffic using their competitors' faster journeys during the summer season. In 1962 they came to an agreement with the two BET subsidiaries to coordinate their schedules and avoid a large measure of this 'creaming off' of summer-only traffic. This agreement initially ran for three years but proved beneficial to both sides and was renewed in 1965.

A crisis faced the company in 1964 when John Wright died. According to the instructions in his will his shares in the business were shared between his children who seemed to be in favour of selling Wright Brothers to the highest bidder. Tom Wright, well into his 70s and long since retired from business, stepped out of the shadows to appeal for family solidarity and his stirring words saved the day. John's son Colin subsequently joined the company's board to represent his branch of the Wright clan.

The route across the Killhope Pass was finally withdrawn in 1967, more for lack of passengers than its challenging terrain. It had already been cut back to run as far as St John's Chapel (where it offered an 'iffy' connection with the Weardale route to Stanhope) and reduced to operate on summer Tuesdays only. With its demise the title for the highest stage-carriage route in England passed to the Alston-Nenthead-Carrshield-Hexham route (which reached 1,998 ft), also operated by Wrights!

The company's first Bedford VAM (LRM 43E) arrived in May 1967 and carried Duple Viceroy bodywork, while two smaller Bedfords arrived in 1969/70 to replace the last of the OBs. One was a Bedford VAS1/Duple Bella Vista from MacBraynes, the other a C5Z1/Duple Super Vista which also started life in Scotland. Another new VAM arrived in February 1970, this one (VRM 100H) a bus version with Plaxton Derwent bodywork which became the regular performer on the Newcastle run. It was followed by the company's first Bedford YRQ, a Plaxton-bodied coach delivered in September 1971.

95

Wrights' service to the Lake District had traditionally been cut short at Penrith during the winter months, with passengers for Keswick using the Ribble/CMS connecting service. As part of the National Bus Company's cutbacks, local services between Penrith and Keswick ceased to run on Sundays in 1971, and as a result the Wrights vehicle began to run through to Keswick on winter Sundays. Another small addition to the timetable was a new fortnightly service from Garrigill to Alston, heavily subsidised by the local authority and resurrecting a route once operated by Hetherington & Renwick (qv).

After the departure of the VAM/Plaxton bus in 1974 (it later served with Hylton Castle and Richards of Moylgrove) all new vehicles were coaches. The branch railway line from Alston to Haltwhistle closed in 1976 (it had avoided Dr Beeching's axe in the previous decade as the parallel road was often closed by bad weather in winter) but the rail replacement service went to Ribble. The Preston-based operator had only served Alston since 1969 when it took over the small United Automobile Services out-station in the town. Many thought that the work should have gone to Wrights.

Despite all of its tribulations over the years the company survived deregulation and continues to operate the Newcastle-Lake District service (now numbered 888) on a daily basis during the summer months, although it has been cut back to one journey in each direction. The Alston-Nenthead service also survives and new routes include a Monday-Friday commuters' express from Alston to Carlisle, and less frequent (market day or schooldays) runs to Brampton and Hexham. Given the atrocious winter weather in their home area, and the desperately low population density along most of their route network, this is little short of a miracle. But Wrights have always had first-class management, and as the saying goes 'God helps those who help themselves'.

Part Two

LANCASHIRE & CHESHIRE

The traditional county of Lancashire was a giant among the shires before being hacked to death by the mental midgets of Westminster. Its northernmost portion included the Furness peninsula (with the major shipbuilding town of Barrow as its local metropolis), Grizedale Forest (which reached up to the shores of Lake Windermere and Coniston Water) and the Morecambe Bay littoral as far east as the seaside town of Grange-over-Sands. The county of Westmorland then claimed the Kent estuary area as its own, leaving this northern portion of Lancashire physically isolated from the rest of the county.

From the seafront at Grange you could look to the south and see the small resort towns of Arnside and Silverdale. The former, the more northerly of the two, was in Westmorland and boasted the magnificent railway viaduct which carried the Barrow to Lancaster line – the glue which held the two parts of Lancashire together. Silverdale was in Lancashire and continuing south-eastwards the roads led to Carnforth (famous for its steam trains both on film and in reality) and to the old county seat of Lancaster with its castle and the Ashton Memorial, both visible by drivers passing the town on the M6 motorway. The River Lune had brought prosperity to the city, but had become less navigable over the centuries. The commercial traffic gradually drifted away to ports closer to the open sea.

One of these was Heysham which became the main port for sailings to the Isle of Man. The town shared a borough with Morecambe, a seaside resort which had its heyday in the 1930s and has been in decline ever since despite its rather feeble attempts to compete with Blackpool's famous Illuminations. Namesake comedian Eric Morecambe once described it as 'a cemetery with lights'. Despite this putdown his statue stands on the seafront.

On the far side of Morecambe Bay is the Fylde peninsula, for decades the holiday playground of people of all social classes – particularly those from the mill-towns of Lancashire and Yorkshire.

Fleetwood at the northern end of the peninsula was traditionally a fishing port, while Cleveleys to the south was mainly a resort which catered for the lower middle-classes. Continuing southwards a rider on the coastal tramway came to Blackpool itself where the middle-classes took their holidays in Bispham and the North Shore area, while working-class visitors swarmed to the less genteel environs of the Central and South Shore. The tramway ended at Starr Gate, at the southern end of the Promenade, where urban sprawl gave way to sand dunes and Squires Gate airport. Beyond these dunes were the posh resorts of St Anne's and Lytham, now much favoured as retirement communities.

The southern edge of the Fylde was provided by the River Ribble which had its lowest bridging point in Preston, the town (later city) which replaced Lancaster as the headquarters of the Lancashire County Council. Preston had grown rich in the engineering industry, and one of the major employers was the Dick Kerr tram factory. This company was merged into the English Electric consortium, which began to produce aircraft during the Second World War, and this led to the manufacture of well-known post-war types including the Canberra bomber and the Lightning fighter. Factory airfields were built at Warton (between Preston and Lytham) and at Samlesbury on the Preston-Blackburn road, and these facilities eventually passed to British Aerospace (or 'BAE Systems' as it prefers to be known these days).

To the south of the Ribble estuary the coast curved around to the major resort town of Southport and then to the Mersey estuary and the great port city of Liverpool, grown fat from the slave-trade. Liverpool was also (until the 1890s) the major port for the importation of cotton bound for the dozens of textile mill-towns in southern Lancashire, and for the arrival of tobacco from other slave-labour plantations. Then the slave-trade was abolished (which reduced profit margins for Liverpool capitalists) and sixty years after that Manchester built the Ship Canal and spoiled everything.

The Lancashire mill-towns had a lot of attractions from an entrepreneur's viewpoint. The area was rich in coal to fuel steam-powered equipment, had fast-running water to supply the needs of production processes, was in at the beginning of both the canal-building and railway construction revolutions, and offered a pool of cheap, semi-skilled, labour (mostly women and children) eager for work and the excitement of urban living. At the centre of this halo of mill-towns was the city of Manchester which inevitably became the *de facto* capital of North West England.

The same River Mersey which flowed along Liverpool's waterfront skirted the southern edge of Manchester, forming the boundary between Lancashire and Cheshire for most of its length. At the western end of this watery boundary, across the river from Liverpool, was the Wirral peninsula – then entirely in Cheshire. The dying seaside resort of New Brighton lay at the mouth of the Mersey estuary, but the major towns of the Wirral were Wallasey and Birkenhead (which had thriving shipyards). On the western side of the Wirral the county boundary was delineated by the River Dee which had reached the Irish Sea after flowing through the county town of Chester, an important administrative centre since the days of the Roman Empire.

Most of Cheshire was flat and agricultural, but the areas around Runcorn and Northwich were known for their salt and chemical works, while Crewe had grown from a small village to a major railway town in less than 20 years. Further to the east Macclesfield was renowned for its production of silk, while in the 'Cheshire Panhandle' which followed the Rivers Tame and Etherow (both tributaries of the Mersey), the cotton industry spilled across the Lancashire boundary into the Cheshire towns of Stockport, Hyde, Dukinfield, and Stalybridge. Several other towns close to Manchester (such as Altrincham, Sale, Cheadle, Bramhall, and Wilmslow) grew rich as 'dormitory' communities for the new Mancunian elite and their senior managers.

For both Lancashire and Cheshire the eastern boundaries were provided by the Pennine watershed, although there were several exceptions to this rule. Yorkshire crossed the hills into the Saddleworth area (north-east of Oldham) and into the Forest of Bowland (north of Clitheroe). These examples of Yorkshire imperialism were countered by a Lancastrian incursion which resulted in some parts of the Yorkshire town of Todmorden being in Lancashire (including half of the Town Hall until the 1880s). In an earlier age the boundaries of Lancashire had reached as far as the town of Skipton, an historical anomaly which Ribble Motor Services would later revive by invading this area of Yorkshire during the 1920s. Lancashire folk have long memories.

Bamber Bridge Motor Services

As already noted in the Introduction to this book, the large village of Bamber Bridge (four miles south of Preston) had received its earliest motorbus service in 1907, courtesy of the Lancashire & Yorkshire Railway. The original route connected the village with Chorley via Whittle-le-Woods and was intended to provide a feeder at Chorley to the L&Y's train services to Manchester, Yorkshire, and beyond. A local connection to Preston was longer in coming, perhaps because of the existing railway service from Bamber Bridge station on the line from Preston to Blackburn, Accrington, and Burnley.

By 1922 Ribble Motor Services was offering a bus at least every half-hour from Bamber Bridge to Preston, but nearly all of these were longer distance routes from Chorley and Wigan, and prone to delays. A local man, John H Cooke, began to offer his own alternative in that year, running into Preston from the Hob Inn at the southern end of Bamber Bridge. The service was a success and by the beginning of 1929 Cooke's fleet had grown to include three 26-seat Guys (CK 3600, CK 3685, and TE 4253) and a Leyland A13 (TC 9719) of identical seating capacity.

In the meantime another citizen of Bamber Bridge, Richard Prescott, had also built a successful business for himself as a bicycle dealer and repairer. He had established his company at the former Methodist chapel on Station Road, and gradually expanded by providing petrol pumps and maintenance for motorised vehicles, including Cooke's buses. In May 1929 he bought Cooke's business, including the Preston service and the four buses, rebranding it as 'Bamber Bridge Motor Services'. The Guys became fleet numbers 1,2, and 4, and the Leyland received fleet number 3. The new proprietor's two sons, Jim and Tom Prescott, were soon active in the company which used the old chapel turned bicycle workshop as its depot.

Frequencies were increased under the Prescott family's ownership and by the end of 1930 there were 36 round-trips per weekday on the route. The company had received its first brand-new vehicle in September when 32-seat LT2 Lion bus TF 2693 had arrived from Leyland. This machine (which replaced the inherited A13 as fleet number 3) lasted until December 1950, a very good innings for a bus of this era. Fleet number 5 was taken up in March 1931 by a fourth Guy, NW 8041, bought second-hand from Samuel Ledgard in Leeds. It would only last for seven months at Bamber Bridge before resale.

An opportunity too good to miss came along in December 1931 when Scout Motor Services of Preston (qv) decided to sell off two recently delivered LT2 Lion buses. Demand had already out-stripped the Lions' seating capacity and they had been replaced by double-deckers on the Preston-Blackpool service. CK 4380/81 became Bamber Bridge's fleet numbers 1 and 5, both replacing Guys. Their purchase helped to bolster the company's presentation to the Traffic Commissioners after Ribble (predictably) objected to Bamber Bridge receiving a licence. With three LT2 Lions (all less than two years old) as the mainline equipment, and the two surviving Guys on stand-by as spares, it was hard for Ribble to portray BBMS as an operator unfit to provide a public service. The combination of this investment and the testimony of local travellers ensured that the Prescotts received their Road Service Licence.

Another new Lion bus (but of the LT5A model and equipped with a 34-seat Burlingham body) arrived in May 1934, registered TJ 5388, and replaced a Guy as fleet number 2. The remaining Guy left the fleet in February 1935 when the company took delivery of its first double-decker, a new all-Leyland TD3 Titan (TJ 8147) which became number 4. A second Titan, of the updated TD4 variant, followed in November 1935 as fleet number 6 (ATD 596). Both double-deckers had lowbridge bodywork, a choice which reflected the roof clearance in the old Methodist chapel used as a garage rather than any height restrictions on the route to Preston. All of the company's double-deckers until the very end were of low-height construction for this reason.

The two ex-Scout LT2 Lions were the next vehicles to be replaced. No 5 went in April 1937 its fleet number transferred to a new LT7 Lion with 35-seat Fowler bodywork (BTF 262). Fowler was a small bodybuilder with a workshop in Leyland and (many years later) would be taken over by John Fishwick & Son (qv). The

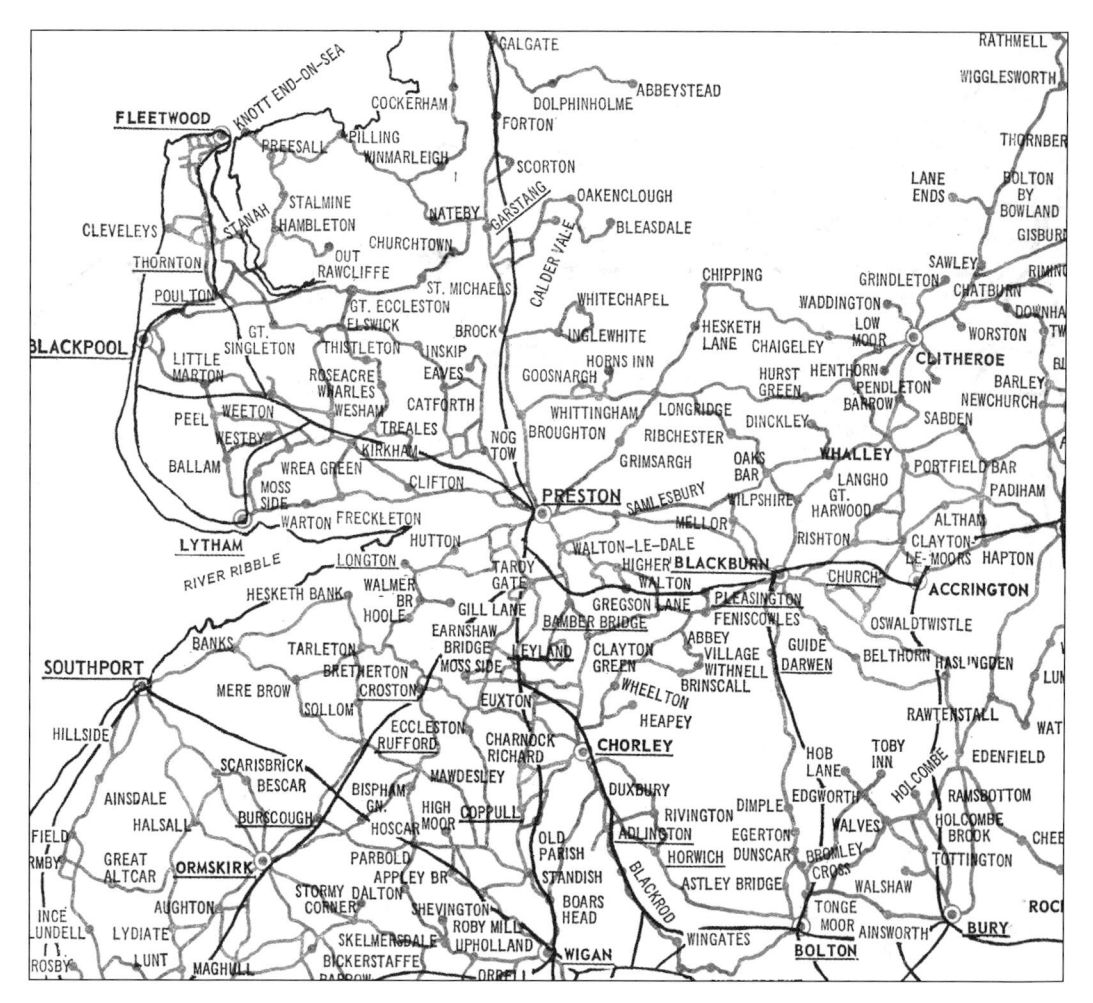

The central part of the Ribble empire, as depicted on a map issued with their 1966 timetables. The map shows many of the routes acquired from independent operators in the post-war era. Scout's main services were already jointly operated with Ribble before the 1961 take-over and run from Blackpool to Preston (via both Weeton and Wrea Green) and then beyond Preston to Burnley and Rochdale, and from Lytham to Preston. Fishwick's routes were also joint with Ribble (and were until deregulation) and can be seen in the triangle bounded by Preston, Leyland, and Chorley. Corless Services' route from Chorley to Wigan and Hart of Coppull's service from Croston to Southport were also jointly operated with Ribble before their respective take-overs. Viking's services ran westwards from Preston to Great Eccleston via Woodplumpton, Inskip, and Elswick, and BBMS's southwards to Bamber Bridge. Also visible are the services in the Clitheroe area acquired from Bolton-by-Bowland in 1955. One route not shown here, having never been operated by Ribble, is the service from Clitheroe northwards to Slaidburn. This route started off with West Riding operators Bounty Motors and Hodder Motor Services back in the 1920s, and passed from Bounty to Leedham of Dunsop Bridge (just inside Lancashire) in 1965. It should also be added that most of the other Ribble services shown on this map were acquired from independents in the 1920s and 1930s – in 1922 the company's heartland was confined to Preston, Blackburn, and Chorley with inter-urban routes reaching out to Bolton, Ormskirk, Southport, and Wigan. *(Author's Collection)*

99

other Scout Lion lasted until March 1938 when the fleet number 1 was painted on a second-hand all-Leyland TD1 double-decker acquired from Preston Corporation, CK 4050. As at Scout, the Lions had become too successful for their own good and had required replacement by something larger. At the outbreak of the Second World War in September 1939 the BBMS fleet was made up of the three Titan double-deckers and three Lion single-deckers.

The only wartime delivery was a Roe-bodied Guy Arab utility bus, FTE 568, which arrived in October 1944 and made the first use of fleet number 7. BBMS celebrated the return of peace by ordering a brand-new (all-Leyland) PD1 Titan double-decker which was delivered in December 1946 as the new fleet number 1 (GTF 418). Up until this point the company had conducted very little private hire work (all of its vehicles had been service buses), but during the post-war boom in coach travel the Prescotts decided to throw their hats into the ring. Four new coaches arrived within three years. The first was the original fleet number 8, an Arab III with Santus bodywork, delivered in December 1947 as HTJ 862. A second Arab III coach (but with Barnard bodywork) came in September 1948 as fleet number 2 (JTF 763), followed by a 29-seat Guy Vixen/Barnard in April 1949 (KTD 979, fleet number 3), and a Leyland PS1 Tiger with fully-fronted Burlingham Sunsaloon body (LTJ 119, fleet number 2) which replaced the second of the Arab IIIs in May 1950.

With three coaches in service the Prescotts turned their attentions back to the stage-carriage part of the fleet. In December 1950 they acquired a second-hand Arab/Strachan utility bus from Reading Corporation (BRD 755) and gave it fleet number 4, previously used by TD3 Titan TJ 8147. The Titan remained on the premises, as did TD4 ATD 596 (fleet number 6) when it was replaced by a new No 6, a Burlingham-bodied TD4 Titan (ATD 776) acquired from Fishwick in 1952. The chassis of the two pre-war BBMS Titans were in poor condition, but their bodywork was better than average. A body-swap was the perfect solution. The new No 4 (Arab BRD 755) received the Leyland body from the old No 6 while the new No 6 (TD4 Titan ATD 776) got the Leyland body from old No 4.

A new Bedford SBG/Duple Super Vega coach (STD 373) replaced the Guy Vixen as No 3 in April 1954, but the biggest shock came in December of that year when BBMS took delivery of a new AEC Regent III double-decker with East Lancs bodywork. This was bought partly as a result of one of the company's drivers being an evangelist for the type (he had driven AEC lorries for many years) and partly as a snub to Leyland Motors who had declined to supply a PD2/12 Titan with their own bodywork as they were closing their in-house bodybuilding operation. Leyland suggested that the Prescotts go to East Lancs for their bodywork, and so they did, but not on Leyland chassis. The new Regent III (UTC 672) became fleet number 4 and replaced the Arab/Leyland hybrid.

A second-hand Bedford SB/Duple Vega coach (BEN 302) was acquired from Auty's Tours of Bury in 1955, and received fleet number 5, previously used by the LT7 Lion/Fowler bus of 1937. The next year's purchases were of greater significance. Fellow Lancashire independent Corless of Charnock Richard (qv) had sold their stage services to Ribble, but the deal had not included the Corless fleet. As a result a pair of Corless PD1/Leyland double-deckers (GTJ 955 and GTF 476) were sold to BBMS in December 1956, becoming fleet numbers 6 and 7 respectively and replacing the wartime Arab and the rebodied (ex Fishwick) TD4. At the end of the year the company's fleet was made up of three PD1 Titans (Nos 1/6/7). Regent III/East Lancs No 4, Bedford SB coaches Nos 3 and 5, PS1 Tiger/Sunsaloon coach No 2, and Arab III half-cab No 8. The latter had lost its Santus body to the rot associated with this coachbuilder, and had received a Burlingham unit originally fitted to a Regal III operated by Premier Coaches of Preston.

The next major change to the coaching side of the business came in December 1959 when BBMS acquired two Royal Tiger/Duple Roadmaster coaches from Scout. Fleet number 2 (DRN 356) was an 8 ft wide version and replaced the 1950 Sunsaloon, while fleet number 5 (DRN 357) was one of the narrower 7ft 6 in variants and replaced the Auty's SB. The Arab III/Burlingham coach No 8 was also withdrawn during 1959, but the new vehicle which took its fleet number was far from being another coach. In November 1960 BBMS startled the local horses by acquiring its first rear-engined vehicle, former Leyland Atlantean/Weymann lowbridge demonstrator 661 KTJ. The new No 8 caused quite a sensation in

Bamber Bridge Motor Services bought this TD4 Titan with Leyland lowbridge bodywork, ATD 596 (fleet number 6) in November 1935. In 1953 its body was transferred to second-hand Guy Arab BRD 755. *(Keith Johnson Collection)*

And this is what BRD 755 looked like when it was acquired from Reading Corporation in December 1950, still carrying its Strachan lowbridge utility body. It operated for several years without a Bamber Bridge fleet number, but became No 4 after being rebodied in 1953. *(Author's Collection)*

101

Bamber Bridge's fourth No 1 was GTF 418, an all-Leyland PD1 Titan delivered in December 1946. Seen here in Starchhouse Square in Preston, in company with Scout PD2s and a PD3, it lasted until June 1966. *(Keith Johnson Collection)*

Arab III coach HTJ 862 (Bamber Bridge fleet number 8) was originally delivered in December 1947 with a Santus body, as shown here. After the Santus unit began to disintegrate it received a Burlingham body donated by a Premier Coaches of Preston AEC Regal III. *(Roy Marshall)*

Preston independent circles, where (by the end of 1960) only Scout – four times as large as BBMS – had entered the Atlantean era. Fishwick received their first Atlanteans in 1963, when BBMS finally received their own second example of the type as No 7 (2295 TE). This was a new machine and replaced one of the former Corless PD1s.

For the first 34 years of its existence BBMS had operated just one (unrestricted) stage-carriage service, the route from the Hob Inn at Bamber Bridge to Preston via the Pear Tree pub and the main A6 road. In 1963 a variation of this route was introduced when one journey per hour was diverted to serve a new housing development on Duddle Lane. The other two journeys continued to travel via the Pear Tree, and to differentiate between the two the company's destination blinds were amended to show the route letter 'D' (via Duddle Lane) or 'P' (via the Pear Tree).

The 1954 Bedford SBG/Duple was withdrawn in March 1963 and replaced by a three year old SB1/Plaxton acquired from Premier of Preston, OCK 169. The final delivery during 1963 was another double-decker which had served as a demonstrator. Albion Lowlander/Alexander 747 EUS arrived in November and replaced the surviving ex-Corless PD1 as fleet number 6. It had a narrow blind aperture which enabled the window-line to continue around the front of the upper-deck, avoiding the ugly 'step up' of the front windows which ruined the appearance of all other Alexander-bodied Lowlanders.

Further second-hand coaches came in 1964/65. The first was another SB1/Plaxton (TNL 322) which came from Galley of Newcastle-upon-Tyne in March 1964 and received fleet number 2, replacing one of the Scout Royal Tigers. The second was a Leyland Leopard/Duple Britannia, GCU 573, which also hailed from the north-east having been new to Hall Bros of South Shields in 1962. It became BBMS's fleet number 3 in March 1965 and replaced both the surviving Scout Royal Tiger and the ex-Premier SB1/Plaxton. As a result the fleet number 5 was now missing from the roster for the first time since 1931.

No 1, the PD1 bought new in 1946, was withdrawn in June 1966. Its replacement was a 12 year old PD2/20 Titan with Weymann Orion lowbridge bodywork (HJN 844) acquired from Southend Corporation. Sadly, this was to be the company's last purchase. In early 1967 there was a horrifying accident at the old chapel which still served as the company's garage. One of the fitters was killed and Tom Prescott was badly burned, leaving him out of action for the foreseeable future. The brothers thought long and hard about the future and decided to retire.

On the 1st of April 1967 Bamber Bridge Motor Services was absorbed by Ribble. The purchase price of £24,400 included the 'goodwill' of the stage services, the two Atlanteans, and the Lowlander, and was quite a small sum to pay for the removal of such an energetic competitor. On the other hand the Prescott brothers wanted 'out' and continued in business with the filling station and garage on the old chapel site, The worst outcome was probably that for the Lowlander which Ribble decided to modify to suit their standard 'Scottish style' destination display. As a result of this surgery it became as ugly as all the other Alexander-bodied Lowlanders in the country. I still picture it in its original form whenever I pass the Hob Inn.

Bolton by Bowland of Clitheroe

As the name suggests, Bolton by Bowland Motor Services had its origins in the small village of that name to the north east of Clitheroe. Under the pre-1974 boundaries the village was actually in the West Riding of Yorkshire (along with the rest of the Forest of Bowland) whereas the nearest market town, Clitheroe, was in Lancashire. The company is included in this volume as it later moved its main depot to Clitheroe and most of the company's stage-carriage revenues were earned in Lancashire.

The early history of the operator is a little vaguer than most. It was founded by Isaac Bleazard of Bolton by Bowland in the years immediately after the First World War. The Bleazards had been farmers in the Bowland area since at least 1809 (with an Isaac in each generation) and had already opened a garage in the village, initially to service motorised farm vehicles and then private cars. The addition of a taxi led to the first bus which operated a weekday service from the village to Clitheroe station along with a market-day service to Settle in Yorkshire.

Details of vehicles for this pioneering period are completely unknown, but the stage-carriage network was gradually expanding and by 1930 the

103

company was operating a far more remunerative cross-town service in Clitheroe from Low Moor in the west to Chatburn in the east. The only other daily service at that time was the operation from Bolton by Bowland to Clitheroe, but there were market-day runs from the hamlets of Lane Ends (to the west of Bolton) and Worston to Clitheroe (on Tuesdays and Saturdays), and from Bolton to Settle (on Thursdays and Saturdays), and a Sunday only route from Clitheroe to Settle. Despite strident objections from Ribble all were granted licences by the new Traffic Commissioners.

The earliest known vehicle, a 14-seat Dodge registered CB 7971, was joined in 1934 by four brand-new Dennis Aces with Dennis 20-seat bus bodywork (YG 6291-94). This shiny new fleet seemed to embolden the proprietor and in 1937 he applied to *reduce* the fares on his Clitheroe cross-town route. Ribble (which also ran along the roads in question) objected strenuously to the proposal. At the subsequent hearing before the North West Traffic Commissioners Bleazard openly mocked the Ribble representative, offering to buy the company's routes if they were worried that the fare reduction might affect their finances. He got the laughter, and lots of favourable publicity, but not the fares reduction.

The only other machine recorded in the pre-war era was a second hand PLSC1 Lion acquired from Ribble (via a neutral dealer!) in October 1938, CK 3831. This and one of the Aces were allocated to the town service, and another two Aces to a mixture of schools runs and the market day routes. It was thus a disaster when three of the four Aces were requisitioned in early 1940 for military use. By 1941 the situation had become so parlous that Bleazard was forced to go cap in hand to Ribble and to ask if they might be interested in buying his business. A deal, at a very low valuation, was negotiated and permission sought from the wartime Regional Traffic Commissioner. This was not forthcoming and the two parties were advised to wait until the end of the war and then reapply to the civilian Commissioners. More helpfully the RTC managed to pull some strings and by the end of the year second-hand Lions had arrived from Burnley, Colne, and Nelson joint committee (three) and Blackburn Corporation (two). Other wartime acquisitions were two Bedford WTB coaches and a Leyland TS7 bus, and these additional wheels were required for works journeys which served a variety of strategic industrial sites, both to the west (the aircraft factories around Preston) and to the east (as far as Burnley and Barnoldswick).

The first new arrival after the war was an Ormac-bodied Bedford, EWW 306, followed by two brand-new Commer Commando coaches with Plaxton bodywork, (FWW 435 and FWW 565) in 1947. In the post-war boom the company's single-deckers were unable to meet the demand for the Low Moor-Clitheroe-Chatburn service without regular (and expensive) duplication, and Bolton by Bowland acquired its first double-decker to solve the problem. This was JX 1787, a 1934 vintage Park Royal-bodied AEC Regent, which arrived from Halifax JOC during 1948. A pair of new Bedford OB/Duple Vista coaches (HYG 23/JYG 418), delivered in 1949/50, left the two Commer Commandos free to operate the market-day services in company with the surviving Dennis Ace, YG 6292. A further OB (BRN 494) arrived from Scout of Preston late in 1949.

By 1949 the main focus of the operation had moved from the original site at Cosy Nook Garage, Bolton by Bowland, to 4, Wellgate in Clitheroe, saving much wasted mileage. In September 1952 the business, which had been under the sole proprietorship of Isaac Bleazard, became a limited company as Bolton by Bowland Motor Services Ltd, registered at the Clitheroe address. With hindsight it is possible that this conversion in legal status was motivated by Mr Bleazard's desire to enjoy his retirement without anxieties about exorbitant death duties.

In February 1953 the ex-Halifax Regent wore out and was replaced by the company's second and last double-decker. This was a lowbridge Regent, DYL 853, which had previously served with London Transport as STL 2220. Second-hand coaches acquired during 1953 included a Bedford OB/Plaxton from Hardwick of Scarborough (EAJ 645), an Austin CXB with rare Booth bodywork (CWH 770), and the company's first Bedford SB/Duple Vega (RTN 999). The following year saw the arrival of a five-year old Bedford OB/Mulliner bus (JWT 24) which had been new to neighbouring operator Ezra Laycock of Barnoldswick. Laycock had fitted the OB with a Perkins P6 diesel engine which made it cheaper to run and ideal for Bolton by Bowland's poorly patronised market day

Fleet number 7, GTF 476, was one of a pair of all-Leyland PD1s acquired from Corless Services of Charnock Richard in December 1956. Both were replaced by more modern vehicles in 1963. *(Roy Marshall)*

In December 1959 Bamber Bridge acquired two Royal Tiger/Duple Roadmaster coaches from Scout of Preston. DRN 357 (BBMS fleet number 5) was a PSU1/11 variant, indicating that it was only 7ft 6 ins wide. The vehicle gave four years of service to the company before passing to a contractor. *(Keith Johnson Collection)*

This Leyland Atlantean with a semi-lowbridge Weymann body, 661 KTJ, started life as a Leyland demonstrator in September 1959. In November 1960 it became Bamber Bridge's first rear-engined vehicle and received fleet number 8. This photograph shows it after the Ribble take-over and RMS fleet number 1966 is just visible to the left of the registration plate. Although still in full Bamber Bridge livery it had received a Ribble style destination display.
(Senior Transport Archive)

Alexander-bodied Albion Lowlander 747 EUS was also built as a demonstrator. After nine months of evaluation by Edinburgh and Glasgow (neither of which ordered any Lowlanders) it was sold to BBMS in November 1963 as fleet number 6. Note 661 KTJ behind it, showing its original destination display. *(Senior Transport Archive)*

routes. The surviving Dennis Ace was withdrawn and the two Commandos were relegated to schools journeys.

Despite such economies (and the relative popularity of the Clitheroe local service) the stage-carriage routes were losing money. In September 1955 they were sold to Ribble Motor Services and all continued to operate for at least another decade as a result. No vehicles were involved in the sale (Ribble was, for some reason, not interested in Commer Commandos, a Perkins powered Bedford OB, or a pre-war AEC Regent), and Bolton by Bowland continued in business as a provider of excursions, tours, private hires, and schools contracts. These did not require the lowbridge STL, which was scrapped.

In 1956 the founder died. None of his surviving relatives were interested in continuing the business and the company was acquired by Stanley Hodgson, the proprietor of Slaidburn based Hodder Motor Services (this operator will be covered in my next book 'Independent Buses in Western Yorkshire'). Hodgson kept it as a separate company and, in 1962, moved the registered office of Hodder from Slaidburn to the Clitheroe address. The first casualties of the change of ownership were the two Commandos, replaced by second-hand heavyweight coaches in the shape of Crossley SD42/Burlingham Sunsaloon GPY 103 and Foden PVSC6/Plaxton Envoy FJF 613 during 1957.

Later purchases were less inspiring, being mainly of standard Bedford coaches (SBs followed by VALs) with routine Duple or Plaxton bodywork. Almost all were second-hand with Mr Hodgson buying a pair of vehicles at a time and registering one to Hodder and the other to Bolton by Bowland. The company survived in this afterlife until the mid-1970s.

Corless of Charnock Richard

In the 1901 census Matthias Corless of Charnock Richard is recorded as a coalminer with two young sons, Albert and Horace. At the outbreak of the First World War he returned to his former regiment and (despite being in his late thirties) volunteered for combat. In the event he ended up as a driver and mechanic, so it came as no great surprise when he used his demobilisation pay to buy a second-hand taxi. In November 1923 he went one step further and acquired a brand-new 14-seat Ford Model T bus (TC 5831), using this vehicle to establish regular services from Charnock Richard to Chorley (via the neighbouring village of Coppull) and Wigan (via Standish).

Within a year demand had out-stripped the Ford's meagre capacity and it was replaced by a 26-seat Leyland A13 (TC 9576). By then Albert Corless had joined his father and shortly after the Leyland's delivery the two routes were linked to form a through service from Chorley to Wigan. This was partly in response to the activities of Ribble, which had become increasingly aggressive since entering the Chorley area in 1921 and had recently deployed 'chasers' against the Corless vehicle. To keep up with the much larger competitor in terms of frequency and modernity, a second vehicle was acquired in October 1927. This was TE 1793, a PLSC1 Lion with Leyland's own 31-seat bodywork, and received fleet number 2. The A13 was retro-actively numbered '1' after the Lion's arrival and lasted until 1936.

The intensifying competition justified the purchase of a second PLSC1 in June 1928 (TE 4349, fleet number 3), and then one of the improved LT1 Lion model (TE 9020, fleet number 4) in August 1929. Another LT1 came to Charnock Richard three months later as TE 9651, fleet number 5. With four very up-to-date Lions in the fleet, and the ageing A13 available as a reserve, M Corless & Son had no problem in securing licences from the new Traffic Commissioners in 1931. Two services from Chorley to Wigan were approved, virtually identical except for the route taken in the Coppull area. At the time of the grant of these licences the Traffic Commissioners expressed the hope that Ribble and Corless would co-ordinate the timings on their competing routes. This was usually seen as a veiled threat to impose coordination if no such scheme was offered voluntarily, but another four years would pass before Ribble accepted Corless as a joint operator.

The company's first ever coach arrived in April 1936 when the Corlesses bought FV 7215. The new number 1 was a Leyland TS7 Tiger with a 32-seat Burlingham body (hence the Blackpool registration). It was followed by two Tiger buses, a TS7 in 1937 (BTE 628, fleet number 7) and a TS8 in 1938 (DTC 393, the second fleet number 4), and then by the company's first double-decker, all-Leyland TD5 Titan ETB 52 (the new number 3).

107

This was delivered in August 1939, weeks before the start of the Second World War, and was soon requisitioned for service elsewhere as was the TS7/Burlingham coach. Their replacements were a 1935 Leyland Cub/East Lancs coach (ATB 347) and a 1929 vintage TS2 Tiger (GU 2317), the latter coming north from a London operator as FV 7215 was going south.

The tatty TS2 received fleet number 6, which had obviously been issued before (or why number the 1937 Tiger bus as '7'?) although its original wearer remains unidentified, while the Cub succeeded the last surviving Lion as fleet number 5. Neither of these specimens survived until the end of the war, so by the time of the German surrender the Corless fleet had been reduced to just the two Tiger buses. As the Chorley-Wigan services had a peak vehicle requirement of two buses something needed to be done quickly to avoid missed journeys. A temporary solution was provided by the acquisition of TS7 Tiger RN 7921 in December 1945. The Spicer coach body on this vehicle had deteriorated during the war and Albert Corless (by then the sole proprietor) sent it to Santus in Wigan to receive a new coach body before entering service in February 1946. It received fleet number 2 but was sold on to a Wigan operator in less than a year.

Despite the desperate shortage of vehicles, Corless refused to take back the two pre-war vehicles which had been requisitioned in 1940. Both were apparently in poor mechanical condition, although the TS7 coach ran for a Luton operator until 1956, and the TD5 Titan was sold to North Western and ran successfully for them until 1954. It was then converted into a racing car transporter and lasted until at least 1958 in this form. In their place came two brand-new Leyland PD1 Titans with lowbridge Leyland bodywork, GTF 476 (fleet number 5, delivered in December 1946) and GTJ 955 (fleet number 1, new in March 1947). They were the last Corless vehicles to receive fleet numbers.

After the sale of the TS7/Santus coach there was a gap of two years before Corless re-entered the coaching market, although the bus fleet (the two PD1s and the two pre-war Tigers) operated the occasional local outing in the interim period. Luxury returned to the fleet in January 1949 with the purchase of a brand-new Crossley SD42/Santus coach, KTB 664. On the debit side the 1937 Tiger bus was withdrawn in June. A second coach, Bedford OB/Duple Vista LTB 907, was acquired in May 1950 from Lamb of Upholland. It was only four months old, but was sold on at the end of the summer season to Penn of Warrington. It survives in preservation.

In December 1950 the Crossley was replaced by a PS2/3 Tiger coach with fully-fronted Santus bodywork, JP 8688. A rather odd addition in July 1951 was a 16 year old LT7 Lion bus, RN 7664, previously operated by Ribble. It was presumably acquired for a contract as it vanished twelve months later, shortly after the arrival of Corless' final vehicle. This was NTJ 985, an all-Leyland Royal Tiger bus, delivered new in May 1952. It replaced the 1938 TS8 Tiger bus and was usually allocated to the infrequent journeys which ran via Coppull Moor.

During the 1950s Ribble embarked upon a policy of connecting trunk services together into single marathon routes across its territory. As part of this scheme they proposed to Corless that the Wigan-Coppull-Chorley services should be connected with the Chorley-Blackburn route and that Corless vehicles should run the full length to Blackburn. Albert Corless decided to give it a try but rapidly became disillusioned with the extended route. He could have easily disengaged from the changes, but he was ready to retire and had no heir apparent at the bus company. His son Horace (named for his late uncle and familiarly known as Harry) had his own career in industry – he later moved to the USA and became the chairman of ICI – while his three daughters were all married to successful businessmen scattered around the country.

When approached Ribble offered a generous price and Corless took the money. The business of M Corless & Son ceased to trade on the last day of 1956. The two PD1s were sold to Bamber Bridge Motor Services (qv) while the Royal Tiger bus ended up in Scotland with Baxter of Airdrie. By 1968 it was serving as a site hut for West Lothian County Council. The Chorley to Wigan services are still making money, currently operated by Arriva's Bolton depot although continuing to use their old Ribble service number '362'.

Photographs of Bolton-by-Bowland's ex London Transport 'STL class' Regent DYL 853 are all but impossible to find, which explains why Roy Marshall bought this poor quality print of the vehicle taken by an unknown photographer. The former STL 2220 came to the company in February 1953 and is seen here on the main cross-town service in Clitheroe. It was scrapped in February 1956. *(Roy Marshall Collection)*

Bolton-by-Bowland's Plaxton-bodied Commer Commando FWW 435 was painted in the two-tone blue coaching livery, and is seen here on the Bolton-by-Bowland to Clitheroe route. It was sold in 1958, passing to Flint of Carr Vale. *(Charles F Klapper via The Omnibus Society)*

This all-Leyland TS8 Tiger bus, DTC 393, was new to Corless of Charnock Richard as fleet number 4 in August 1938. After withdrawal by them in 1952 it passed to Bryn Melyn of Llangollen for further service, giving the Welsh operator a further three years of front-line service. *(Roy Marshall)*

Corless Services' PD1 Titan GTF 476 (fleet number 5) is seen here in Wigan bus station, awaiting its departure on the service to Chorley jointly operated with Ribble. After Corless sold out it went to Bamber Bridge, as shown in an earlier photograph. *(Roy Marshall)*

110

Fishwick of Leyland

At the beginning of 1907 John Fishwick was working for the Lancashire Steam Motor Company of Leyland. The company would soon change its name to Leyland Motors, but by then Fishwick had decided to go it alone, buying a steam lorry from his former employers and setting himself up in business as a haulage contractor. Things went well and in 1910 he bought a second vehicle, a petrol-powered Leyland X type originally configured as a flatbed lorry. In common with many small hauliers, Fishwick was anxious to maximise the utilisation of his assets, and in 1911 bought a demountable char-a-banc body for the Leyland. During the week it carried freight, but on Saturdays it opened a passenger service from Eccleston to Preston via Leyland. Two more 'convertible' Leyland Xs were acquired in 1914, but any further expansion of stage-carriage routes was delayed by the start of the First World War.

In 1916 a further Leyland was acquired, this time of the RAF type which was an evolution of the X series modified to suit military specifications, and a second example of this variant followed in 1919. A more important purchase during that year was fleet number 8, a Leyland S5 with a 20-seat body, which was Fishwick's first purpose-built passenger vehicle. By this time two of the founder's sons, William and Bernard, had joined the business and a period of rapid expansion followed. Between 1920 and the end of 1922 four more Leyland S5 buses joined the fleet and daily services were commenced from Leyland to Preston and Chorley, along with a market day route (on Thursdays) to Ormskirk.

The BET/BAT subsidiary Ribble Motor Services was also spreading its wings during these years, and to avoid expensive conflict Ribble, Fishwick, and another Leyland operator (Bridges), agreed to co-ordinate their services between Preston and Leyland. The three operators accepted each other's return tickets, produced jointly funded publicity and timetables, and formulated a schedule acceptable to them all. Some other operators on the route, notably Singleton of Leyland and Dallas Services (originally of Earnshaw Bridge, later of Preston), declined to join the scheme and were declared 'fair game' by the consortium. All three allied operators deployed small 'chaser' buses to discourage their uncoordinated competitors, Fishwick's contribution being four Leyland A9s acquired in 1923/4.

The Fishwicks were determined from an early stage to match Ribble's equipment on the joint services (which operated between the two towns on four different routes) and in March 1926 two brand-new PLSC1 Lions made the short journey from the Leyland works to the Fishwick depot. They were followed in 1927/8 by eight of the slightly longer PLSC3 version. More money was spent during 1929 to buy five TS2 Tigers, which replaced one of the S5s and all of the A9s. The haulage business continued, but by the end of the 1920s the company's fleet was made up of 14 buses and only six lorries.

Meanwhile Bridges had sold out to the Yarrow Motor Co of Eccleston in 1927, giving that company access to Preston for the first time. Yarrow declined to join the Leyland Motor Bus Service consortium, which disintegrated as a result, but despite the end of the formal alliance Ribble and Fishwick continued to co-operate against their common enemies on the Leyland-Preston and Leyland-Chorley corridors. Yarrow must have felt particularly victimised after Ribble acquired the neighbouring business of the Eccleston Motor Co in 1928, bringing it into conflict with the rest of Yarrow's route network. Despite this animosity Fishwicks acquired four vehicles from Yarrow in September 1930, two PLSC1 Lions (one of them new to Bridges, the other sold off by the Eccleston Motor Co before its own absorption by Ribble) and two PLSC3 Lions which had been new to Yarrow only two years previously. It appears that the competition from Ribble was hurting Yarrow badly and the Fishwicks were willing to take advantage of the situation to buy some fairly new vehicles on the cheap.

In 1930/1 Fishwicks applied to the new Traffic Commissioners for licences for its entire network of existing services, consisting of operations from Leyland to Preston (via three main routes), from Leyland to Chorley (via two routes), the market day runs to Ormskirk (via two routes), and a Sunday only service from Leyland to Bamber Bridge (later incorporated into one of the Preston services). All were granted, as were similar services applied for by Ribble. More annoyingly, from the viewpoint of Fishwick and Ribble, Yarrow were also licensed for their Eccleston-

Leyland-Preston route (along with their other services from Eccleston), while Leyland-Preston licences were granted to Singleton and another Leyland operator, Parkinson.

Nevertheless, the news from the Traffic Commissioners was good enough to justify an order for three Leyland TD1 Titans, the company's first double-deckers, which were delivered in June 1931. By the time of the founder's death in 1934 his company had become one of the leading independent bus operators in the North West of England. The business was continued by a partnership of his four sons, William, Bernard, Vincent, and James.

In August 1935 the Fishwick brothers agreed to join with Ribble to purchase the stage-carriage services of both Singleton and Parkinson, leaving Yarrow as the only 'uncoordinated' competitor on the Leyland to Preston routes. Their reward was an unprecedented two-thirds share of the Preston and Chorley traffic, with Ribble accepting the remaining third with apparent good grace. This was quite possibly the only joint operating agreement in the entire country where a 'Combine' company played second fiddle to a locally owned independent operator. The Fishwicks celebrated by acquiring another three double-deckers, TD4s with Burlingham bodywork, delivered in December 1935. Four similar vehicles (but with TD5 chassis) followed in June 1937.

The final pre-war deliveries, four all-Leyland LT9 Lion saloons, arrived in January 1939 and replaced the remaining PLSC1 models of 1926-28 vintage. Three months later Fishwick and Ribble jointly acquired the Yarrow Motor Co, eliminating their final competitor on the Leyland-Preston routes. Another consequence was that Fishwick vehicles began to run through to Wigan for the first time, operating their share of Yarrow's Preston-Leyland-Eccleston-Standish-Wigan service. J Fishwick & Sons entered the war with a fairly modern fleet, and as a result received no allocations of utility vehicles despite the presence of an enormous strategic employer (Leyland Motors), literally on the company's doorstep. The war did, however, bring tragedy to the Fishwick family when brother James was killed in an air crash.

The Post-War Years

By the end of the war most of the fleet was in serious need of refurbishment and most of this work went to a small Leyland-based bodybuilder, WH Fowler & Co. Fowler had produced a relatively small number of bus and coach bodies to their own designs during the 1920s and 1930s. They would play a major part in the Fishwick story some twenty years later. The need to take vehicles off the road for essential refurbishment left the fleet temporarily under strength, and new vehicles were sought with some urgency.

The first to arrive, towards the end of 1946, were two PS1 Tiger saloons with Burlingham bodywork and two all-Leyland PD1A double-deckers. Two more PS1/Burlingham single-deckers arrived in the late summer of 1947 and by the end of that year the Fishwick fleet was made up of 12 double-decker buses, 21 single-deckers, and just four lorries. By then Fowler had completed the rebuilding programme, allowing a slow and measured replacement of the pre-war rolling stock. Two all-Leyland PD2 double-deckers were delivered in February 1949 (followed by a third in January 1950), and two more PS1/Burlingham saloons arrived in October 1949. These deliveries allowed the retirement of the TD1s and PLSC3s.

By 1951 the company's coffers were replete with profits from the post-war travel boom and the surviving Fishwick brothers went on a shopping spree at their local bus factory. The biggest surprise was an order for six HR44 Olympic single-deckers and for two of the slightly shorter HR40 version, delivered between March and October of 1951 and eliminating all the remaining pre-war saloons. There were also three all-Leyland PD2/12 double-deckers (to lowbridge layout), which arrived in November, and then a long pause before the delivery of two more PD2/12s (but to highbridge configuration) in July 1954. The PD2/12s replaced the pre-war Burlingham-bodied TD4/5 double-deckers, leaving Fishwick with a modern fleet in which the oldest vehicle had yet to reach its eighth birthday.

The Fishwicks found that this modern fleet was extremely economical to operate and decided to spend more money to maintain the low age profile. In November 1957 the company took delivery of a batch of six LW1 Olympians (the lightweight successors to the Olympic), allowing the retirement

A pre-delivery Leyland Motors shot of B 8851, a Leyland S5 which became Fishwick's fleet number 8 in December 1919. It was the operator's first 'purpose built' bus – previous machines had been lorries with removable passenger bodies. The vehicle wears Fishwick's original livery of pale green with black trim. It lasted as a bus until 1929 and then gave four more years of service to the company after its conversion into a flatbed lorry. *(Roy Marshall Collection)*

Fishwick's fleet number 25 (TE 2331) is also shown in a Leyland Motors shot. It was an all-Leyland PLSC3 Lion, new in January 1928, and illustrates the first version of the two-tone green livery. The vehicle was eventually withdrawn from service in December 1947. *(Roy Marshall Collection)*

After several deliveries of all-Leyland Titans, Fishwicks turned to Burlingham for their double-deck requirements in 1935/37. This is fleet number 18 (CTC 267), one of four Burlingham-bodied TD5s delivered in 1937. *(Keith Johnson Collection)*

Fishwick's Leyland HR44 Olympic MTD 516 (fleet number 27) was one of eight Olympics delivered to the company during 1951. In this shot it had just left Fishwick's Fox Street bus station in Preston, bound for the Queens Hotel in Leyland. *(Senior Transport Archive)*

The Olympics were followed by a batch of six LW1 Olympian service buses in November 1957. 524 CTF was originally fleet number 15, but in 1963 it received a cosmetic front panel grille, 40 dual-purpose seats in place of its previous 44 bus seats, and was repainted in Fishwick's new grey and white coaching livery as 'C5'. Sister vehicle 523 CTF was similarly treated and is illustrated in the colour section. *(Roy Marshall)*

Left: Fishwick's fleet number 32 (GTF 282) was an all-Leyland PD1A Titan delivered in December 1946. It is seen in Wigan bus station on the service to Preston via Eccleston and Leyland, jointly operated with Ribble who used the route number 113 for their share. Fishwicks later relinquished their mileage to Wigan and Southport in exchange for more timings on the Leyland-Preston services. *(Keith Johnson Collection)*

A slightly different angle on 'cover girl' 528 CTF (fleet number 5), taken when the PD2/40 was already in preservation and awaiting its departure from the British Commercial Vehicle Museum in Leyland during a running day. *(Author's Collection)*

Fishwick's semi-lowbridge Weymann-bodied Atlantean ATB 597A (fleet number 30) was one of four delivered in October 1963. 'A-suffix' registrations were rather rare, particularly on buses and coaches, as most local authorities went over to the suffix system with 'B' in 1964. *(Alan Murray-Rust)*

of the PS1/Burlingham saloons. Five months later, in March 1958, it was the turn of the double-deck fleet when six PD2/40s with lowbridge Weymann Orion bodywork were acquired.

With the fleet thoroughly renewed the company settled down to the everyday tasks of carrying passengers and making money, and no further purchases were made until 1963 when Fishwicks acquired the coaching business of Singleton of Leyland (having already jointly acquired their stage services in 1935). Singleton's garage at Chapel Brow was retained, but their entire fleet was sold off to a dealer and replaced by brand-new vehicles. The first to arrive was the rarest, a 36ft long Leopard with 49-seat Duple (Northern) Dragonfly bodywork delivered in May 1963. Only eight of the centre entrance Dragonfly bodies were built, and six of these were supplied to Samuelson of London on AEC Reliance chassis. Fishwick's example started a new fleet numbering series for coaches as 'C1'. The only other Leopard/Dragonfly built, demonstrator 750 TJ, would later pass to Fishwick after service with Leyland's Sports and Social Club. Fleet numbers C2 and C3 were taken by a pair of Albion VT21L Victors with Duple (Northern) Firefly bodies which were significant as the first 'non-Leylands' ever owned by Fishwick, although Leyland did own Albion and the vehicles had Leyland engines. C4 and C5 were even more of a surprise, the numbers being allocated to two of the 1957 LW1 Olympians which had their 44 bus seats replaced with 40 coach seats! Like the Duple (Northern) products they were painted in a new coach livery of grey and white.

The surprises kept coming. In October 1963 the first of five rear-engined Leyland Atlantean double-deckers (with semi-lowbridge Weymann bodywork) was delivered. All except the last of the batch carried 'A' suffix registrations, which were rare enough on private cars and extremely rare on public service vehicles, as most local authorities changed over to the new suffix system with 'B' in 1964. The next shock followed in March 1965 when another Atlantean, Alexander-bodied SGD 669, was acquired. This had been built for Glasgow in 1962 (hence the registration) but rapidly returned to Leyland for use as a demonstrator. Its stylish Alexander 'A type' bodywork made the flat-topped Weymann-bodied examples look rather frumpish in comparison. Three more of the frumpy version joined the fleet in 1966.

Vehicles were not the only purchases during 1966, as Fishwicks acquired the business of WH Fowler & Co in August. By that stage almost all of the bodybuilder's work involved refurbishment or repair, although a small number of lorries and vans had been equipped with specialist bodywork. Fishwicks' reason for buying Fowler was not immediately clear, although the company did build a minibus body for its new parent in March 1968 on a Ford Transit chassis. This became 'C12' in the coaching sequence.

By 1969 the 1951 Olympic single-deckers were in need of retirement. The first replacement vehicle was another former Leyland demonstrator, Panther Cub/Park Royal JTJ 667F, which entered service in April. Three months before that Fishwick had bought a brand-new PSUC1/12 Tiger Cub chassis from Leyland, but this would not enter service until March 1970 when it emerged with a body built by Fowler of Leyland – their first full-size PSV body for more than 30 years! It was followed at the end of the year by three Fowler-bodied PSU4 Leopard single-deckers. An even more ambitious Fowler project saw the light of day in August 1972 when the bodybuilder produced its one and only double-decker. This was built on a 1969 PDR1/3 Atlantean test chassis which Fishwick had acquired from the manufacturer and – it has to be said – was probably the ugliest double-decker in the country. I have heard it referred to as a monstrosity, and if this seems a little unkind I suggest that the reader takes a look at the picture of it in the colour section of this book!

Everybody agreed that Fowler should stick to single-deckers, and in 1973/4 five bodies were built on SRL6 Fleetline chassis for Fishwick. The next double-deckers were a pair of East Lancs-bodied AN68 Atlanteans delivered in 1974 (joined by a third example of the same combination in 1976). The possibility of further Fowler-bodied single-deckers was eliminated in 1975 when Fishwick bought its first Leyland National. In the next decade this would become the standard saloon with a total of 20 bought new (eight of them the improved National 2) and another four acquired on the second-hand market.

On the double-deck front the 1980s were the age of former Leyland demonstrators. In 1981 the company bought an AN69 Atlantean prototype which featured engine shrouds similar to those on London Transport's 'DMS B20' Fleetlines. It received an ECW body, the first to be bought by Fishwick. Next (in 1982) came all three Leyland B15 Titan/Park Royal demonstrators, cast into the outer darkness for failing to attract any new orders in more than a year. They were followed in 1984 by another AN69 Atlantean prototype, a 33ft long version which was given an 83-seat ECW body to the design more usually associated with NBC Olympians of the period.

The story of Fishwicks after deregulation is outside of the scope of this book, but (to summarise) the company successfully defeated many new challengers and at one stage used the brand-name 'FishKwik' for a fleet of minibuses employed as the modern equivalent of 'chasers'. The business is still in the hands of the founding family, although the current principals are descended from Fishwick daughters so this might not be apparent at first glance. The Leyland Nationals have finally gone and have been replaced by a modern fleet of low-floor Wright-bodied DAF saloons, but the company remains dedicated to preserving its past. Both of the rather peculiar AN69 Atlanteans have survived and other company vehicles in preservation include one of the 1957 LW1 Olympian single-deckers, one of the 1958 PD2/40s, and at least two of the 24 Leyland Nationals. Very few independent bus operators have been in business for more than a century and the extended Fishwick clan have survived with style. Combine this fascinating company with a visit to the British Commercial Vehicle Museum, and there are still two very good reasons to visit the town of Leyland.

A complete history of the Fishwick fleet (including all fleet numbers and registration marks) can be found in 'John Fishwick & Sons 1907-1997' by David Prescott (Senior Publications, 1997). The book is out of print, but still widely available.

Grange Motor & Cycle Co of Grange-over-Sands

Grange-over-Sands, like so many British seaside resorts, owed its prosperity to the arrival of the railway. The Ulverston and Lancaster Railway opened for business in 1857 and Grange was the first stop to the north of the Arnside viaduct which crossed the estuary of the River Kent. Within 40 years a sleepy fishing village had been turned into a genteel Victorian resort, much favoured by middle-class holidaymakers who appreciated its proximity to the scenery of the Lake District. Fortunes were made by local landowners, among them the Blackhurst family.

On the 23rd of June 1914 Richard Blackhurst established the Grange Motor & Cycle Co Ltd to sell and repair the two means of transport named in its corporate title. The timing was, perhaps, not ideal as the First World War started shortly after the formation of the company, but the Blackhursts had the capital to persevere until trading conditions improved. Immediately after the end of the war the business added another string to its bow by purchasing a trio of char-a-bancs and offering excursions to visitors. The first known vehicles were a Leyland (TB 1070), a Ford Model T (TB 2082), and a Fiat (TB 8886). The latter was delivered in March 1922.

In June 1922 a larger, 28-seat, Leyland C5 char-a-banc was acquired (TC 434), while in January 1923 an eight-seat Crossley X (TC 1972) joined the fleet to cater for the private party market. The business expanded significantly in 1925 when three vehicles were acquired. The first, delivered in May, was a new 20-seat Albion PF24 chara, followed by a twelve month old Lancia (FR 5856) in July. The Lancia had previously been operated by the Blackhurst family's coaching business in Blackpool, established in 1913. August saw the arrival of the company's first service bus, a brand-new (but sadly unidentified) Leyland C9.

The bus had been acquired to start a regular service from Grange-over-Sands to Barrow-in-Furness via Newby Bridge and Ulverston, competing with the parallel railway service at much lower fares. It was an instant success, particularly during the summer months when the shipwrights of Barrow found that Grange offered a welcome break from their arduous working lives. The char-a-bancs were sometimes employed as duplicate vehicles in high season, and also offered a wide choice of Lakeland excursions. The most profitable of these was to Ambleside at the northern end of Lake Windermere, operated at least twice daily in the summer, and it was predictable that this route would become GM&CC's second stage-carriage service in 1928.

Fleet number 33 went to this 36 ft long PSU3 Leopard with Weymann dual-purpose bodywork, STC 359C, new to Fishwick in 1965. *(Roy Marshall)*

XTB 728N (fleet number 18) was an AN68 Atlantean with East Lancs bodywork, one of a pair delivered in 1974. A third, identical, machine arrived in 1976. *(Keith Johnson Collection)*

Fishwick subsidiary Fowler provided the bodywork for this single-deck Daimler SRL6-36 Fleetline, WTE 485L (fleet number 10), new in 1973. *(Alan Murray-Rust)*

Fishwick assembled a large fleet of Leyland Nationals in the 1970s, so I am forced to include them in this book! This is fleet number 29 (XCW 956R), a 49-seat 11.3m version, new in 1977. A picture of sister vehicle XCW 955R can be seen in the colour section. *(Keith Johnson Collection)*

This AN69A Atlantean prototype, complete with 'London B20 style' engine shrouds, was sold to Fishwick in 1981 as GRN 895W (fleet number 23). It was fitted with a slightly modified version of ECW's Atlantean body design and is now preserved. *(Keith Johnson Collection)*

A second experimental AN69 chassis was acquired in 1984 and was a longer wheelbase version originally intended for the export market. A462 LFV (fleet number 2) was fitted with an 83-seat ECW body, similar to the design fitted to Olympian double-deckers but with an extra short window bay inserted amidships. It is also preserved. *(Keith Johnson Collection)*

In April 1928 the business took delivery of a brand-new 32-seat PLSC3 Lion (TE 3240) to cater for the demand on the route to Barrow. A 24-seat Albion PFB26 coach (TE 4138) followed in May, a four year old Lancia chara (FR 5862) in July, and a new 20-seat Dennis G bus in August. The latter was used on a new local service to the Cartmel peninsula and on the Ambleside service during the winter months when the char-a-bancs were less than ideal from the viewpoint of passenger comfort. Various members of the family had become active in the business by this point, including the founder's son, Richard Edward Blackhurst.

The success of the stage-carriage services inevitably attracted competition in the years before Road Service licensing. To combat this intrusion two more buses were acquired during 1929 to act as 'chasers' and frighten off the competition. WT 7241 was a five year old Leyland A13 with 26 seats acquired from Heald of Normanton in the West Riding of Yorkshire. It had gone within a year. The other (unidentified) vehicle was a 20-seat Daimler which had a similarly short stay in Grange-over-Sands, both being replaced by new deliveries during 1930. The first three arrivals in that year were all service buses, a 26-seat LT1 Lion (TF 769) in March and two 30-seat TS2 Tigers (TF 869/870) in May. There were also three coaches, two 20-seat Commer Invaders in July (one of which was TF 2927) and a 30-seat TS3 Tiger with Burlingham bodywork (TF 3559) in December. They replaced the last of the char-a-bancs.

The TS3 Tiger was one of four delivered in 1930/1. Two of these were 30-seat Leyland-bodied buses (TF 3358, delivered in February 1931, and TF 4728 in April) and the other a second Burlingham-bodied coach (TF 5319) which arrived in June. This considerable investment paid dividends as the company was licensed for all of its stage-carriage routes by the new Traffic Commissioners despite opposition from the railway company, and from Ribble Motor Services which had acquired several of GM&CC's competitors including Furness of Ulverston and the Kendal company. A co-ordination agreement with Ribble was finally signed in September 1938.

A pair of Leyland KP3 Cub coaches with Plaxton bodywork (TJ 1132/33) arrived in 1933, and then there was another hiatus in vehicle procurement until 1935 when the company acquired a 14-seat Dodge coach (ATB 300), a year old Commer Centaur coach (YG 7030), and a trio of six year old all-Leyland TS1 Tiger buses from Plymouth Corporation (DR 5815/16/32). The Tigers arrived as 31-seaters with dual doors but had their rear doors removed (allowing four more seats) before entering service at Grange-over-Sands. By comparison 1936 was a quiet year, with the only acquisition being a new TS7 Tiger/Plaxton coach (ATJ 259) in June.

There were two new vehicles during 1937. The first was BTJ 366, a Plaxton-bodied Leyland LZ2 Cheetah coach which arrived in May. The second was rather more unusual. CTB 820 was a Dodge car chassis fitted with a 7-seat 'miniature coach' body which was a one-third scale replica of the bodywork fitted to the full-size Plaxton-bodied coaches. It was used to attract publicity and as a mobile booking office on Grange promenade, but was licensed as a public service vehicle and made occasional outings on private hires. Unfortunately, no photographs of this fascinating vehicle have emerged, although I will probably receive several after this book has gone to the printers. It always happens!

Deliveries returned to more normal dimensions in 1938 with the arrival of a new TS8 Tiger/Plaxton coach (DTB 407) and a second-hand AEC Regal with a Duple coach body (FV 8194) which had been new to Leamington of Blackpool the previous year. A more expensive purchase was that of 'Lymehurst', a large house in Grange which had been built for the wealthy Ward family of Northern Quarries. The founder moved into the house itself and built a coach station for the excursion business in the grounds of the property. This liberated the smaller house next to the company's garage for occupancy by RE Blackhurst, who had married in 1928 and had a family of his own.

The company's operating area included the wartime aerodrome at Cark on the Cartmel peninsula, and the demand from the military population of the base resulted in the allocation of three additional vehicles during the Second World War. Dates are uncertain (such information was classified!), so in alphabetical order the new arrivals were BGH 300 (a 1934 LT5A Lion with Beadle bus bodywork), CM 9562 (a 1930 TS2 Tiger/Burlingham coach), and GM 2586 (a 1936 TS7 Tiger/Burlingham coach). Further capacity was achieved when four pre-war vehicles

(TF 869/70 and DR 5815/32) received new Burlingham 'utility bus' bodies for the journeys to Cark and for another important contract to the Vickers shipyard at Barrow.

The scarcity of new vehicles in the years after the war meant that GM&CC had to wait until 1948 for fresh deliveries in the shape of two PS1 Tiger/Plaxton coaches, JTE 58 and JTE 822. Most of the post-war fleet renewal process took place in 1949/50 when the company received a motley collection of a Guy Vixen with Samlesbury bodywork (KTE 765), a Commer Avenger/Plaxton (KTF 18), four Vulcan 6PFs with Dutfield bodywork (KTF 671-74), two PS2/3 Tigers with fully-fronted Dutfield bodies (LTE 227 and LTJ 783), two AEC Regal IIIs with identical Dutfield bodies (LTF 111-12), and a Guy Wolf with a 16-seat body by KW of Blackpool (LTE 228), All of these vehicles were for the coaching fleet, leaving the stage-carriage services in the hands of pre-war vehicles. To disguise the age of their chassis TF 3559 and BGH 300 received new 35-seat Burlingham bus bodies in 1950/1. Another rebody was of TS8 coach DTB 407 which had its pre-war Plaxton unit replaced by a fully-fronted Samlesbury coach body.

The lack of investment in the bus fleet reflected the fact that most of GM&CC's income now came from two sources, selling cars and operating coach excursions. To continue with the stage services the Blackhursts would have had to buy some expensive new underfloor-engined saloons – Royal Tigers or similar – to replace the pre-war stock. They reluctantly decided not to bother and sold the stage-carriage licences to Ribble with effect from the 1st of July 1951.

The company continued as a car dealership and coach operator, but in December 1957 the coaching business was also sold to Ribble. As might be imagined, Ribble declined the company's vehicles in both acquisitions. 'Lymehurst' was also sold in 1957, later becoming an hotel. The Blackhursts kept the car dealerships, later renamed as Grange Motors, until the 1970s when they were sold to the Batemans Toyota group.

Hadwin of Ulverston

Edgar Nelson Hadwin was born in 1884, the son of a coal miner from Dalton-in-Furness. Not wishing to follow his father 'down the pit' he found work at Vickers shipyard in Barrow, and after the First World War established a garage in King Street, Ulverston. He soon acquired his first char-a-banc, a pre-war Argyll, and began to offer excursions from Barrow, Dalton, and Ulverston to various destinations in the Lake District. This business proved so lucrative that further char-a-bancs were acquired, most of them built on unidentified war surplus lorry and ambulance chassis. The Argyll was also used to start a daily stage-carriage service from Ulverston to the village of Urswick. This remained as the only bus service operated by Hadwin until the Second World War.

Fleet details for the period before 1939 are rather meagre. Confirmed vehicles include 1935 AEC Regal/Duple coach ATF 574, 1937 Leyland Tiger coach CTJ 867, and 1938 Bedford WTB/Duple DTC 863. The only known wartime delivery was a TS2 Tiger/Burlingham coach, CM 9563, an identical twin to the vehicle allocated to Grange (qv). The TS2 was acquired to operate a service from Ulverston to the prisoner-of-war camp in Grizedale forest, and Hadwin continued to run this service on a stage-carriage licence after the camp had closed, as it had proven to be popular with local people and tourists alike.

Post-war deliveries were a mixture of new and second-hand. The new vehicles included two Bedford OB/Duple Vista coaches (GTC 651 and JTC 487), a Maudslay Marathon III coach with ACB bodywork (KTF 381), and two Harrington-bodied AEC Regal III coaches (LTB 39 and LTB 157). Other acquisitions were a pre-war Regal coach from Pearson of Liverpool (KF 8680) and a post-war Regal III/Santus coach from an operator in Herefordshire (EVJ 807). The company also acquired its first bus, a wartime Bedford OWB (BBN 746), which came with the business of Johnson of Bardsea. The Johnson purchase included a stage service from Bardsea (a coastal village on Morecambe Bay) to Ulverston. A second OWB, CVJ 61, was acquired by Hadwin to provide a back-up vehicle for the services to Urswick and Bardsea, while the Grizedale service was usually operated by Regals KF 8680 and EVJ 807.

In the early 1950s Hadwin began to operate extended coaching holidays with a pair of luxurious AEC Regal IVs. NTB 299 had Harrington bodywork with only 33 seats, while NTJ 744 had a Plaxton Venturer body with 34 seats. A third Regal IV, PTC 327, also had Plaxton

Venturer bodywork but with 37 seats in a more normal lay-out. The next coach to arrive was UTC 698, a Commer Avenger II with Plaxton bodywork, in 1954. It would be followed by a pair of Avenger IIIs (both with Plaxton bodywork), a pair of Avenger IVs (one Duple, one Yeates), and three Ford Thames Traders (two with Burlingham bodies and one with Harrington) before the Duple-bodied Bedford VAL14 became the standard Hadwin coach in 1964.

By then the stage-carriage services had long gone, having been sold to Ribble in July 1956. In 1973 the Hadwin business was sold to Barrow-in-Furness Corporation which wanted to expand into the coaching market Four years later the councillors decided that this had been a bad idea and sold the company to Shaw of Silverdale on the far side of Morecambe Bay. The combined business (originally known as Shaw-Hadwin Coaches) survives to the present day, still owned by the Shaw family and trading as 'The Travellers Choice'. Mr Hadwin died in 1979 at the grand old age of 94.

Hart of Coppull

Compared to most bus-owning families the Harts were quite wealthy, almost royalty by the modest standards of their home village of Coppull to the south-west of Chorley. The Harts lived at Blainscough Hall, owned the Coppull Coal Co and the Blainscough Colliery, owned farms and a stables, and had expanded (via their coal business) into road haulage. In July1929 they entered the bus industry, trading as Oliver Hart & Sons, and opened a stage-carriage service from Croston to Southport via Tarleton and Hesketh Bank. Their initial equipment was a pair of brand-new LT1 Lion buses registered as TE 8779/80.

One question which remains unanswered despite extensive research is the reason for their choice of route. Croston, the nearest point on the route to their home base, is a good half hour's drive from Coppull and an enormous amount of 'dead mileage' was involved. In the modern age one might detect the hand of an expensive consultant, but in 1929 it would have been the Harts who made this curious choice.

Oliver Hart Sr had his hands full with the family's coal business, so from the beginning the bus company was under the control of the 'Sons'. These were Oliver Jr, Ronald, and Stanley, with Oliver Jr taking the leading role. All three Hart brothers were speedway riders as well as entrepreneurs, with Oliver Jr gaining some degree of national fame in the sport between 1933 and 1952. Stanley Hart was less fortunate and died in a speedway accident in 1937.

With licensing by the Traffic Commissioners imminent, Ribble made a concerted effort to drive the upstart company off the road. The Harts responded by acquiring three second-hand vehicles during 1931 to shadow Ribble departures. The vehicles involved were a 26-seat Leyland A13 (TC 9576, new to Corless of Charnock Richard in 1924), a Leyland TS1 Tiger bus (DB 5293, new to North Western in 1929), and a 24-seat McCurd (CW 7829, new to Wood of Burnley in 1928). These 'chaser' vehicles became fleet numbers 3-5 and achieved their goal when Hart received a licence for the Croston to Southport route.

Fleet number 6 (TF 7892), delivered in March 1932 was another Lion bus, but of the improved LT3 model. It replaced the McCurd. The next purchase was a second-hand TS1 Tiger bus, DR 5824, acquired from Plymouth Corporation in 1935 when it was six years old. No fleet number has been recorded, although it might be conjectured that it took the number of the Leyland A13 it replaced. Unfortunately, this guesswork doesn't help as the A13's fleet number is unknown!

In late 1938 Hart finally signed a co-ordination agreement with Ribble. As a result the company was allowed to buy two 1930 vintage TS2 Tiger buses from the larger operator in March 1939. CK 4329 and CK 4315 became Hart's fleet numbers 7 and 8. As Hart still only had the one route and frequencies remained unchanged, it can be surmised that the Hart family were already convinced that war with Germany was unavoidable and wanted to 'stock up the larder' before the conflict began. A third Tiger bus, TF 9050, came from Ribble later in the year. This one was a TS4 and had been new to the Yarrow Motor Co in 1932. Ribble acquired it with the Yarrow business in April 1939, but passed it straight on to the Hart brothers. Fleet numbers fell into disuse at this point, although the numbers 9 and 10 would later be allocated to two double-deckers (but none to several others).

The Grange Motor & Cycle Co bought three six year old TS1 Tiger buses from Plymouth Corporation in 1935. When acquired they had 31-seat dual entrance Leyland bodies, but Grange eliminated the rear doors before placing them into service. DR 5816 was withdrawn from use in December 1950 and scrapped. *(Keith Johnson Collection)*

LT5A Lion BGH 300 was new to a London coach operator (Brickwood) in July 1934, and was equipped with this 32-seat Beadle body. By 1938 it was operating for Lowland Motorways in Glasgow, and then passed to Grange during the Second World War. In early 1951 the company had it rebodied by Burlingham as a 35-seat bus, but a few months later the stage services went to Ribble and the Lion was sold to Armstrong of Ebchester. *(Keith Johnson Collection)*

This 1936 Duple-bodied TS7 Tiger coach, GM 2586, also came to Grange from Scotland during the war. It had been new to Hunter of Wishaw. The vehicle was retained by Grange after the bus services had gone and was eventually sold to a Cheshire operator, lasting until 1959. *(Keith Johnson Collection)*

Hart of Coppull operated several second-hand double-deckers on works services, but this was the only new one in the history of the fleet. JTC 912, an all-Leyland PD2/1 Titan, was delivered in May 1948. After the Croston to Southport route was abandoned it went to Turner of Brown Edge (Staffordshire), surviving in that company's yard – in derelict condition – as late as 1982. Sadly, by then it had deteriorated quite badly and could not be saved for preservation. *(Roy Marshall Collection)*

Two Bedford OWB utility buses arrived during 1942 (FTC 531 and FTC 626). They were the only wartime acquisitions. To make up for this lack of newcomers the Harts went on a minor spree in 1946, acquiring TSM B10A/ECOC bus DB 5254 in February (new to North Western in 1929, although rebodied in 1935), TD3 Titan/Massey double-decker FM 8936 in May (new to Chester Corporation in 1934 and Hart's first ever double-deck vehicle), TS4 Tiger GTD 444 in September (new to United Auto in 1932 as an ECOC-bodied bus, but rebodied by Santus as a coach and re-registered before entering service with Hart), and TD3 Titan/MCCW RB 9307 in October (new to Chesterfield Corporation in 1933).

The double-deckers were needed because of the enormous increase in traffic to Southport during the post-war travel boom. This continued in 1947, necessitating the purchase of another double-decker. TD1 Titan/Cowieson GG 925 had been new to Glasgow Corporation in 1930 but came to Coppull from its second owner, Young of Paisley. The other purchase during 1947 was also significant as it was Hart's first (all new) coach. GTJ 318 was a PS1 Tiger with Santus bodywork and was delivered in March ready for the summer season.

The Scottish TD1 was at the very end of its life, and in May 1948 was replaced by a brand-new (all Leyland) PD2 Titan, JTC 912. It received fleet number 10 and became the main vehicle on the Southport route, backed up by assorted pre-war Titans. As the post-war boom fizzled out, and duplicates became less of a regular occurrence, Hart began to bid for works contracts to keep the second-hand double-deckers busy. As a result pre-war Titans would remain a feature of the fleet almost to the end. The only other new arrival during 1948 was Bedford OB/Pearson coach JP 6921 which entered the fleet in September.

From Easter 1949 the stage-carriage route was extended to operate from Standish to Southport as a joint service with Ribble (Ribble used service number 106 for the route). When Ribble's managers had first suggested the idea this extension must have seemed like a gift to the Harts as Standish was considerably closer to Coppull than Croston and much dead mileage could be avoided. Traffic on the long rural leg between Croston and Standish was negligible, however, and for the first time Hart started to lose money on the stage service.

Another rebodied pre-war coach was placed into service in May 1949. BWB 88, a TS7 Tiger, had been new to Sheffield Corporation in 1935 as a Cravens-bodied bus. Hart had the original body removed and replaced by a fully-fronted Bellhouse Hartwell unit which disguised the vehicle's true age far more efficiently than a Northern Ireland registration. Many customers must have thought that it was entirely new. The TS7 was followed, in 1950/1, by three pre-war TD5 Titans. BBN 178 and BBN 193 had Massey bodywork and had been new to Bolton Corporation, while ERA 79 (which, for no apparent reason, was given fleet number 9 by Hart) was another refugee from Chesterfield and had Leyland bodywork. The trio replaced the earlier TD3s on the works contracts.

The Hart brothers received their only underfloor-engined vehicle in July 1951. NTC 445 was a PSU1/15 Royal Tiger with a flamboyant Bellhouse Hartwell Landmaster coach body. It replaced pre-war TS4/post-war Santus coach GTD 444, so the registration was rather appropriate. The delivery of a brand-new coach might have suggested that Hart was doing well, but any money made by the coaches and the contract work was being swallowed up by the loss-making route to Southport. The Harts approached Ribble, wanting to revert to the original route, but Ribble's managers were unsympathetic. Instead they offered to operate the entire service but were unwilling to give the Harts any money for this, claiming that they would be doing them a favour.

The Harts were no fools, and knew a scam when they saw one, but the Southport service was losing money hand over fist. Eventually they capitulated and in May 1953 they handed their share of the service to Ribble, free of charge. Oddly, as soon as this happened, Ribble decided to cut the service back to run from Croston to Southport. If anybody can supply the name of the Ribble manager who came up with this nefarious scheme, let me know so that I can shame him in public. It was out of character for Ribble in the regulated era and one can only suspect that the perpetrator was after promotion and thought that defecating on a joint operator was the way to achieve this.

After the stage service ceased the PD2 was sold to Turner of Brown Edge in Staffordshire.

The contract double-deckers stayed in place and two more pre-war Titans were acquired in 1954. AFY 960 was a TD3 with English Electric bodywork, new to Southport in 1934, while HG 3228 was a TD4 with a Leyland body, new to Burnley in 1935. Hart lost the contract during 1955 and the remaining double-deckers were all sold to dealers. The business was visibly dwindling, and in 1955/6 all of the coaches were sold except for the 1951 Royal Tiger. This soldiered on until February 1958 when it was sold to the well-known Scottish operator McLennan of Spittalfield and all operations by Oliver Hart & Sons came to an end. The family is still active in the haulage industry and the DAF trucks of James Hart can be seen at most events at the British Commercial Vehicle Museum in Leyland.

Hollinshead of Scholar Green

The history of this company is more obscure than most, despite its accessibility (on the northern edge of the Potteries and within an hour's driving time of Manchester) and its obvious attractions to bus enthusiasts (Fodens anyone?). Even the PSV Circle, usually guaranteed to know the fleet details of the tiniest and remotest of operators, has an intermittent record of its vehicles. Perhaps Scholar Green is like Brigadoon.

Kelly's Directory for 1928 lists the Hollinshead Brothers as 'motor engineers and char-a-banc proprietors' of Kent Green (the next village to Scholar Green), while their sister Lucy is described as a 'shopkeeper' of the same village. In 1931 John Hollinshead is listed as a sole proprietor when applying for licences to the North West Traffic Commissioners, and the more familiar address in Scholar Green is given on the applications. These were for excursions and tours from the Scholar Green area, for a daily works service from Kent Green to Congleton via Scholar Green and Astbury, and for a weekly (Thursday) market day service from Mow Cop to Sandbach.

Fleet details are also sporadic. Between 1931 and 1945 only two vehicles have emerged from my research. These were LG 8655, a 1933 Dennis Dart with a 24-seat coach body by local builder Lawton and VT 7642, a 1932 Albion PM28/Lawton bus acquired from Rowley of Bignall End in 1939 (or, according to one source, 1944!). Perhaps these were the only vehicles then operated but it seems unlikely.

In the post-war era we are on firmer ground. In 1946 the company acquired one of the Bedford OWB utility buses imported to Britain from Northern Ireland (GZ 1188). Then, in 1948, the company bought a 1934 Dennis Lancet bus with Willowbrook bodywork (AEH 702) from Rowbotham of Harriseahead, and acquired a brand-new Bedford OB/Pearson coach (KMA 93). All new vehicles from 1949 to 1953 were Foden coaches, delivered at the rate of one each year. The first to arrive was a PVSC6 with fully-fronted Plaxton bodywork (LTU 511), followed by a PVFE6/Metalcraft FC37F (MMB 861), and then by rear-engined PVRF6/Metalcraft NTU 125, PVRF6/Plaxton Venturer OMB 501, and PVRG6/Bellhouse Hartwell Landmaster PMB 915.

The picture of the stage-carriage services is also blurred. The service to Congleton, although granted as a restricted works service back in 1931, seems to have been opened up to the public during the Second World War and to have retained that status after the conflict. There is a personal reminiscence on-line from someone who used this service to get to and from school during the war and was often joined by their mother on the return journey after she made a shopping trip to Congleton. I have also spoken to several enthusiasts who travelled on the afternoon (outbound) journey from Congleton during the 1950s, just for the experience of riding on MMB 861. Their money was taken without difficulty, but despite these anecdotal accounts I can find no trace of the Traffic Commissioners approving a change in the service's status.

Similarly, with the Thursday service from Mow Cop to Sandbach, it seems that it changed from a stage-carriage route to a weekly excursion some time in 1964. Hollinshead already held a parallel excursion licence for the route, so there was no legal problem with the change, but (as far as the Traffic Commissioners records are concerned) the stage-carriage version was never officially withdrawn and was still listed as a current licence as late as 1978!

After the Fodens the fleet became a lot less interesting, with acquisitions being an ongoing procession of new Bedford coaches with either Plaxton or Duple bodywork from 1954 until 1960. These were followed by second-hand Bedfords from 1962 until 1966, the most interesting of which were a 41-seat SB5/Burlingham Gannet (5700 WD) and a 29-seat C5Z1/Duple Super Vista (XWD 769), both acquired from Black and White of Harvington in May 1962. The Gannet was only a few months old. The C5Z1 replaced the Irish OWB which lingered on at the depot until it was scrapped in January 1964. Some of the Fodens were still in service despite the influx of Bedfords, with PVFE6/Metalcraft MMB 861 and PVRF6/Metalcraft NTU 125 surviving well into the 1970s. The reward for their longevity was preservation.

The first new vehicle since 1960 appeared in 1968 and signalled a change in policy. GTU 119G was a PSU3 Leopard with Duple Commander bodywork and its purchase seems to have exhausted the company's resources as no more vehicles were acquired for several years. By 1971 the business had become a partnership of John, William, and Lucy Hollinshead and the Congleton service appeared to have ceased, although (again) I can find no reference to this abandonment in the Notices and Proceedings of the Traffic Commissioners.

In 1985 the Hollinshead family sold the business to Biddulph businessman David Haydon, a livestock haulier. Four years later he formed a limited company, Hollinshead Coaches Ltd, originally at his haulage company's Biddulph address and then later in the nearby village of Knypersley. Mr Haydon died in 2009, but the Hollinshead Coaches business survived him and by 2010 was operating a new stage-carriage service, the H1, which was a (Thursday) market day run from Kidsgrove to Sandbach. The route (except for the extension to Kidsgrove) was very similar to that operated by the company before 1964 but, sadly, there were no Fodens in evidence.

Leedham of Dunsop Bridge

The village of Slaidburn, to the north of Clitheroe in the Forest of Bowland, has around 300 inhabitants. Until 1974 the village was in the West Riding of Yorkshire but Clitheroe (in Lancashire) was the nearest market town. Although the village was relatively small there were two bus companies in residence before 1956. Bounty Motors was owned by the Walker family and Hodder Motor Services by the Hodgsons (both of these operators will be covered in my next book, 'Independent Buses in Western Yorkshire'). The two businesses competed for the modest traffic to Clitheroe and when national Road Service licensing was introduced in 1930/1 both firms applied for licences to continue their competing stage-carriage routes.

The Traffic Commissioners must have seen the absurdity of two operators vying for such a tiny prize, but their hands were tied by the legislation. Both businesses had been operating the route for the same length of time, both operated vehicles which were mechanically sound and well maintained, and both were run by individuals of adequate character and ability. Both received their licences.

Hodder dropped out of the contest in 1956 after owner Stanley Hodgson bought the much larger Bolton-by-Bowland Motor Services (qv) and moved his centre of operations to Clitheroe. Bounty persisted with their route until 1965 when they announced to a startled community that they had decided to call it a day. The Walkers preferred to arrange a replacement bus service before they retired from business and a committee was formed to produce a solution. Its members included a representative of the Walkers, the village grocer, a directory of a brewery who lived in Slaidburn, and garage proprietor James Leedham from the neighbouring village of Dunsop Bridge.

Dunsop Bridge was just across the boundary in Lancashire (and lays claim to being the geographical centre of Great Britain) but the Slaidburn-Clitheroe service passed through the village and provided its only public transport link. It was eventually agreed that Leedham's Garage would provide a daily bus service on behalf of the community. In July 1965 the Walkers sold one of their two remaining vehicles, 1951 Albion Victor/Scottish Aviation coach GET 600, to James and Mary Leedham for a token sum and arranged for the transfer of the stage-carriage licences.

The near loss of their only link to the outside world seemed to arouse the local communities. Business improved slightly, eliminating the downward spiral in traffic experienced over the previous 15 years, and in November 1968 the ageing Victor was replaced by a 1959 Bedford SB3 with Yeates Europa bodywork (NWH 947) acquired for another token sum from Stanley Hodgson's Bolton-by-Bowland Motor Services. The Bedford was no more suited to one man operation than the Victor had been, but the

Hollinshead of Scholar Green bought this 37-seat Foden PVFE6 coach with a fully-fronted Metalcraft body, MMB 861, in 1950. After the company's Bedford OWB was scrapped in 1960 it became the regular performer on the stage services. The vehicle remained in almost daily use until the early 1970s and is believed to be preserved. *(Peter Tulloch)*

When Leedham of Dunsop Bridge acquired the Slaidburn to Clitheroe service from Bounty Motors in July 1965, this 1951 Albion Victor coach came with the route. GET 600 had a 31-seat Scottish Aviation body and stayed with Leedham until November 1968. *(Roy Marshall via The Omnibus Society)*

passenger loads were still relatively low so speed of boarding was not really affected to any noticeable degree.

The original SB3 was replaced by another in February 1975. This second Bedford, 831 STC, was two years younger than the first and carried a Duple Super Vega body. Like its predecessor it came from Bolton-by-Bowland at a very low price and lasted until the early 1980s. The Leedhams' third and final Bedford was the first with a diesel engine. OND 11H was an SB5 with Plaxton bodywork and had been new to Finglands of Manchester in May 1970.

At the time of deregulation the Leedham family decided not to register the route as a commercial service, having been advised by local councillors that it would almost certainly qualify as an essential route which would be supported by the local authority. After more than 20 years of hard work providing their village with a bus route for next to no reward they felt more than justified in handing the responsibility to the wider community. The service is still in operation on a daily basis (as a tendered route) and has been extended at the Slaidburn end to the Yorkshire market town of Settle. Leedhams Garage is also still in business, and the current partners (David Leedham and his wife Brenda) operate a minibus on a contract service to a local Catholic high school.

Mayne of Manchester

At the time of the General Strike in 1926 more than two dozen coach operators began services into central Manchester from suburban locations. Roughly half of these continued their operations after the strike ended and details of many of them can be found in the Introduction to this book. One deliberately omitted from the earlier section was a service from Droylsden to Manchester (Hilton St Garage) which started in November 1927, eighteen months after the strike ended. This was operated by James Albert Ferrington.

Like the other 'return ticket' services Ferrington's ran as a non-stop express from the Manchester city boundary to its terminus on private land in the city centre. When the various corporations reacted to the incursions by independent operators by creating their own 'Co-ordinated Motor Bus' network, one of the municipal routes ran along Ashton New Road (in competition with Ferrington's service) and then continued across the city centre to Stretford. In June 1928 Ferrington applied to Stretford council for a licence to extend his own service to the town. This was summarily refused after Stretford councillors were lobbied by Manchester transport officials.

Ferrington's existing service was then subjected to a campaign of harassment by the Manchester constabulary, and in early 1929 he decided to sell the service and to concentrate on his other business interests. The purchaser was Arthur Mayne & Son of Bradford, an inner city suburb on the east side of Manchester. The Mayne family had gone into business in the late 19th century, running a general store and a furniture shop in the Bradford area, and the founder's son (Arthur Mayne Jr) had joined the business in 1909 as an apprentice. Various horse-drawn conveyances were used to deliver the company's furniture, and in 1920 the company purchased its first motor vehicle, a Ford Model T van.

It would not have been Arthur Mayne Jr's choice of vehicle. During his military service in the First World War he had driven and repaired many AEC lorries and thought very highly of the marque for its ruggedness and dependability. In 1923 he arranged the purchase of an AEC Y type lorry to supplement the Model T on furniture delivery duties. The cost of the AEC was justified by the fact that it could be fitted with a removable char-a-banc body and used for excursions on Saturdays and Sundays. Considering the condition of most roads at that time these day trips ranged far and wide, regularly visiting such destinations as Blackpool, Buxton, and Southport during the summer months.

Purpose built 'all-weather' coaches followed in 1925 in the form of an AEC 416 and a smaller AEC 509 (both acquired from an Essex dealer), and these vehicles started a timetabled express service (in summer only) from the eastern suburbs of Manchester to Blackpool, using the trading name 'Mayne's Premier Motors'. In the following May the General Strike took all municipal buses and trams off the road (and many buses belonging to the larger company operators) and for the ten days of the strike Maynes offered a replacement service from the Bradford and Clayton areas to the city centre. This operation ended when the strike did, but Arthur Mayne Jr had experienced local bus services and had developed a taste for them. When Ferrington's business came onto the market he was ready with his cheque-book. The Droylsden to Manchester route changed hands in February 1929 and Mayne's extended it to Audenshaw at the eastern end.

The deal with Ferrington included four buses, a Dennis and three Warwick-bodied Crossley Eagles. All had 20 seats and later in the year the Mayne fleet was increased to seven by the addition of a new AEC Model 660 Reliance. The company endured the traditional harassment from Manchester police for more than a year and then applied to the new Traffic Commissioners for a Road Service Licence to continue the route. This was initially refused in May 1931 (despite Mayne's having the support of Droylsden Urban District Council) but the service continued pending an appeal. The appeal was considered in June 1932 and a licence was granted, but with four restrictions. Mayne's could not carry passengers on journeys entirely within the city boundary, its fares were to be determined by the Traffic Commissioners (and would no longer be allowed to undercut the municipal operators), its timetable was to be co-ordinated with those of the other operators (this was fairly meaningless given the high frequency of services along Ashton New Road), and the city centre street terminus was to be agreed with Manchester City Council.

Arthur Mayne Jr celebrated the decision and then immediately filed an application for another service, a local route in Droylsden from Edge Lane (the main cross-roads in the centre of the town) to Greenside Lane. This was granted in January 1933 and extended to Medlock Street in March 1935. Meanwhile, a selection of good quality second-hand vehicles had arrived to supplement the fleet, including a 32-seat Dennis E bus (built in 1927 and acquired from Yorkshire Woollen District (YWD) in October 1932), a similar vehicle from the same source in December 1933, a Leyland Lioness coach from Bracewell of Colne, and two AEC Regal/Duple coaches from Hanson of Huddersfield. The Regals apparently made a good impression as a brand-new example of the same chassis/body combination was acquired during 1933.

Manchester Corporation and the other competing operators received a nasty shock in November 1934 when Mayne's first double-decker arrived. This was an AEC Regent with Park Royal bodywork (AXJ 496) which made everything the municipalities had in stock look very dated by virtue of its forward entrance complete with a door. It also had seats for 60 people at a time when a typical double-decker carried 51/2. This was achieved, of course, by reducing the leg-room between seats to the bare legal minimum (making them profoundly uncomfortable for anyone taller than five feet), but the route was relatively short and given a choice between being left at the bus-stop, standing all the way, or sitting in an uncomfortable seat, most passengers chose the uncomfortable seat. And it did have a futuristic forward entrance *with a door!*

An identical vehicle followed in August 1935, followed by a third Dennis E from Yorkshire Woollen in October. In December of the same year Arthur Mayne Sr died, leaving the bus and coach operations to his eponymous son. Shortly afterwards the business became Arthur Mayne & Son Ltd. Two more forward entrance Regent/Park Royals arrived during 1936 and these vehicles managed to cram an additional two passengers into their interior. Perhaps people were significantly shorter back then. The only other purchase during 1936 was a 20-seat Albion PKA26 bus, acquired from United Automobile in July for use on the Droylsden local service.

A fourth and final Dennis E bus was acquired from YWD in March 1937, but only lasted until October. During its brief stay Mayne's renewed their coaching fleet with the addition of three new Regal/Duple coaches. A more unusual purchase at the end of the year was an old-fashioned rear entrance Regent double-decker from Nottingham. The reason for this purchase became apparent in early 1938 when the eight year old vehicle was sent to Park Royal and received a new 62-seat forward entrance body. A similar transplant was planned for a 1931 Regent acquired from Exeter Corporation in 1938, but with war on the horizon Park Royal was forced to decline the order. As a result the vehicle was used as a 'spare' with its original (Brush H48R) body until something could be arranged.

Since the take-over of Ferrington the vehicles had been housed in the Beswick area of eastern Manchester, but in 1939 the company established a new purpose-built depot on Ashton New Road in Clayton – roughly at the half-way point of the main stage-carriage route. The Second World War began within weeks of the new garage's opening.

By 1943 the bodywork on the Exeter Regent was beginning to fall apart and Mayne's received authorisation to have it rebodied by East Lancs in Blackburn. The Ministry probably expected that it would emerge with a standard utility body but Arthur Mayne Jr somehow persuaded the bodybuilder to give it a forward entrance unit very similar to those on the pre-war Park Royal machines! As a sop to the powers-that-be it operated in grey primer for the rest of the war – 'yes, it has a front entrance, but we didn't paint it'. The company was impressed by East Lancs' standard of craftsmanship (and willing collusion in this wartime scam) and in 1945/6 three of the pre-war Regents were sent to Blackburn to receive new 58-seat forward entrance bodies.

Back to the rear entrance

The two Regents which retained their pre-war bodies were withdrawn in 1949 and replaced by two brand-new Regent IIIs with East Lancs bodywork. The restrictions on the Audenshaw-Manchester service had been lifted during the war and as a result the company was carrying far more passengers on short journeys. Traffic congestion had also increased compared to the pre-war era and passengers preferred an open rear entrance so that they could join or leave a bus at a point of their own choosing. Mayne's noted these factors (alongside the equally pertinent fact that customised bodywork was more expensive) and the new Regents were equipped with standard rear entrance bodies.

The company's coaching activities had expanded rapidly during the post-war boom (full details can be found in the book listed at the end of this essay) and the stage-carriage services accounted for less than 30% of the business's income by 1950. The Audenshaw-Manchester route had a peak vehicle requirement of four buses, so the remaining (rebodied) pre-war Regents and the two 1949 machines were more than adequate. The only addition to the service bus fleet in the early 1950s was LXJ 318, a military style Bedford SB/Mulliner saloon acquired for the Droylsden local service. It was unpopular with the public and sold after only four years to an operator in Cornwall. The vehicle would later return to the North West in the hands of McGregor of Ambleside (see Part One).

Park Royal had noticed that Mayne's were no longer giving them any bodybuilding work and in September 1954 they attempted to 'prime the pump' by selling a former demonstrator to the operator at a knock-down price. This was 7194 H, an AEC Regent III with a prototype lightweight body, and was less than a year old when it came to Mayne's depot in Clayton. The company were clearly impressed by the gesture as its next double-deckers (three AEC Regent Vs delivered in July 1957) received standard, rear entrance, Park Royal bodies. No double-deckers were withdrawn in exchange as Mayne had applied for a new limited stop service from Sunnyside Road in Droylsden to Stevenson Square in the city centre. The Traffic Commissioners ignored Manchester Corporation's objections to the application, agreeing with Mayne that it was unfair for them to carry passengers on the local service in Droylsden and then watch them board the next vehicle (probably a corporation bus) to continue their journey to the city centre. It was also more expensive from the customer's viewpoint as they had to pay two separate fares to complete their journey. Mayne's got their licence, but were forced to share the service with Manchester Corporation which provided one bus to Mayne's two. Manchester allocated the route number 46 to the service and Mayne followed suit. The Audenshaw-Manchester route (which was still forced to use the isolated Dale Street terminus allocated by the city council in 1932) remained unnumbered.

The surviving forward entrance Regents were withdrawn at the end of 1961 and replaced by three new Regent Vs with Park Royal bodywork. These machines arrived with a new bodywork design which the most kind-hearted person in the world would have considered extremely ugly. Park Royal received no more orders from Mayne and the next pair of Regent Vs (the famous 8859/60 VR, both of which survive in preservation) had bodywork by East Lancs. They arrived in 1963. Three basically similar machines were acquired in 1965 although the bodywork was built by Neepsend of Sheffield, a subsidiary of East Lancs.

In 1966 Manchester and Ashton-under-Lyne Corporations withdrew their jointly operated trolleybus services along Ashton New Road, and applied to the Traffic Commissioners for replacement bus service licences. The boot was

133

AEC Regent CNB 1 was delivered to Mayne of Manchester in March 1936, and was the third of the company's five pre-war forward entrance double-deckers. The original Park Royal body was replaced by the East Lancs unit shown here after the war. *(Keith Johnson Collection)*

Regent FJ 7821 was new to Exeter Corporation in 1931 with a Brush rear entrance body. Mayne bought it in 1938, and after its original body had suffered blast damage from a Luftwaffe bomb they sent it to East Lancs for a replacement. The Blackburn bodybuilder ignored wartime restrictions on acceptable bus designs and gave it a forward entrance body. It remained in this all-grey colour scheme until the end of the war. *(East Lancs via Roy Marshall)*

Post-war double-decker deliveries had open rear entrances until the arrival of the Fleetlines in 1976. This East Lancs-bodied Regent III, KNA 876, was one of a pair delivered in 1949. After withdrawal in 1967 it remained at the depot for five years before entering preservation. It was later scrapped. *(Keith Johnson Collection)*

Park Royal attempted to recover Mayne's business by selling them this Regent III demonstrator in September 1954. 7194 H carried a prototype lightweight body and was the last of Mayne's Regent IIIs to be retired, in 1972. An attempt to preserve the vehicle was unsuccessful due to the condition of its chassis, but some parts from the bus were donated to a former Bury Regent III, BEN 177. *(Roy Marshall)*

The Regent IIIs were followed by 30ft long Regent Vs with Park Royal bodywork. UNF 12 was the last of a trio delivered in 1957, and is seen leaving the city centre for Sunnyside Road in Droylsden. This was not as attractive as the name suggests. *(Keith Johnson Collection)*

In the early 1960s Park Royal switched to this visually offensive 'Orion lookalike' design, which used the same upper deck as the company's products on AEC Bridgemasters. Mayne's Regent V 6974 ND, one of three delivered in December 1961, is seen in Stevenson Square, Manchester. *(Roy Marshall)*

now on the other foot and Mayne's objected to the new applications. Manchester were advised that Mayne's were likely to win and sought a compromise. It was agreed that Mayne would assume sole ownership of route 46 (at an increased frequency) in exchange for ceasing to operate the original Audenshaw-Manchester service and raising no further objection to the changes proposed by Manchester. The changes took effect from the 1st of January 1967. In July 1968 Mayne's service 46 changed its number to '213', partly to liberate the number 46 to be reused by Manchester on the Wilmslow road corridor and partly because the new number dovetailed with the former trolleybus services 216/218, now operated by corporation motor buses.

The new arrangements required fewer buses, and the two 1949 Regent IIIs were withdrawn in 1967. One of them (KNA 876) remained at the Clayton depot as a staff dining room, and entered preservation in 1972. After a couple of years on the rally circuit it disappeared and has probably been scrapped. The former Regent III demonstrator 7194 H (withdrawn in 1972) was also earmarked for preservation until it was discovered that its chassis was in very poor condition. It was also scrapped, although some of its parts live on in the Manchester Museum of Transport's Bury Corporation Regent III, BEN 177.

The Regent V fleet maintained the stage-carriage route (and a number of contract services) unchallenged until 1976 when the next batch of new double-deckers arrived and Mayne's finally entered the rear-engined double-decker age. The newcomers were five Roe-bodied Fleetlines which replaced the six earliest Regent Vs. They were the last new vehicles to wear Mayne's distinctive double-decker livery of dark red with pale blue relief. All future deliveries would carry the medium red and cream colour scheme traditionally worn by the coaching fleet.

In 1978 the company switched its allegiance to Bristol chassis when three VRT3s arrived. The vehicles had 70-seat ECW bodies with luxurious high-back seating and replaced an equivalent number of Regent Vs. Two more VRT3s arrived in 1980 to replace the last of the rear-loaders. The Bristols were the regular performers on a new Mayne's stage-carriage route, the 209 from Stevenson Square to Droylsden and Littlemoss, which started on the 17th of December 1979. In November 1980 this new route was extended to Hartshead on the northern outskirts of Ashton-under-Lyne after Mayne's took advantage of Norman Fowler's partial deregulation of local bus service licensing.

Arthur Mayne Jr died on the 11th of November 1980, aged 85. Control of the business passed to his second wife, Olive, and the couple's younger son, Stephen Mayne, who had been a director since his 21st birthday in 1971. An older son, Andrew (born in 1947) had also been involved in the company at one time, but had decided to go into teaching instead. He later became a professional poet.

The next double-decker was a second-hand Fleetline, one of London Transport's prematurely withdrawn DMS class, which arrived from the capital in 1982. Two more of these vehicles joined the fleet in 1985, both having served with Staffordshire operators between leaving London and coming to Manchester. Many more would follow after deregulation as Mayne's spread its wings and extended its route network into the Pennine hills at Mossley and Glossop. There were also many new double-deckers (including Scania N113s and low-floor Dennis Tridents), but this period of the company's history is outside of the remit of this book.

Regardless of the enormous increase in local bus service mileage, this aspect of the business was becoming dwarfed by the ever expanding coach operations. In 1982 the Mayne family (as opposed to Arthur Mayne & Son Ltd) had acquired Barry Cooper Coaches of Warrington and maintained it as a separate corporate entity albeit with sub-titles which showed it to be 'Part of the Mayne Group'. Seven years later the Manchester-based coaching operations moved out of the Ashton New Road premises to a new base in Fairclough Street, Clayton, adjacent to the future site of the Manchester Velodrome. The Ashton New Road garage continued in use as the base of the bus fleet.

In 1998 the Warrington company became Mayne Coaches Ltd, and the Manchester-based coaches were also transferred to this new entity. Early in the new century Stephen Mayne's three children let their father know that they were no longer interested in pursuing the local bus business and would prefer to concentrate on the Mayne Coaches operation. On the 21st of January

2008 the bus company, which had resisted forceful overtures from (in turn) Manchester Corporation, SELNEC, and Greater Manchester Buses) was willingly sold to Stagecoach Manchester. The coach business continues to the present day, currently operating 94 high-specification coaches from Fairclough Street in Manchester (56 vehicles) and Marsh House Lane, Warrington (38 vehicles).

With the takeover by Stagecoach imminent the old bus fleet premises on Ashton New Road were demolished in December 2007 and the site was redeveloped as an Aldi supermarket. Stephen Mayne died on the 28th of July 2012 at the tender age of 62. He was survived by three children (Tina, Christopher, and Sarah) and two grandchildren (Ben and Harry). The Mayne family are still very much in control of Mayne Coaches.

A complete history of Mayne's, including a comprehensive fleet history with full registration details, can be found in '75 Years of Mayne's Buses and Coaches' by Mark Hughes, published by Venture in 1995. The book is out of print but can be found in many public libraries and (usually at a price much lower than displayed on the cover!) from second-hand booksellers.

Naylor of Stockton Heath

The village of Stockton Heath, to the south of Warrington on the road to Northwich, was the southern terminus of Warrington Corporation's tramway network. Villagers from further afield were left to walk the remaining distance until August 1921 when Mr W Dean of The County Motor Co started a daily bus service from Stockton Heath to Stretton, Great Budworth, and Pickmere. This pioneering service appears to have ended fairly swiftly (possibly because of the introduction of a Warrington to Northwich route via Stretton by the Mid-Cheshire company), and in 1922 the service to Pickmere was reintroduced by another local entrepreneur, taxi-cab proprietor George Naylor. The Pickmere route was reduced to operate on summer Sundays only, but to compensate for this Mr Naylor opened new services from Stockton Heath to Arley (via Appleton Thorn) and to Great Budworth (via Comberbach). These new services operated on Wednesdays and Saturdays, which were Warrington's market days, and on Sundays.

Later in the decade further new services commenced from Great Budworth to Northwich (via Marston, Wincham, and Lostock Gralam), and from Stockton Heath to Warrington (on Sunday mornings when the trams did not operate). Details of the early fleet are minimal. Photographs used in John Dunabin's excellent article on the company (in Omnibus Society magazine No 432) show what appears to be a Ford Model T, and another unidentified vehicle registered TU 1064. The first two vehicles listed by the PSV Circle were registered LG 5161 and VR 7354 (both of which are 1930 registrations), but nothing else is known about them.

The existing services were all granted licences by the new Traffic Commissioners in 1931. By then the proprietor of the business (which then traded as 'Stockton Heath Motor Services') was Mr John Forshaw Naylor of Hall Cafe Garage, Victoria Square, Stockton Heath. It is believed that the business was started by his father, George, who had been a commercial traveller. In May 1932 he sold his two Great Budworth services to North Western for £700, leaving him free to concentrate on the route to Arley.

The first fully identified vehicle owned by Naylor was CED 663, a new Bedford WTB with Waveney C24F bodywork, acquired in April 1939. The outbreak of the Second World War brought a great deal of misery, but also some fresh opportunities. A major new Fleet Air Arm aerodrome (known to the Navy as 'HMS Blackcap') was built at Stretton, along the line of the Arley service, and the thousands of military and civilian personnel involved were soon complaining about the lack of a direct bus service to Warrington. The corporation was forced to comply and from February 1943 Naylor's vehicles began to appear in the town on weekdays on a new joint service. A Bedford OWB utility bus, DED 588, was allocated to Naylor to help meet the demand. Warrington's share of the route was usually operated by LT7 Lion ED 9468, acquired with the business of Suburban in February 1939.

The through service from Arley to Warrington via Appleton Thorn and Stockton Heath continued after the war (and the aerodrome at Stretton remained in use), but demand for the service reduced as the Navy started to operate its own staff buses for the benefit of military personnel. Civilian employees were still dependent upon the joint Naylors/Warrington route, latterly allocated the service number 12 by the corporation. The reduction in frequency meant that only one vehicle was required and the joint operators got around this by dividing the route into two 'shifts'. The first covered Monday to Saturday daytime departures, the second the evening and Sunday timings. The two operators alternated between shifts on a weekly basis.

Naylor's new coaches in the post-war period included two OB/Duple Vistas (EED 618 in June 1947 and FED 767 in May 1949) and a Windover-bodied Guy Arab III with a Meadows engine (LLG 579, which arrived in March 1949). In May 1950 Naylor bought a new Commer Avenger coach with Beccols bodywork (MMB 114), but the company's major investment came in May 1951 when it acquired Arab III/Massey L55R double-decker NMB 314. This replaced the OWB and meant that Naylor's service had spare seats on offer between Stockton Heath and Warrington. In peak periods this produced a lot of extra revenue, much to the corporation's annoyance.

In March 1953 an Avenger II/Plaxton coach was delivered (PTU 772), and this was followed two months later by a second-hand Commer Commando with Beccols bodywork (DBA 936). The Commer theme continued in 1955 with the delivery of a new Avenger III/Plaxton coach (UTU 364) in May. The aerodrome at Stretton closed in 1958, but by then a considerable amount of new housing had been built along the route, which lessened the blow. There were some further service reductions, however. In 1960 the extensions from Appleton to Arley were withdrawn on Thursdays and Sundays, and in October 1963 all Sunday timings were abandoned. The problem, as always, was the increasing level of private car ownership.

In 'Commercial Motor' for 29th May 1964 it was announced that Naylors (now being run by the founder's grandson, John Wynne Naylor) had sold its stage service to Warrington Corporation. The hand-over took place on the last day of the year and the Arab III double-decker was sold for scrap in the New Year. Naylors continued as a coach company with a variety of new Duple and Plaxton-bodied Bedfords, and in 1965 acquired the well-known coach operator Sykes of Warrington. A respite from the hegemony of standard coach designs came in 1970 when Naylor's acquired two second-hand vehicles for schools contracts.

These were an all-Leyland PD2/10 double-decker OTD 577 (which came from Darwen Corporation in May) and Bristol LS6G/ECW coach OFM 669 (acquired from Crosville in October).

In August 1977 Naylor's Motor Services was sold to Barry Cooper Coaches of Warrington, itself later to be acquired by the Mayne family of Manchester (see above). Part of the proceeds was used to buy a 1947 vintage Bedford OB with SMT 'Vista lookalike' bodywork, FDV 548, which was painted in full Naylor's livery and appeared at many rallies and other events over the next few years. It was a fitting tribute to a fascinating company.

Reliance of Kelsall – see West of Kelsall

Roberts of Crewe

William Roberts of Crewe began his coaching business in the early 1920s. His vehicles during that decade included a Crossley, a Dennis G, and a Chevrolet. In the 1930s he standardised on the Dennis Lancet, acquiring at least four of the type. Excursions and private hires provided the bulk of the revenue, and while the majority of these headed for coastal resorts or other tourist attractions there were also excursions to market towns closer to home. The most popular of these market day runs were the weekly outings across the border to the Shropshire towns of Market Drayton and Whitchurch.

When national Road Service licensing was introduced by the 1930 Road Traffic Act Roberts initially applied for excursion licences for these market day operations along with the rest of his day trip destinations. Before the hearings he was advised that it would be wiser to make applications for express stage-carriage services on the Shropshire journeys, as other operators who were providing similar routes might (successfully) object to the excursions on principle – the principle being that excursions were not allowed to divert traffic from stage services. An express service, on the other hand, could claim 'grandfather rights' if it was in operation before the passing of the RTA, and this would place his application on an equal footing with the likes of Crosville. Roberts followed this advice and was awarded licences for routes from

Crewe to Market Drayton (via Nantwich and Audlem) and from Crewe to Higher Heath (via Nantwich and Whitchurch) in October 1931. The Market Drayton service was withdrawn in 1938 after a decline in traffic, but the Whitchurch route (although suspended for the duration of the war) continued until the early 1960s.

Military leave contracts kept the cash-flow moving between 1939 and 1945, with Roberts' vehicles particularly active on services connecting airfields in Shropshire (Hinstock, Shawbury, and Ternhill) to the mainline railway stations at Crewe and Stafford. Two second-hand Lancets joined the fleet to cater for this traffic. Just before the end of the war, in April 1945, Roberts acquired the business of another local coach operator, Farrell of Crewe. The Farrell purchase included five vehicles; a Gilford 168OT (DG 1911), an AEC Regal (HG 610), two Bedford WTBs (CLG 665/66), and a Maudslay SF40 (CTU 522), almost doubling the size of the fleet.

Interesting vehicles in the latter half of the 1940s included three Guy Arab IIIs with Santus bodywork, a Barnard-bodied Guy Vixen (LLG 42), two Foden PVSC6s with Burlingham bodywork (LMB 68/69), and a Crossley SD42, also bodied by Burlingham (LMB 557). In 1948 Roberts Coaches became a limited company and ownership was transferred from the founder to Les Gleave, a well-known Cheshire coach dealer.

In 1952 the Gleave group made a series of applications for express military leave services from the Shropshire airfields to replace the contracts previously granted by the armed forces themselves. Les Gleave & Son Ltd, at that time based in Nantwich, applied for routes from RAF Stoke Heath to Leeds, Monmouth, Nottingham, and Sheffield, and from RAF Ternhill and RAF Hinstock to London, while Roberts Coaches Ltd applied for services from RAF Shawbury to Birkenhead, Birmingham, Crewe, Derby, and Preston. The Gleave applications were withdrawn in October after the Traffic Commissioners ruled that a coach dealer was ineligible to be licensed. The Roberts Coaches applications were later refused and the military leave services were divided among several Shropshire operators.

As one might expect from a coach company with a coach dealer as its owner, there was a high turnover of second-hand rolling stock. Vehicles operated by Roberts during the 1950s included two Austin CXDs, two Commer Avengers, two Dennis Falcons, three Foden PVFE6s with Bellhouse Hartwell bodywork (acquired from Smiths of Wigan in 1953), two more Foden PVSC6s, a Leyland Comet, and two Royal Tigers. The purchases from Smiths of Wigan were particularly notable as they brought that company to Les Gleave's attention. In 1958 the Gleave group acquired both Smiths and its associated company Websters. Subsequent purchases brought three Morecambe area coach companies into the Gleave empire. Vehicles transferred from Smiths to Roberts between 1958 and 1963 (when Gleave sold Smiths and Websters to the Blundell Group of Southport) included a Plaxton-bodied Avenger III (VVT 20), two Commer-Beadle T48 Rochesters (CEK 461/2), eight Tiger Cub/Plaxton coaches, and an Albion Aberdonian/Plaxton, as well as a veritable horde of Fords with an assortment of Burlingham, Duple, and Plaxton bodywork. Other transfers to Roberts included five Bedford SB1s from the Morecambe part of the group.

In early 1962 Les Gleave decided to lengthen six ten year old Royal Tigers to the newly permitted length of 36 feet and then to have them equipped with new Plaxton Panorama bodies. One of these conversions, 501 WLG, was allocated to Roberts. It was the last interesting delivery before the service to Whitchurch ceased, a victim (as was always the case) of increased private car ownership. Les Gleave began to sell off his interests during the 1960s. The sale of the Wigan operators has already been mentioned, and Roberts was the next to go, being sold to Salopia Saloon Coaches (ironically, of Whitchurch) in 1969. Its identity was then submerged into that of Salopia. Les Gleave & Son Ltd moved its registered office to Morecambe, where Gleave had acquired a retirement property and was eventually wound up in 1988.

Scout Motor Services of Preston

The Watkinson family founded a farm produce business in Preston in the early 20th century, using horse-drawn vehicles to collect crops from farmers in the surrounding area which were then re-sold to shops in the town itself. In 1919 James

Naylor's Massey-bodied Guy Arab III, NMB 314, was new to them in 1951 and is seen here arriving at Bridgefoot, Warrington, on the service from Arley and Appleton Thorn. When Naylor gave up its share of the stage service at the end of 1964 the Arab went to Warrington Corporation, which immediately sold it for scrap. *(Roy Marshall)*

This Plaxton-bodied Thames Trader, 5 HLG, was one of four delivered to Roberts Coaches of Crewe in July 1959. In 1961 the batch was replaced by four similar vehicles transferred in from Smiths of Wigan, another Les Gleave company at that time. *(Author's Collection)*

Watkinson decided to embrace the new internal combustion engine and acquired two Leyland lorries. These were relatively expensive and to justify the purchase the firm diversified into general haulage and furniture removals, using the fleet-name 'Scout Motors'. Further expansion came in the following year when Watkinson acquired three Daimler CK flatbed lorries and a similar number of removable 24-seat char-a-banc bodies produced by Buckingham. These were used as lorries during the week and then for excursion and private hire work at the weekends.

A fourth Daimler and a 30-seat Leyland were added in 1921, followed by a fifth (second-hand) Daimler in 1922, making Scout a major player in the Preston coaching scene. Two more Leylands joined the fleet in 1923, and these second-hand machines came from Charles Smith Jr, a Blackpool coach operator who would play a major role in the continuing development of the business. The company's final two char-a-bancs were acquired in 1924, another Leyland and a short-lived Guy which was sold in the following year. At the end of 1925 Scout Motors had eight char-a-bancs in its fleet, five on Daimler chassis and three on Leyland, the 1921 Leyland having been sold in 1923. The fleet then stabilised until 1928 when the first 'all-weather' vehicles were delivered. A PLSC1 Lion with Leyland bus bodywork and a pair of PLC1 Lionesses with coach bodies produced by Burlingham then replaced an equivalent number of char-a-bancs.

In 1927 Scout had acquired the lease of Foxhall Garage in Blackpool, initially for use by the furniture removals part of the business. From May 1928 it was also used as a base for coach excursions, incurring the wrath of the local coach owners' association by charging lower fares than the members of this price-fixing cartel. This work dried up at the end of the summer, and to keep its vehicles occupied over the winter Scout offered a selection of extended tours from both its Blackpool and Preston bases. These were not a success and Scout began to look for other alternatives.

The famous Blackpool coach operator Walter Clinton Standerwick had started a weekly express coach service from Blackpool to London on the 23rd of March 1928. Another Blackpool firm, Wood Brothers (trading as John Bull Coaches) followed suit on the 16th of April. Standerwick and John Bull also began express services to Manchester and Liverpool, in competition with the existing services of Charles Smith Jr's company C Smith Motors. Smith was overwhelmed by this competition and on the 1st of July 1928 he sold his company to Joseph Bracewell, already a major coach operator in the Colne and Nelson area of eastern Lancashire. Bracewell retained the Smith fleet and used it to open a third express route from Blackpool to London only fifteen days after buying the Smith business. The Bracewell route called at Preston and Scout Motors became their local booking agent.

Scout goes to London

James Watkinson watched the bookings flooding in and decided that he wanted a larger piece of the action. On the 3rd of December 1928 Scout began its own service from Preston to London, offering 'feeder' coaches from Blackpool, Blackburn, and Darwen. As all of these options were already available from Bracewell, it was inevitable that Scout would lose their booking agency as a result. This was unfortunate as Scout's new London service was forced to close on the 9th of January for lack of demand. The poor patronage might well have been accounted for by the fact that the two Lioness coaches in use had no heaters and it was a very cold winter!

Undaunted, Watkinson ordered two new TS2 Tigers with Leyland coach bodies (and heaters) and restarted his service as a daily operation in July 1929, altering the routing so that the service ran from Blackpool to London via Preston and Birmingham. The fares on the amended operation undercut those of Standerwick, John Bull, and Bracewell by a considerable margin and the resurrected service was an instant success. Six additional TS2 Tigers (but with Spicer bodies) were added to the fleet in 1930 to cover the demand.

With money flooding into the company's coffers James Watkinson and his two sons (Ernest and James Charles Watkinson) began to look for further opportunities, and found one closer to home. In April 1930 the LM&S Railway, acting on behalf of Ribble Motor Services, acquired two prominent Preston independents, Empress Motors and Majestic Motors. Empress had been founded by former employees of Pilot Motors, made jobless when Ribble had swallowed up the company in October 1926, while Majestic was owned by local councillor Matthew Wade (known for his hostility to Ribble) and also employed many former Pilot personnel. The two companies (which acted jointly) had developed a network of routes from Preston to Longridge, Lancaster (via Garstang), Blackburn (via Walton), and Blackpool (via Kirkham).

In the spring of 1929 Ribble had begun a ruthless counter-attack using its County Motors subsidiary, cutting fares to a ridiculous level, and within a year both Empress and Majestic were on the brink of bankruptcy. They still refused to sell out to Ribble on principle, but agreed a sale to the LM&S Railway as an intermediary. Nearly all of the employees of both companies lost their jobs, many of them for the second time in three and a half years and for the same reason. The redundant personnel had hundreds of friends and relatives, none of them fooled by Ribble's 'County Motors' ploy, and with Ribble's name firmly in the ordure the Watkinsons spotted the opportunity they had been looking for.

Challenging a Monopoly

First, in May 1930, they rented the former Majestic garage on Starchhouse Square in Preston and moved the coaching side of their business into the premises. Then, in June, they applied to both Preston and Blackpool councils for a licence to operate a stage-carriage service over the former Empress/Majestic route from Preston to Blackpool via Kirkham and Wrea Green. At the same time another Preston operator, James Davis Ltd (owned by Charles Smith Jr), applied for an identical licence along with other services from Preston to Blackpool via Kirkham and Weeton, and from Preston to Blackpool via Warton, Lytham, and St Anne's.

Given the public mood, Preston Council had no problem with granting licences to both operators. The town had a generally liberal attitude towards independent operators and the chance to give Ribble a good kicking was too good to miss given the Combine company's recent antics. Blackpool Council's Watch Committee, with similar predictability, refused both applicants point-blank. The two operators had the Watch Committee's decision referred back to a full meeting of Blackpool Council for reconsideration, but before this could happen the Watch Committee changed its mind and granted a licence to the Watkinsons on the 25th of July 1930. James Davis Ltd also received the licences it had requested, but not until the full council meeting on the 6th of August. By then Charles Smith Jr had already sold his vehicles to the Watkinsons and had lost interest in stage-carriage licences. A cynic might suggest that he had only applied for them in the first place to provide the Watkinsons with a 'Plan B'.

Scout's new route to Blackpool started in the middle of August, operating half-hourly. Ribble's directors were only a little short of furious as Blackpool's decision left Scout as an existing operator when the Road Traffic Act came into force only four months later. When the Traffic Commissioners met to consider Scout's application for a Road Service Licence later in 1931, Ribble's representatives tried to claim that they were such a latecomer to the route that they could not be considered as an 'existing operator'. The Watkinsons answered this by saying that they were merely continuing an existing route, operated by Empress and Majestic for several years. The Commissioners ruled in Scout's favour, and Ribble also lost their appeal. For the next thirty years there would be competition on the road to Blackpool.

The six vehicles acquired from Charles Smith Jr, a mixture of ageing Lancias and Leyland Lionesses, were totally unsuitable for stage-carriage work and were quickly replaced by five brand-new LT2 Lion service buses, delivered in late 1930 and early 1931. Demand for the service made larger vehicles necessary almost at once. During 1931 four of the LT2 Lions were traded back to Leyland in exchange for five TD1 Titans with 48-seat lowbridge bodywork. They were Scout's first double-deckers. The end of the year saw further investment when the London express service was 'refreshed' by the addition of seven new TS2 Tiger coaches.

A sixth new double-decker, this time an updated TD2 Titan, arrived in early 1932 and replaced the last of the LT2 Lions. It was followed by four all-Leyland TS4 Tiger coaches for the London route. Up until this point James Watkinson had been the sole proprietor of Scout Motors (his two sons were technically his employees), but in December 1932 he transferred his assets to a new limited liability company, Scout Motor Services Ltd. He became the new company's chairman while Ernest and James Charles Watkinson were appointed as directors. It was also rumoured that Charles Smith Jr had been granted a minority shareholding in exchange for services rendered, but the company's shareholder register is long gone so this is impossible to confirm and may have been a slur circulated by miffed Ribble managers.

Deprived of their monopoly on the lucrative Preston-Blackpool routes, Ribble expanded elsewhere in the vicinity. With the backing of fellow T&BAT subsidiaries Midland Red and North Western they acquired all three of Scout's competitors on the Blackpool-London service. The Standerwick company was the first to sell out, in October 1932, followed by the Wood Brothers' 'John Bull Coaches' and the Bracewell operation (still using the trading name of 'C Smith Motors') in February 1933. All three were combined into a new Ribble subsidiary which used the well-known WC Standerwick name. Despite this change in status from being one of four roughly equal competitors to being the sole surviving underdog, Scout continued to make an enviable income from their London express route. For the remainder of the 1930s the company's coach fleet was regularly modernised by the addition of TS6, TS7, and TS8 Tigers, LT5A and LT8 Lions, and a pair of Leyland Cubs acquired for private hire work.

The double-deck fleet was similarly updated. Another TD2 Titan (this time a former demonstrator) was acquired in 1934, and two TD4 variants in 1935/37. With nine double-deckers in service the company was able to provide duplicates as required, and in the summer months this was more often than not.

War and Peace

Relations between Scout and Ribble remained fraught for several years, but the declaration of war in September 1939 forced them to fight on the same side. From the 20th of September the Preston to Blackpool services of both operators were placed into an operating pool with mileage and revenue divided – 60% to Ribble and 40% to Scout. In peacetime Ribble had operated four journeys per hour and Scout only two, so this seemed more than fair. Part of Scout's increased share came from joint working on the version of the route which ran via Weeton (previously Ribble territory) and this was made necessary by the construction of a large new army camp close to the village.

On the negative side the London express service (placed into a pool with the Standerwick routes in September 1940) were completely suspended in June 1941 when the coaches previously used on both companies' services were redeployed to 'military leave' contracts. These were usually reimbursed at 'cost', but the lost income was largely replaced by revenue from the stage-carriage services. High demand for these resulted in the allocation of three more double-deckers to Scout, an 'unfrozen' all-Leyland TD7 in 1941, a Guy Arab utility bus in 1943, and a similarly spartan vehicle built on a Daimler CWA6 chassis in 1944. Both of the utility buses had Duple bodywork. In 1945 the two TS6 Tiger coaches delivered in 1934 were rebodied as double-deckers by Northern Counties, adding still more capacity to the bus fleet.

After the war ended Ribble and Scout decided to retain their pooling agreements, although these were modified and expanded. Scout's original service from Preston to Blackpool via Wrea Green was equally divided between the two companies (and received Ribble route number '155', soon shown by Scout vehicles as well), while the route via Weeton (Ribble's 158) was also evenly split. From 1949 further income came from the nuclear fuel processing factory at Salwick (east of Kirkham and within the 'pooling' area) which required many works services to Blackpool, Preston, and elsewhere.

Post-war fleet renewal began quite modestly in 1946 with the delivery of two PD1 Titan double-deckers (which replaced a pair of TD1s) and a single PS1 Tiger/Duple coach. The pace increased in 1947 when Scout received six more PD1s, six more PS1 coaches, a solitary Daimler CVD6/Duple coach, and 11 Bedford OBs, a total of 24 new vehicles in a single year. Another 14 Bedford OBs were delivered in 1948, along with six more PS1 coaches, and by the end of the year the only pre-war vehicles left in the fleet were the two rebodied TS6 double-deckers and a single (1931 vintage) TD1 Titan which somehow soldiered on until 1950.

Leyland Motors arranged this line-up of Scout vehicles for a publicity shot. The operator's Starchhouse Square premises in Preston provide the backdrop for (from left to right) Burlingham-bodied LT5A Lions CK 4901 and CK 4900, TD4/Leyland RN 7576, TD1/Leyland CK 4603, TD2/Leyland CK 4654, and two other unidentified Titans. (*Roy Marshall Collection*)

Scout received two brand-new Leyland PD2/12 Titans with Leyland bodywork in early 1952. ECK 869, fleet number 22, is on its way to Blackpool from Rochdale on the long 158 service via Edenfield, Haslingden, Blackburn, Preston, Kirkham, and Weeton. *(Author's Collection)*

Scout's former Leyland Motors demonstrator STC 887 (fleet number 20) was widely listed – and still is in some places – as a PD2/20 Titan. Photographic evidence suggests that it was in fact a PD2/12 (with an open radiator grille as shown here), although I have also seen it listed as a (slightly shorter) PD2/3. It survived in Scout's latter-day 'pseudo Ribble' livery as S20 until the end of Scout as a separate subsidiary in 1968. *(Keith Johnson Collection)*

Scout's Blackpool-Preston-London service was placed into a pool with Standerwick's similar operations after the war. In this view at Victoria Coach Station in London Scout's DRN 359, a 1951 PSU1/15 Royal Tiger with Duple Ambassador bodywork, stands next to all-Leyland Royal Tiger coach FFR 690 of Standerwick. *(JT Williams Collection)*

FCK 568 was another PSU1/15 Royal Tiger, but with Duple Coronation Ambassador bodywork, delivered to Scout in 1953. It lasted long enough to receive fleet number S40 from Ribble in 1961. *(JT Williams Collection)*

The Coronation Ambassador mutated into the Duple Elizabethan design, seen here on Scout's PSUC1/2 Tiger Cub FRN 983 which was one of six delivered in 1954. It became fleet number S45 in 1961. *(JT Williams Collection)*

The next deliveries for the express services were four PSUC1/2 Tiger Cubs equipped with Duple Britannic bodies which arrived in 1956. The Britannic was basically a centre entrance alternative to the front entrance Britannia design which replaced the Elizabethan. From the following year the name was dropped and both versions became Britannias. JCK 686 was the first of the quartet and became S48 after the Ribble take-over. *(JT Williams Collection)*

Ten more Bedford OBs were acquired in 1949/50, bringing the total number acquired to a staggering 35. No more than 20 were in service at any given time and all of them had gone by 1954. Other deliveries during this two year period included three more PS1 coaches and three of the new (eight feet wide) PD2/3 Titans, which replaced the rebodied TS6s and the final TD1. The rapid disappearance of the Bedford OBs was a result of a large delivery of new coaches in 1951/52. No fewer than 19 underfloor-engined PSU1 Royal Tiger coaches were acquired. The bodywork order for this veritable armada was split between Duple (three Roadmasters and 11 Ambassadors) and Bellhouse Hartwell (five Landmasters). A shorter term investment brought three Bedford SB/Duple Vega coaches into the fleet – like the smaller OBs they had all gone by the end of 1954. There were also three more PD2 double-deckers which replaced the wartime vehicles.

In 1953 Ribble decided to link some of its services to Blackpool with routes extending further inland. The 158 (jointly operated with Scout) was reduced to an hourly frequency but revised to reach all the way to Rochdale, to the north of Manchester. A new version of service 154 (Burnley-Preston) was extended westwards to Blackpool, replacing the 'missing' departures on the 158. This was also placed into the Ribble/Scout pool and as a result of these changes Scout's double-deckers began to appear in many towns in eastern Lancashire. The independent's double-deckers were also given a share of Ribble service 167 from Preston to Lytham. It was all a very far cry from the days when Ribble wanted Scout's blood on its sword.

The only double-decker addition during 1953 was a second-hand PD1, but the year also saw the arrival of three more Royal Tiger coaches. These vehicles carried Duple Coronation Ambassador bodywork and were the last of the rather heavy PSU1 chassis to be delivered. The following year's new coaches were six of the much lighter PSUC1/2 Tiger Cub chassis with Duple Elizabethan bodies. A rather mysterious double-decker, formerly a Leyland demonstrator, was also delivered in 1954. This was STC 887, which has been variously described as a PD2/3, a PD2/12, and a PD2/20. It had an 'open' radiator grille (see the photograph in this section) which seems to rule out the concealed radiator PD2/20 variant, but opinions vary! It definitely had a Leyland body.

There were no new deliveries at all during 1955, but in 1956 the company received four new Tiger Cubs with the short-lived (and comparatively rare) Duple Brittanic body. This was basically a Duple Britannia with a centre entrance and from 1957 was described as such rather than by a separate name. Two more Tiger Cubs coaches followed in 1957 with front entrance Britannia bodies.

The Final Years

By 1958/59 the company's double-deck fleet was in need of renewal. The early post-war PD1s were replaced by five of Leyland's new PD3 Titan which were 30 feet long and could carry 72 passengers. The new double-deckers carried forward entrance Burlingham bodywork and were similar to the fully-fronted versions then being built in bulk for Ribble. The new deliveries in 1960 also brought some surprises. The four Tiger Cubs acquired in that year had Duple (Midland) Donington bodywork with a far more basic exterior than previous Duple specimens including relatively shallow side windows. An even bigger shock came when OCK 500 was delivered. This was Scout's first rear-engined Leyland Atlantean double-decker and carried a Metro-Cammell body 'finished by Willowbrook'. I put this into inverted commas as I'm still not sure what it means. It appeared to be a standard Met-Cam product.

Four more Met-Cam-bodied Atlanteans arrived in 1961, one of them a former demonstrator, the other three brand-new. That year's new coaches were five Leyland Leopards which carried the final (much improved) version of the Donington body design with deeper windows. They also had a toilet compartment, a fixture made necessary by the company's use of the new M1 motorway which considerably reduced the journey time to London. The company's next order for coaches was for the longer (36ft) PSU3 Leopard with Duple (Northern) Continental bodywork, but these vehicles were destined never to wear Scout's traditional livery.

On the 5th of December 1961 the Watkinson family sold Scout Motor Services to Ribble for a figure believed to be in the region of £300,000 (ten times that in today's money). The deal included the fleet as well as the licences, but not the premises in Starchhouse Square, Preston. Ribble retained the Scout fleet-name (but not the colour scheme) and operated the business as a wholly-owned subsidiary until 1968 when the surviving Scout machines received Ribble titles. They were a splendid bus company and I still miss them.

A history of the Scout fleet can be found on line in the 'Local Transport Histories' section of Peter Gould's excellent website www.petergould.co.uk There is also a fleet list in the book 'Standerwick and Scout' by Peter and Judith A Deegan, published by Venture in 1994. Long out of print, but still easily accessible on Amazon or eBay or from second-hand booksellers.

Viking of Preston

In 1919 Mr C Whiteside of Great Eccleston (a village on the main road from Blackpool to Garstang) started a bus service to Preston via Elswick, Inskip, Catforth, and Woodplumpton, using the fleet-name 'Royal Blue'. His service proved to be popular and members of the Tootell family noted that fact as his vehicles passed through their home village of Woodplumpton. The Tootells were probably the most influential family in their community and each generation of the clan since at least the 18th century had been headed by an individual named Richard Ashton Tootell. This can be very confusing to historians who might wish that English families would adopt the American system of adding a number to the recurring name.

In 1920 James Tootell decided to start a competing bus service from Woodplumpton to Preston, as Whiteside's vehicles were often full by the time they passed through the village and left intending passengers behind. His original vehicle remains unidentified, but in July 1922 he acquired a war surplus Daimler chassis and had it converted into a 20-seat bus registered CK 3472. Whiteside decided to fight back against this upstart by adding another vehicle to his Royal Blue fleet, and on busy days this was deployed as a duplicate which started picking up passengers at the point where the first bus became full.

By the following year James Tootell was losing money and decided to withdraw, passing the business to his father and his brother. Both were named Richard Ashton Tootell, the younger of the two having been born in 1890 and taking the leading role in the enterprise. He retained the fleet-name of 'Viking', which had already been painted on the side of the Daimler, and in May 1924 the two RA Tootells formed a limited company to continue the business as Viking Motors (Preston) Ltd.

Other local people were offered shares in the business (a proposal made more attractive by the fact that shareholders travelled free of charge) and the money thus raised was used to purchase two additional vehicles, a 1919 Leyland (B 8912) and a 1921 Daimler (WA 5397). These acquisitions enabled the Tootells to extend their own service to run from Great Eccleston, competing with Whiteside over the full length of his route. A period of cut-throat competition proved costly to both companies and by 1926 they had agreed to co-ordinate their services to mutual advantage.

Viking's next vehicle was CK 3727, a brand-new 26-seat Guy B, which arrived in March 1926 and replaced Daimler CK 3472. Three more new Guys were acquired in 1928 (CK 3910/1/3966) and these replaced the two second-hand machines which had arrived in 1924. Whiteside was forced to respond and acquired two new buses for his own fleet in the summer of 1929, a 30-seat LT1 Lion (TE 8195) and a 26-seat Vulcan Duchess (TE 9039). Both of these vehicles, along with four older Whiteside machines (Leylands TD 296, TD 979, TD 9127, and CW 8135), passed to Viking in November 1929 when the two companies merged. Whiteside was paid in shares and became Viking's company secretary.

Five further Leyland Lions were acquired between 1930 and 1935 (CK 4556/610/79/772 and RN 7570), along with a single Morris Dictator/Northern Counties 32-seater (CK 4578). These were followed in the summer of 1936 by the amalgamated company's first two coaches, an LZ2 Cheetah (RN 7958) and an SKPZ2 Cub (RN 7959). Work for these luxurious vehicles proved harder to find than had been imagined, and in October 1936 Viking rectified this situation by acquiring Lockett & Lonsdale, a Preston-based coach operator. Viking was only interested in the company's excursion traffic and its two elderly vehicles (a 1928 Dennis G and a 1929 Star Flyer) were instantly discarded.

Viking's final acquisitions before the start of the Second World War were a TS8 Tiger coach in 1937 (RN 8248) and a 32-seat LZ2A Cheetah/

In 1958/59 Scout received five new PD3 double-deckers with 72-seat Burlingham bodies which were basically the same as Ribble's contemporary buses, but without the full-width fronts. They were far more visually attractive than their fully-fronted counterparts. MCK 369 (fleet number 23) was the first of the 1959 trio. After the take-over it became S23 and then passed to direct Ribble ownership in 1968 as fleet number 1976. *(JT Williams Collection)*

Scout's first PDR1/1 Atlantean, OCK 500 (fleet number 1) arrived in 1960. Its 77-seat MCCW body appeared to be standard but was apparently 'completed by Willowbrook'. In 1961 it became S1 and then passed into Ribble ownership as fleet number 1969 in October 1968. *(JT Williams Collection)*

It is a great shame that no colour images of the Viking fleet could be found. Here, in their two-tone blue and white livery, is all-Leyland LT7 Lion bus RN 7570 (fleet number 7), new in July 1935. It served with Viking until the end and then gave further service to two Scottish independents. *(Roy Marshall Collection)*

Viking's third fleet number 2 was RN 8483, an LZ2A Cheetah with a 32-seat Burlingham bus body, delivered in March 1938. In August 1949 it was sold to a dealer in Inskip and also ended up in Scotland. *(Roy Marshall)*

Burlingham bus in 1938 (RN 8483). A second new TS8 coach arrived in May 1940 and also had a Burlingham body (ACK 259). The construction of a new military aerodrome at Inskip increased Viking's traffic three-fold and resulted in the allocation of two Bedford OWB utility buses in 1942 (ACK 685/6) and two Daimler CWA6s with lowbridge bodywork in 1944 (ACK 813/37). The CWA8s were the company's first double-deckers.

This is perhaps the appropriate point to give some details of Viking's fleet numbering system. In pre-war years this had been slightly haphazard with some vehicles carrying no fleet numbers and at least one case where the same number was worn by two different vehicles simultaneously for at least a year! For the record the numbers in use at the end of the war were 1 (RN 8248), 2 (RN 8483), 3 (CK 4679), 4 (CK 4610), 5 (ACK 847), 6 (CK 4772), 7 (RN 7570), 8 (ACK 259), 9 (RN 7958), 10 (ACK 685), 11 (ACK 686), and 12 (ACK 813). Fleet number 13 was not used and the first post-war vehicle, PS1 Tiger/Burlingham bus ARN 528 (delivered in August 1946) became fleet number 14.

Two new double-deckers arrived in December 1946 in the shape of all-Leyland PD1 Titans BCK 100 (which carried fleet number 10 alongside the OWB with the same number until the latter was sold in 1949!) and BCK 191 (fleet number 15). The next arrival was one of the 'never used' Daimler CVD6/Burlingham coaches discarded by Western SMT in early 1949, CAG 791, which became fleet number 11 (the OWB which had previously worn this number had been sold in 1947). Two more CVD6s were delivered in March 1949, but these were brand-new double-deckers with Strachan bodywork (CRN 58/59, fleet numbers 16/17).

This apparent prosperity belied the fact that Viking was losing money. One of the problems was that more than a hundred people held shareholder's passes and travelled for nothing. These minor shareholders, collectively, owned more shares than the Tootell and Whiteside families, so there was little chance of the shareholders' privileges being withdrawn as turkeys rarely vote for Christmas. With the gradual running down of the aerodrome at Inskip (it later became a forest of radio masts used to communicate with Royal Navy submarines), the number of fare-paying customers was plummeting.

Nevertheless the directors (most of them now small shareholders, including the chairman) continued to spend money. In the summer of 1949 two brand-new PS1 Tiger/Santus coaches were acquired (CRN 662/715, fleet numbers 18 and 2) but these would be the last arrivals at Woodplumpton. By 1950 it was obvious to the most self-interested of shareholders that the company was going down the pan. Frantic representations were made to Ribble, but the larger company was reluctant to become involved as the terms and conditions of the shareholder's passes stated that they would be honoured (for the lifetime of the holder) by any company which acquired Viking.

Eventually, with Viking on the verge of declaring itself bankrupt, Ribble relented and acquired the company's Great Eccleston to Preston route in November 1952 for the relatively paltry sum of £3,000. This was probably around half the potential value of the stage-carriage service had the company not issued free passes as if they were confetti. Viking was left with its fleet (which Ribble did not want) and the sale of these vehicles barely covered the company's debts and other liabilities. PD1 Titan BCK 100 passed to Scout (qv), and twin sister BCK 191 went to The Delaine in Lincolnshire. The CVD6 double-deckers ended up with AA Motor Services of Ayr (CRN 58) and Culling of Claxton (CRN 59), while the single-decker buses and the coaches were scattered far and wide. Viking might well have been a financial disaster on wheels, but it will be well remembered by people of a certain age who adored its style and its friendly service.

Webster of Alvanley

Alvanley is a small village on the south-eastern side of Helsby which is a larger community on the main road between Warrington and Chester. Helsby has a railway station as does the neighbouring village of Frodsham. For many years the main employer in the area was the Helsby cable works, while in more recent times the Stanlow Oil refinery has been a major source of employment. Helsby Hill rises above the village, and on the crest of the next (slightly higher) hill to the southeast is the hamlet of Kingswood. At the beginning of the 20th century two tuberculosis hospitals were built at Kingswood, the Liverpool

Sanatorium and the Manchester Sanatorium, the latter more commonly referred to as 'The Crossley Sanatorium' as it was funded by William Crossley, the well-known Manchester industrialist.

Norman William Webster owned a garage in Alvanley and by the late 1920s was providing a bus service from Helsby railway station to the hospitals at Kingswood. This was for the benefit of visitors to the two sanatoria and operated on Wednesdays, Saturdays, and Bank Holidays. Journeys were suited to the train times and the hospitals' visiting hours, departing from Helsby at 1.15pm and 2.30pm.

The first known vehicle was a new 20-seat Bedford WLB, LG 9082, delivered in June 1932, while the second was a 32-seat Bedford OWB utility bus (HMA 69) which arrived in December 1944 to provide more capacity. The two hospitals could house up to 150 patients, so visitor numbers were substantial, and a part of the site was used for additional patients incapacitated whilst serving in the war. After the war Mr Webster decided to buy a coach to expand the private hire side of his business. The pre-war WLB was replaced by an unidentified Bedford WTB with Duple bodywork in May 1949, and this was replaced by a second-hand OB/Pearson coach (CWH 640) in July 1955. The wartime OWB remained 'quarantined' as the vehicle of choice for the hospital runs throughout the 1950s.

An 11-seat Austin J2BA joined the fleet in November 1959 and was used for small private-hires. It would be succeeded by two similar BMC products over the years. A more substantial vehicle was acquired from Crosville in July 1960 when Bedford OB/Duple Vista coach KFM 435 came to Alvanley. It became the front-line private hire machine, while the Pearson-bodied OB was demoted to the hospital service, and the OWB was sold for scrap.

A larger Bedford SB with a Duple Super Vega body (TWE 86) was acquired from a Sheffield operator in May 1962, bringing the fleet strength to three coaches and one minibus. The next change came in May 1967 when 960 EMB, a 1958 Bedford SB3 with the 'butterfly grille' variant of the Super Vega body, arrived from neighbouring operator Reliance of Kelsall (qv). The older SB then became the regular hospital bus, while the Pearson-bodied OB was withdrawn. In the late 1960s the sanatoria were closed, but quickly reopened as 'The Crossley Hospital' (a name which covered both sites), specialising in geriatric care. Old people had visitors too, so the Helsby-Kingswood service continued after a short break.

In April 1970 the OB/Vista coach was replaced by a Bedford VAS5 with Duple Bella Vista bodywork, KRF 670F, acquired from a Staffordshire operator, while in July 1971 a Bedford SB5 coach with a Plaxton body (NMA 597D) replaced TWE 86. It came from Naylor of Stockton Heath (qv). Plaxton bodywork was also worn by Bedford VAS5 AMB 851M, which came to Alvanley in May 1974 and was Webster's first new 'full-size' vehicle since 1944.

During the 1970s the stage-carriage route was amended, both in route and schedule. On Wednesdays and Saturdays it ran from Frodsham station to Kingswood, and on Sundays from Helsby. The reasons for these changes are unknown, but could have something to do with railway schedules at that time. The early 1980s saw another change of use for the Kingswood site when it became a psychiatric hospital. In 1985 it closed and the bus service came to an end. Mr Webster was by then in his early eighties and decided to retire.

West of Kelsall

Kelsall is on the A54, which heads eastwards from Chester to Winsford and beyond. The village was the home of the Reliance Iron Works, and when George West opened a filling station on a site close to the foundry he called it the Reliance Garage. Like many garage owners, West expanded into private hire work, at first with taxis and then with char-a-bancs. A side-view exists of one of these charas, but the vehicle is partially obscured by people so that even the make is impossible to ascertain.

Details of the earliest vehicles are completely unknown, but in 1931 West applied to the Traffic Commissioners to continue his existing stage-carriage services from Kelsall and Tarporley to Helsby cable works (restricted to employees) and from Cotebrook to Chester (available to all). The latter service consisted of two journeys on Saturday evenings and ran non-stop from Kelsall to the Queens Hotel in the city centre – its terminus from the days when it needed to use private ground to avoid Chester's Watch Committee. Crosville objected strenuously to the granting of the Chester licence, but it was an existing service and West got his pieces of paper,

All-Leyland PD1 Titan BCK 100 was one of a pair delivered to Viking in December 1946, and was given fleet number 10 even though that number was already allocated to a wartime OWB which remained in the fleet until April 1949! When Viking closed down BCK 100 was sold to Scout – based in Starchhouse Square, Preston, where this photograph was taken in happier days. *(Roy Marshall)*

After the two PD1s Viking bought a pair of Strachan-bodied Daimler CVD6s in March 1949. Fleet number 4 (CRN 59) is seen in Starchhouse Square alongside vehicles of Scout and BBMS. After Viking's demise the vehicle served with Culling of Claxton (Norfolk) and Morley of Whittlesey (near Peterborough). It was last licensed in 1959, as was sister machine CRN 58 which went to AA Motor Services in Ayrshire, suggesting that the Strachan bodywork on the two buses was of that company's usual poor quality. *(Author's Collection)*

The first two known vehicles were a 1930 Dennis G acquired from a Southport operator (WM 4109), and a 1927 Albion which came from Stoke-on-Trent Motors in 1933 (EH 9566). The latter vehicle became fleet number 1 in the post-war era and remained in service until March 1949. It lingered in the garage yard for another decade before being sold for further service as a hen-house. The only other vehicle recorded during the 1930s was West's first new coach, a Duple-bodied Bedford WTB (ELG 455).

The Chester route was suspended for the duration of the war, but the Helsby works services continued. Second-hand arrivals during the conflict were a 1928 Albion with a 25-seat Strachan coach body (TU 5958), an LT5A Lion from Richardson of Buckley (DM 9662, post-war fleet number 2), a Wilmott-bodied Commer (BYE 259), and a Crossley (HA 7665). Two Bedford OWB utility buses were allocated to the company in 1943/44 (HMA 16 and HMA 468, fleet numbers 4 and 3 respectively). A very rare Alexander-bodied Leyland Gnu is also rumoured to have served with West for a few months during the war, but this has proven impossible to confirm from the documentary or photographic record. It might well have been hired from a dealer as the record cards for the only two built make no mention of West.

The first post-war arrival was a 1932 Dennis Lancet, RF 9908, acquired from a Potteries operator in early 1946. It became fleet number 5. Fleet numbers 6-8 were taken up by KLG 670 (a Bedford OB/Pearson coach delivered in November 1947), and 1948 deliveries LMA 174 (an OB/Duple Vista), and LLG 688 (a Dennis Lancet J3 coach with Burlingham bodywork). Another 1932 Dennis Lancet acquired in 1949 (XJ 757) and became fleet number 9, while fleet number 10 was taken up in the following year by a brand-new Tilling-Stevens Express coach with Dutfield bodywork (MTU 745). This rare machine served the company until January 1964.

The fleet numbering system introduced in 1946 had been completely logical until this point, but things started to get slightly surreal in 1952 when a new Bedford SB/Duple Vega coach arrived (OMB 217) and was also given fleet number 10! Both vehicles were in service, side-by-side, for another twelve years with the same fleet number. Another pointless duplication came in the following year when Bedford OB/Mulliner bus GWW 612 arrived from Longstaff of Mirfield and became another fleet number 8. The original number 8, LLG 688, served alongside the second one for at least four years.

Sanity returned in 1954 when new Bedford SBG/Plaxton coach KCA 352 arrived as fleet number 11. It was the first of many coaches acquired with the assistance of Hanmer of Southsea, hence the Denbighshire registration. According to one anecdotal story Hanmer had a good relationship with Bedford dealer Vincent Greenhous and received a substantial discount on new coaches. Hanmer then split the difference with his friend George West, but to avoid annoying the Cheshire area Bedford franchisee the vehicles had to be registered in Wrexham. This may or may not be true, but no better explanation has emerged.

Increased demand for the Helsby works services resulted in the arrival of three second-hand AEC Regals during 1954. The first of these, GN 2104 (fleet number 12), had previously been operated by London Transport as T283. Fleet number 13 was not used, for superstitious reasons, and the next used Regal (ACX 368 from Hanson of Huddersfield) became fleet number 14. The third Regal was the longest lived of the trio which migrated to Kelsall. HG 819 had been new to Burnley in 1931 and after the war had been sold to Charles Holt of Whitworth who had it rebodied by Harrington as a coach. It became fleet number 15 and ran until January 1965. Meanwhile, the second use of the fleet number 6 came in 1956 when the Pearson-bodied OB was sold and replaced by a second-hand OWB bus acquired from nearby operator Coppenhall of Sandbach. HMB 236 ran for West until February 1965. Fleet number 16 followed in 1957 and was a PS2/3 Tiger with a Harrington 'dorsal fin' coach body very similar to that on HG 819. GDM 494 had been new to Wakley of Northop (Flintshire) in 1950 and stayed at Kelsall until 1967. The vehicle is currently preserved in 'Classique' livery.

George West (as a sole proprietor) had been using the fleet-name 'Reliance Motors' on the rear panels of his vehicles since the beginning, and in November 1957 the business became a limited company as Reliance Motor Services (Kelsall) Ltd. Many vehicles delivered after this date continued to display the word 'West' on their front panels or

George West of Kelsall (Reliance Motor Services) bought this wartime Bedford OWB, HMB 236, from fellow Cheshire operator Coppenhall of Sandbach and gave it fleet number 6. It would appear that Coppenhall had rebodied the vehicle after the war as this is either a Duple Mk II body or a virtually identical Mulliner 'Mk III'. The bus was finally withdrawn from use in February 1965. *(R Winter via The Omnibus Society)*

This Duple (Midland)-bodied Bedford SBG bus, OUN 592, came to Kelsall from George West's friend Walter Hanmer of Southsea (near Wrexham) and received fleet number 16. This was a pointless duplication as the fleet number 16 was already worn by PS2 Tiger/Harrington coach GDM 494. It is seen here outside Chester General railway station, across the road from the Queens Hotel terminus of West's stage service from Cotebrook. The vehicle was sold in August 1966. *(Roy Marshall)*

in the eyebrow apertures. In the years immediately after the change in legal status fleet numbers 17-20 were taken by four new Bedford SB3/Duple Super Vegas delivered in 1958 (960 EMB), 1960 (VCA 100), and 1962 (1930 UN and 3562 UN). After this fleet numbers were rarely used and the next two arrivals, second-hand Bedford OB/Duple Vista coaches GJF 73, and MPP 245, remained unnumbered. A third OB/Vista, EVH 664, became the third wearer of fleet number 8.

In 1964 Reliance bought two second-hand Bedford SBs from Hanmer of Southsea. OUN 592 was an SBG with a Duple (Midland) 40-seat bus body, acquired so that the two Helsby services could be amalgamated into one route. It also became the regular performer on the Chester runs. Rather perversely it was painted as fleet number 16, a number which was still worn by Tiger/Harrington GDM 494! The other Hanmer vehicle was another SB3/Duple coach, RCA 296. A further OB/Vista coach came in May 1965 when LRR 601 was acquired from a Nottinghamshire operator. Second-hand deliveries during 1966 were a pair of Duple-bodied Bedford SB5s from operators in north-eastern England (VNL 45 and 212 UP), while the SBG bus was sold in August to an operator in South Wales. The rise of the private car had made its capacity superfluous and the stage-carriage services reverted to operation by Bedford OBs, or (on busy days) the larger coaches.

The following year saw the arrival of two very different vehicles. JCA 288E was a brand-new Bedford VAM14 coach with a 45-seat Duple Viceroy body, while EX 6666 had started life as a war-time Bedford lorry before being modified to PSV standards and fitted with a 29-seat Duple Vista coach body. It came from the well-known independent Osborne of Tollesbury and was the final acquisition to appear on the Chester service before the route was abandoned in 1968. Reliance continued with the works services and as a coach operator, and seems to have ceased trading in the early 1980s.

The best known of the company's later vehicles was RFE 461, a 1961 Bristol MW6G with a 43-seat ECW semi-coach body, acquired from Lincolnshire Road Car in March 1977 for use on the Helsby services. It received fleet number 31 with Reliance and lasted until the end of operations. It then passed to Neston Air Cadets on the Wirral for use as a private transport, and by 1991 was in use as a mobile home in County Cork having been re-registered in September of that year as BVL 654A. It is believed that the vehicle still exists in the hands of travellers.

STOP PRESS

While this book was in the editing process I discovered the photograph of the Leedham (of Dunsop Bridge) Bedford shown to the right, and by a happy coincidence there was enough 'white space' left at the end of the text to include it at the last minute. It really sums up the 'deeply rural' aspect of the Clitheroe to Slaidburn route, which survives to this day as a tendered service.

This left just half a page to fill, and although the Altrincham Coachways Tiger may seem to be a little out of place in a book about independent bus operators, there is a tenuous link. Norman Juckes, who founded Altrincham Coachways after the Second World War, had operated a stage service from Altrincham to Trafford Park until 1939 when the licence passed to Manchester Corporation. Photographs of Altrincham Coachways vehicles in the 'pre-North Western' era are also quite rare, which was another good reason to include the image. It was this or another Whitson observation coach!

This 1970 SB5 with Plaxton Panorama bodywork, OND 11H, was the last of three Bedford SB variants acquired by Leedham of Dunsop Bridge for their Clitheroe service. As the operator had only two destinations, a simple solution was found to avoid the need for an expensive route blind. It did the job! *(Author's Collection)*

Leyland PS1 Tiger/Duple FC33F HOU 868 was one of four identical vehicles which passed from Basil Williams' Hants & Sussex company to Altrincham Coachways in July 1951. It's stay was short-lived as all four of the fully-fronted Tigers were sold to Spencer of Oldham in January 1953. *(Author's Collection)*

Part Three

NORTH WEST ENGLAND IN COLOUR

Independents in the region selected a wide range of liveries, usually chosen to make it easier for passengers to distinguish their vehicles from those of the larger operators. In Cumberland all four of the 'area agreement' firms which had services in the county (Cumberland MS, Ribble, United Auto, and Western SMT) used differing shades of red, so Blair & Palmer used two-tone green and Ernie Hartness pale blue and cream. Further south in the Lake District, where Ribble reigned almost supreme, Robinson of Appleby also used two-tone green while Dallam swung the other way and chose a plum and white colour scheme with some vehicles (the two Seddons) having additional dark cream relief. At a distance it was similar to Ribble's livery.

Down in Lancashire Bolton-by-Bowland Motor Services used dark blue and cream, although some of its coaches were in a two-tone blue scheme. Both contrasted nicely with Ribble's cherry red and cream. Following the river westwards Preston was a very colourful place in the late 1940s. The dark red Ribble and Corporation buses were relieved by the maroon, black and white of Scout, the bright red, black, and white of Bamber Bridge, the two-tone green of Fishwick, and the two-tone blue and white of Viking.

In eastern Manchester the dark red and pale blue of Mayne's double-decker fleet added an interesting note to the visual symphony of municipal colour schemes already on offer, while in Warrington the pale blue of Naylor's Guy Arab made a pleasing contrast to red (the Corporation, LUT, North Western, and St Helens), Tilling green (Crosville) and deep blue (Leigh). In rural Cheshire Reliance of Kelsall chose red and cream (often with maroon relief) to make its vehicles stand out from the drab ranks of Crosville's Bristols. If you wanted a bus in the North West you could have it in any colour you liked!

After Ernie Hartness's death his premises in Penrith were used for a variety of purposes but eventually became derelict and were demolished. The site was given over to a new (local authority) bus station and a block of low-cost flats called Sandgate Court. The clock from Ernie's bus station was saved and affixed to the wall of the new housing where it remains to this day. A very nice memorial to a great local character. **(Keith Johnson Collection)**

The 'Commer' badge on the front of Blair & Palmer's UHH 877 was not entirely truthful. As with the previous home-made service bus, NHH 482 (see photograph in Part One), the chassis was a Commer Avenger IV, but this machine had an eight cylinder Albion engine beneath its floor in place of the original front-mounted TS3. It entered service in June 1962. According to PSV Circle records its 43-seat body incorporated parts from a Scottish Aviation unit acquired from Glasgow but this is unconfirmed. *(Geoff Lumb)*

Atkinson PL745H Alpha coach VS 6440 came to Blair & Palmer from Doig of Greenock in April 1963, and carried a 41-seat Duple Elizabethan body. In June 1967 it returned to Scotland with McRae of Fortrose. *(Geoff Lumb)*

Geoff Lumb has produced thousands of excellent photographs over the years, but this one is my personal favourite. Ernie Hartness's 1947 Daimler CVD6 GAO 399 started life with a pre-war ECW single-decker body from North Western, but soon received this new double-decker body from Roe. It was retired in November 1965. **(Geoff Lumb)**

The Daimler CVD6 in the foreground of this view, GAO 201, was another early 1947 delivery and Hartness initially gave it an MCCW single-decker bus body donated by a pre-war Ashton-under-Lyne Crossley Alpha. In 1949 it received a new Plaxton coach body as shown here. To the left in the yard at Penrith is one of the CVD6s fitted with fully-fronted Roe bus bodies in 1954, and to the left of that a four axle ERF tipper lorry of Harrisons of Penrith. **(Geoff Lumb)**

This Bedford OB with SMT 'Duple Vista lookalike' bodywork, GRM 914, was new in January 1948 to Mandale of Greystoke. It was later sold to Askew of Grange-in-Borrowdale, one of the partners in the Keswick Borrowdale Bus Service, and is seen here on the Keswick to Seatoller service with Mr Askew at the wheel but no visible passengers. *(Geoff Lumb)*

Like several of the operators covered in my earlier book on North Wales, Robinson of Appleby went through a 'Bristol phase' in the late 1970s. This 45-seat Bristol RELH6G/ECW coach, ATA 104B, came from Western National in February 1977 and was withdrawn from use in December 1985. *(JT Williams Collection)*

After the end of the Spadeadam rocket range contracts, Sowerby of Gilsland kept a few double-deckers for other works services. Seen here awaiting employees of the Champion Spark Plug factory are BAG 102 (an ex-Glasgow CVG6 with Alexander bodywork, acquired from Blair & Palmer in December 1965), and all-Leyland PD2/1 Titans JCD 90/91 which came from Southdown in March 1966. A clumsy attempt has been made to disguise the Blair & Palmer livery on BAG 102 with black and yellow paint. *(Geoff Lumb)*

This 1949 Burlingham-bodied Crossley SD42 coach, FUN 319, was new to EG Peters of Llanarmon-yn-Ial but came to Wright Brothers of Nenthead from a Midlands operator in May 1959. After a long service career with Wrights it was retained as a 'heritage vehicle' and remains in preservation in the company's livery as seen here at a rally. *(JT Williams Collection)*

The fourth wearer of Bamber Bridge fleet number 4 was UTC 672, an AEC Regent III with lowbridge East Lancs bodywork, new in December 1954. After the Ribble take-over it went to an operator in the Forest of Dean before being saved for preservation. A fixture in the Manchester Museum of Transport for many years, it is now an active PSV again with Cumbria Classic Coaches and wears full BBMS livery with additional titles. This shot was taken in the early 1960s at BBMS's premises in Station Road, Bamber Bridge. *(Geoff Lumb)*

BBMS's second semi-lowbridge Atlantean, 2295 TE, was delivered in January 1963 and became the third fleet number 7. The location is Starchhouse Square in Preston and in the background are two Scout vehicles in the 'Ribble subsidiary' livery, a PD3 and an Atlantean. The BBMS machine became Ribble fleet number 1967 (in 1967!) and gave them another 12 years of service. *(Geoff Lumb)*

165

Two of the six LW1 Olympians delivered to Fishwick in 1957, 521 CTF (fleet number 7) and 522 CTF (fleet number 8) are seen here at the company's main depot in Leyland. The Olympians lasted until the beginning of the Leyland National era in the early 1970s. 521 CTF was then sold to Williams of Chirk and in 1975 passed to Warstone Motors (Green Bus) as fleet number 14. After a long second career with the well-known Staffordshire company it is now preserved. *(Alan Murray-Rust)*

When 523 CTF was delivered in 1957 (as fleet number 11) it was identical to the machines shown above, but in 1963 it was converted into a 'semi-coach" and painted into Fishwick's grey and white coach livery as fleet number 'C4'. Demoted back to bus work a few years later, it kept the 40-seat lay-out and the decorative front grille, but reverted to bus livery as fleet number 14. *(Alan Murray-Rust)*

Alexander-bodied Atlantean SGD 669 started its life with Glasgow, but was quickly bought back by Leyland Motors for use as a demonstrator. In March 1965 Leyland sold it to Fishwick and it became fleet number 34. The rear end to its right belongs to single-deck Fleetline WTE 484L (fleet number 9), one of five Fowler-bodied examples delivered in 1973/74. *(JT Williams Collection)*

This Park Royal-bodied Panther Cub, JTJ 667F (fleet number 1) was another former Leyland demonstrator and was sold to Fishwick in April 1969. By the time of this photograph its centre exit had been removed by Fowler in a somewhat ham-fisted fashion. Can you tell where it used to be? *(Alan Murray-Rust)*

167

Fowler's first full-size PSV body since the 1930s was fitted to this late model Tiger Cub, VTD 441H, which entered service in March 1970 as Fishwick's fleet number 12. *(Geoff Lumb)*

Yes, it is a complete abomination, but it had to be shown! This is Fowler's only ever attempt at a double-decker body, fitted to Leyland's prototype PDR1/3 Atlantean chassis and delivered to Fishwick in August 1972 as MTE 186K, fleet number 6. The 'experiment' was never repeated. *(Alan Murray-Rust)*

Single-deck Fowler-bodied Fleetline WTE 485L (fleet number 10) of 1973 stands next to Weymann-bodied PD2/40 Titan 532 CTF (fleet number 21), 15 years its senior. Note the slightly different versions of the two-tone green livery – this could vary from one batch to the next with the lighter green sometimes coming close to a 51st shade of grey. *(JT Williams Collection)*

I feel compelled to show a colour view of a Leyland National, even though I have despised the things for more than 40 years. This one is XCW 955R (Fishwick fleet number 24), an 11.3m version new in 1977. From this point on write your own caption for it! *(JT Williams Collection)*

In 1982 Fishwick bought all three of Leyland's remaining B15 Titan demonstrators. BCK 706R, built in 1977, had first come to Fishwick on loan from Leyland in 1980, receiving fleet number 3 after its purchase two years later. *(JT Williams Collection)*

I have no evidence that Hollinshead used this magnificent 1951 Foden PVR/Metalcraft coach (NTU 125) on its stage services, but it was the regular vehicle on its schools run from Alsager to Sandbach during the 1960s. The coach is now preserved by Roger Burdett. How about bringing it up to a Yorkshire Dales Running Day, Roger? Us northerners would like a ride! *(David J Stanier)*

This pre-war AEC Regent with Weymann bodywork, CUS 812, was one of a pair which passed from Glasgow Corporation to Mayne of Manchester in January 1953. A third machine from the same batch followed in 1956 for use as spares. *(Geoff Lumb)*

By the late 1960s service 46 to Sunnyside Road had been renumbered as the 213. East Lancs-bodied Regent V CXJ 522C, one of three delivered in 1965, is seen here at the Stevenson Square stand previously used by corporation trolleybuses. *(GMTS Archive)*

171

The five Roe-bodied Daimler Fleetlines delivered in 1976 were the last new vehicles to wear the distinctive cherry red and pale blue livery. The second of the batch, LRJ 211P, is seen at the Stevenson Square terminus of service 213. It was later repainted into the livery shown below. *(JT Williams Collection)*

The next new double-deckers were three Bristol VRT3s, delivered in 1978 in the red and cream colour scheme already used by the company's coach fleet. The VRs had standard ECW bodies but featured 'dual purpose' seating, which has led some optimists to describe them as double-decker coaches. VJA 665S was the first of the 1978 trio. A further two identical machines joined the fleet in 1980. *(JT Williams Collection)*

Good quality colour photographs of Scout vehicles are very hard to find – I do have several colour shots of their Atlanteans but none were good enough to include alongside this atmospheric shot of all-Leyland PD2/3 Titan DRN 365 (fleet number 9). The period cars are very nice too. *(Roy Marshall)*

George West (Reliance) of Kelsall was still buying second-hand Bedford OBs in the mid-1960s. This Huddersfield registered example with Duple Vista bodywork, EVH 664, became fleet number 8 and was mainly used on schools services and local private hires. *(Vic Nutton)*

173

Brownrigg of Egremont used this PS2 Tiger with Burlingham Sunsaloon bodywork, KAO 542, on a works service to the Leyland National factory in Workington during the early 1970s. For some reason the saying 'pearls before swine' comes to mind. **(Geoff Lumb)**

This is the third of the Regal IIIs delivered to the Belfast Steam Ship Co in 1954, PKD 590, in its later configuration with a full front and an added luggage compartment. The drastic modification enabled the company to dispose of their separate baggage vans. In 1966 the Regals were retired and replaced by Liverpool Corporation's equally strange-looking 'Airporter' conversions. **(Vic Nutton)**